MW00678101

SCHOOL SITING AND
HEALTHY COMMUNITIES

SCHOOL SITING AND HEALTHY COMMUNITIES

Why Where We Invest in School Facilities Matters

Edited by Rebecca Miles,
Adesoji Adelaja, and Mark Wyckoff

Michigan State University Press
East Lansing

Copyright © 2011 by Michigan State University

♾ The paper used in this publication meets the minimum requirements of ANSI/NISO Z39.48-1992 (R 1997) (Permanence of Paper).

Michigan State University Press
East Lansing, Michigan 48823-5245

Printed and bound in the United States of America.

18 17 16 15 14 13 12 11   1 2 3 4 5 6 7 8 9 10

LIBRARY OF CONGRESS CATALOGING-IN-PUBLICATION DATA
School siting and healthy communities : why where we invest in school facilities matters / edited by Rebecca Miles, Adesoji Adelaja, and Mark Wyckoff.
        p. cm.
        Includes bibliographical references.
ISBN 978-1-61186-013-9 (pbk. : alk. paper) 1. School sites. 2. Cities and towns. 3. School facilities—Design and construction. 4. Educational change—Government policy. I. Miles, Rebecca. II. Adelaja, Adesoji. III. Wyckoff, Mark A.
LB3220.S45 2012
371.6'1—dc22
2011006522

Cover design by Erin Kirk New

Book design by Scribe Inc. (www.scribenet.com)

green press Michigan State University Press is a member of the Green Press Initiative and is committed to developing
press INITIATIVE and encouraging ecologically responsible publishing practices. For more information about the Green
Press Initiative and the use of recycled paper in book publishing, please visit www.greenpressinitiative.org.

Visit Michigan State University Press on the World Wide Web at:
www.msupress.msu.edu

Contents

PART 1

Why Where We Invest
in Schools Matters

Introduction and Problem Context
School Siting and Healthy Communities

REBECCA MILES

ONE OF THE DOMINANT POPULATION TRENDS IN RECENT DECADES IN THE UNITED States is the movement of people from urban areas to suburban and rural areas. Important changes in where we invest in schools have accompanied this population shift: existing schools, mainly in urban areas, have been closed and new schools have been built in suburban locations. School construction and closures have followed population shifts but may also have contributed to population growth and distribution. New schools have been getting larger and farther from the residences where students live. These trends have left many school facilities in cities to deteriorate, and many are now in need of upgrading or modernization (ASCE 2009).

A growing chorus of critical voices suggests that current school siting decision making is inconsistent with efforts to reduce sprawl, encourage compact growth, and increase the sustainability of our built and natural environments (Agron 2009; Ewing and Greene 2003; Kouri 1999; Salvesen and Hervey 2003). The built environment includes all buildings (e.g., schools, workplaces), homes, roads, and other components of transportation systems, utilities (i.e., electrical transmission lines, water, and waste disposal systems), parks and recreation areas, fixtures, and other spaces created or significantly modified by humans.

Furthermore, current school siting practices may be contributing to a vicious cycle of families moving to the suburbs to avoid bad schools and neighborhoods with bad schools deteriorating into bad neighborhoods, which then increase the suburbanization trend. The desire for "better schools" is often cited as a motive for moving farther out to the suburbs, and the race and socioeconomic dimensions of this migration have contributed to the resegregation of urban schools and some inner ring suburbs (Orfield et al. 1997; Frankenberg and Lee 2002; de Souza Briggs 2005). The important role of schools in the residential location decisions of families suggests that schools represent a significant factor in shaping the landscape of communities.

There is also a compelling economic rationale for a new approach to school siting. Proponents argue it would save school districts money (Ad Hoc Coalition for Healthy School Siting 2008). Schools located adjacent to or within neighborhoods cut down on the funds needed for infrastructure such as roads, water, sewers, and utilities. Schools sited to maximize walking and cycling to school or riding mass transit can reduce the need for school buses and therefore cut down on school transportation expenses. They also reduce the acreage needed for parking lots and therefore decrease land costs.

A lack of coordination between school capital investments and land use planning processes may represent an important part of the problem, but by no means is it the only part. In his systematic investigation of school board decision making in Michigan, R. K. Norton (2007) finds that state and local governments rarely work with school districts on decisions related to siting, building, and renovating schools and that school board decision making is largely driven by competition with neighboring districts and demographic shifts. In fact, state law puts local schools outside the jurisdiction of local land use planning.

The responses that are taking shape as part of movements focusing on smart growth, sustainability, livability, or healthy communities, all call for both a shift in the way we think about school siting and a change in the strategies we use. Their overarching goal is to balance objectives related to producing the most up-to-date educational programs and facilities as possible, with strategies designed to produce communities that are more environmentally sound (e.g., policies that support alternatives to automobile transport and preserve historic buildings); are "communities of opportunity" (that provide access to good schools, public services, and economic prospects; de Souza Briggs 2005, 8); and are socially equitable (i.e., where access is not determined by race, religion, or class).

The strategies recommended by these various movements typically encourage citizen and stakeholder participation and call for issues to be addressed in a way that recognizes their interconnectedness. For example, it is now accepted that land use decisions have important consequences for transportation systems and vice versa. When local governments allow low-density developments in open, green areas at a distance from existing settlements, they consider the implications for road construction in collaboration with transportation departments. If the planning is done well, it includes stakeholders from groups affected by both land use and transportation decisions including environment advocacy groups.

Strategies to create "healthy communities" have drawn attention to the consequences of decisions such as these on the health of those who live in the communities. For example, land use and transportation patterns that contribute to an increase in the use of motor vehicles and in distances traveled cause an increase in air pollution and countless cases of respiratory illnesses in children. The definition of health used here refers to "a state of complete physical, mental and social well-being and not merely the absence of disease or infirmity" (WHO 1948).

The movement promoting healthy communities has been active around the world for several decades. It began with a focus on healthy cities and has evolved to address healthy and sustainable communities more broadly. Trevor Hancock, one of the pioneers of the healthy communities movement, defines healthy and sustainable communities as "communities where natural and historic resources are preserved, jobs are available, sprawl is contained, neighborhoods are secure, education is lifelong, transportation and health care are accessible, and all citizens have opportunities to improve the quality of their lives." (2000, 152) The movement encompasses a number of major national and international initiatives including the International Healthy Cities Foundation, which supports the International Healthy Cities Movement, the U.S. Housing and Urban Development (HUD) Healthy Communities Transformation Initiative and the Ontario Healthy Communities Coalition in Canada. It also includes hundreds of local initiatives whose work falls under the "healthy communities" umbrella. Among other goals, these movements seek to introduce objectives related to the protection of human health into public decision making with the ultimate goal of creating environments for health.

In the absence of a healthy communities approach, the health consequences of particular school locations or investments are not likely to be taken into consideration when deciding where to build new schools and whether to renovate existing facilities. For example, when schools are located far from residences, they make it impossible for children and other members of school communities to walk or bike to school and thereby deprive them of an opportunity for physical activity as part of daily routines. And when schools are sited near a freeway or high-traffic roadway, an industrial facility, an underground gasoline pipeline, a former land-fill, a waste disposal facility, or other environmental hazards, they threaten the health and safety of children as well as teachers, administrators, and others who work at schools through their impact on air and water quality. The costs of these problems are shifted to the health sector and therefore are seldom considered by either school districts or local governments.

TRENDS IN SCHOOL SIZE AND LOCATION

Whether by design or not, current school siting practices often produce schools only accessible by car. Public schools have also been increasing in size and drawing students from larger areas. In the second half of the twentieth century, the total number of elementary and secondary public schools fell by 69 percent, and their average enrollment increased more than four times (Walberg 1992, 3). Large new schools typically are placed in outlying areas because sites are available and land prices are low.

Concern about the increasing size of schools and their location in places far from residences arises out of two additional perspectives: concern about preventing loss of rural open space and concern about revitalizing deteriorating urban places (Norton 2007, 478). Schools contribute to urban sprawl and the loss of rural open space even if they do not cause it.

A number of people have written about the extreme inequality in spending on schools (Kozol 1991; Lewis 2008). Unequal allocation of funds to schools influences the quality of neighborhoods around the schools, which in turn influences the quality of schools—a downward spiral exacerbated by the draw of new schools being built in suburbs and exurbs (Baum 2004; Clapper 2006). Schools become part of the infrastructure that gives value to new developments. They help attract professionals with children to the district. A new school also may induce families with children to move out of neighborhoods with older schools in the same district and relocate near the new school.

FACTORS INFLUENCING SCHOOL LOCATION DECISION MAKING

Few studies exist that systematically investigate the factors influencing school district decisions about whether to upgrade or expand existing schools and where to locate new schools. These may include federal and state mandates and standards, concerns about traffic safety at the site or possible land use conflicts, and whether or not there is any coordination between school districts and local governments. Much of the evidence for the effect of these on school siting is anecdotal, with the exception of Norton (2007); N. C. McDonald (this volume); and Emily Lees and others (2008).

There are a number of federal and state mandates that address issues of health, safety, and rights of access that may influence school siting. Some affect the design of school buildings and others affect the methods or processes required during construction or renovation of schools. School construction standards may also influence school siting decisions in that they tend to make it less costly to construct new buildings than to renovate older ones (Beaumont 2003; Beaumont and Pianca 2000; Gurwitt 2004). Furthermore, minimum acreage standards for elementary, middle, and high schools may favor certain locations as they often can only be met in open areas at the outskirts of urbanized zones.

In addition, in most cases, little or no coordination exists between local governments and school districts regarding schools or infrastructure planning (see discussion in Norton 2007, 480). Only a few states such as Maryland and Florida have "adequate public facilities ordinances." In general, sites actually chosen may be the best of a set of far-from-ideal options. They could have been donated, required as a condition of development approval, obtained from another governmental unit, or any number of circumstances that did not consider health factors or other socioeconomic considerations.

POTENTIAL HEALTH CONSEQUENCES OF CURRENT SCHOOL SITING PRACTICES

Physical Activity

Schools not located near residences make it impossible for most children to walk or bike to school, thereby missing an opportunity for physical activity as part of daily routines. Regular physical activity reduces the risk of a number of chronic diseases, helps control weight, and improves mental health, all of which results in less use of health services (U.S. DHHS 1996). National data indicate that only one-third of all American youth met current recommended levels of physical activity (Eaton et al. 2008). Body weight in children and adolescents continues to increase, with the prevalence of overweight reaching 17.1 percent in 2004 (Ogden et al. 2006).

Public health researchers and practitioners look to walking for transportation as a new opportunity to increase levels of physical activity and help control weight. Over the past twenty-five years, national trends in cigarette smoking, high blood pressure, and high blood cholesterol have been positive whereas levels of obesity and physical inactivity have not improved (DHHS 1996). A recent analysis of trends over time showed a 70 percent decrease in walking or biking to school across all grade levels between 1969 and 2001 (McDonald 2007).

Studies have shown that people in general are more likely to adopt and sustain moderate physical activity routines such as those involving walking than vigorous exercise regimes. Therefore, public health recommendations have moved from emphasizing fitness and exercise programs of vigorous intensity to emphasizing physical activity of moderate intensity such as walking for transportation. The most recent Centers for Disease Control and Prevention and American College of Sports Medicine (CDC-ACSM) guidelines recommend that all adults perform thirty or more minutes of moderate-intensity physical activity five days a week—if not every day of the week (Haskell et al. 2007). The fact that the guidelines now include the option of accumulating the minimum of thirty minutes per day in multiple sessions lasting at least eight to ten minutes also makes them more applicable to community settings and walking for transportation (U.S. DHHS 1996). The guidelines for children and adolescents ages six to seventeen recommend one hour or more of physical activity daily; in addition, youth should include vigorous-intensity activity in this one hour at least three days a week (Haskell et al. 2007).

Traffic Safety

When schools are located within a road network with multilane roadways, no sidewalks, higher speed limits, and complex intersections, parents are unlikely to allow their children to walk or bike to school unless they have no other option. As more parents drive their children to school there is an increase in automobile congestion around the school and a less safe environment for the children who are walking and bicycling (Dumbaugh and Frank 2007). Another result of the growing distance between schools and homes is that many high school students now drive themselves to school, increasing the frequency of crashes and further contributing to traffic congestion.

Respiratory Health

As congestion increases, so does the amount of idling fumes around the school, which in turn leads to an increase in respiratory symptoms and diseases such as asthma (Bae et al. 2007; Samet et al. 2000). Furthermore, over 30 percent of public schools in the United States fall within a quarter mile of a major roadway, thereby resulting in a potentially increased risk for asthma and other chronic respiratory problems (Appatova et al. 2008). There are also concerns about the health risks of locating schools near other potential sources of air, soil, and water contamination (U.S. EPA 2009).

PURPOSE OF THE BOOK

The main goal of the book is to help planning and public health professionals, public decision makers, and citizens understand why it is important for government and school districts to work together on school siting and capital expenditures and how this will contribute to better health and quality-of-life outcomes for localities and regions. By addressing the likely consequences of current practices for human health and the health of community environments, it draws attention to compelling issues that are seldom considered when making decisions such as where to locate new schools, whether to upgrade existing facilities, or whether to create magnet programs in underenrolled schools.

ORGANIZATION OF THE BOOK

School Siting and Healthy Communities brings together in one volume recent work by researchers investigating a broad set of links between school siting and capital planning and the health, livability, and sustainability of communities and looking at the policy and governance issues involved. Most of the work featured here was originally presented at a Critical Issues Symposium on School Siting and Healthy Communities, convened by Drs. Rebecca Miles and Ruth Steiner and funded by the Florida State University (FSU) DeVoe L. Moore Center. The symposium was held in April 2008 at FSU in Tallahassee, Florida.

In "Health Impacts of School Siting: An Analytical Framework," Miles develops a framework for analyzing the potential health impacts of school siting practices. It is designed to support the decision making of parties seeking to balance the objective of producing the most up-to-date educational programs and facilities as possible with the desire to protect the health of school populations and surrounding communities. It includes two main tools: the web of associations, which portrays the interconnected factors that affect the health of school populations, and scenarios depicting typical school siting processes and the associated health impacts. In "School Siting in Suburban Areas," McDonald compares school planning practices in Maryland and northern Virginia, two states that are demographically similar but differ sharply in their land use policies. Although neither state had minimum acreage standards for schools, all districts had policies requiring relatively large sites, particularly for high schools. McDonald finds that school planners favored larger sites because of construction contingencies, the need to accommodate future growth in student enrollment, decreasing land availability, and the belief that the community wants schools to provide ample recreational fields. This suggests that recent efforts to eliminate state acreage guidelines will have no effect on siting practices in suburban areas. Her findings also indicate that the presence of Adequate Public Facilities Ordinances gave school planners leverage in their negotiations with developers and institutionalized collaboration between school and county planners. This was reflected in schools having a strong voice in development approval and comprehensive plans with more realistic pictures of future school needs.

In "School Construction Investments and Smart Growth in Two High-Growth States: Implications for Social Equity," Vincent and Filardo focus on capital outlay for school facilities in California and Florida and investigate school construction spending, a long-lived and spatially fixed strategic infrastructure investment. Building on previous research that finds tremendous growth in public school construction spending nationally due to enrollment growth, aging buildings, federal and state mandates, and changes in education, they examine the scale, scope, and distribution of public school facility investment in two high-growth states, California and Florida. Both states have had high enrollment growth, have increasingly diverse student bodies, and together have spent nearly $45 billion (in 2005 dollars) for construction costs. Their findings show substantial disinvestment in school facilities in lower-income and minority urban areas and suggest that this is yet another factor driving families with children from core cities and older suburbs.

Two of the chapters focus on Michigan, a low-growth state, which despite its economic decline, spawned a school building boom in the suburbs that masked massive school closures in urban centers and most rural parts of the state. In "The Implications of School Location Change for Healthy Communities in a Slow-Growth State: A Case Study of Michigan," Wyckoff, Adelaja, and Gibson argue that new school construction in the suburbs appears to be largely responding to sprawl driven by migration of families from the urban core and first-tier suburbs and a variety of institutional changes intended to improve school choice for parents of school-age children. In "Population Effects on School District Structure and School Size in Michigan," Adelaja, Gibson, and Hailu examine the relationship between population movement and the structure of schools in Michigan. They analyze in particular the roles of population, income, housing value, employment, poverty, race, and urban character in defining the structure of schools and school districts (school size and number of schools per district) by estimating two equations that explain school district structure. Their findings suggest that in general, school districts more readily respond to growing population by expanding the size of existing schools than by building new schools. High-income districts, however, tend to lean more in the direction of having more schools. The discovery that more expensive neighborhoods tend to feature smaller schools but more schools suggests that rising income may contribute to school proliferation in an attempt to avoid school overcrowding in high-income communities.

Three of the chapters focus on the consequences of school capital investment decisions and investigate the aspects of the built environment that play a role in parents' decisions about how children will travel to school. In "School Trips: Analysis of Factors Affecting Mode Choice in Three Metropolitan Areas," Ewing, Zhang, and Greenwald provide new evidence on the relationship between school location, the built environment around schools, and student travel. Based on data from three metropolitan areas, they find that students with shorter walk and bike times to school prove significantly more likely to walk or bike—which provides additional support for prioritizing neighborhood schools. Students who have access to sidewalks along main roads are also more likely to walk, a finding that confirms the importance of the sidewalk improvement projects included in many Safe Routes to School programs.

In "Policy Impacts on Mode Choice in School Transportation: An Analysis of Four Florida School Districts," Steiner et al. examine the transportation effects of coordinated planning policy in four Florida school districts in the Tampa Bay and Orlando areas. They argue that overlaps between three types of planning—transportation, land use, and school—represent three areas of coordinated planning: (1) multimodal planning, (2) coordinated school planning, and (3) Florida's Safe Ways to School. Using geographic information system (GIS) and survey analyses, they investigate how policy decisions about school siting and school attendance zones affect the number of children walking or bicycling to school. They find that Orlando-area school districts (Seminole [13.4 percent] and Orange [15.8 percent]) have greater numbers of students walking or bicycling than Tampa Bay–area school districts (Pasco [11 percent] and Hillsborough [7.6 percent]) among sampled schools. Preliminary results suggest that school districts with longer histories of coordinated school siting and multimodal planning tend to have more students walking and bicycling to school.

In "Where to Live and How to Get to School: Connecting Residential Location Choice and School Travel Mode Choice," Yang et al. focus on environmental factors that have the potential to increase the probability of children walking or biking to school and include the degree to which parents' preference for active school travel affects both their choice of where to live and their decisions about their children's travel to and from school. Based on survey data from approximately 1,200 households with young children attending elementary schools, their findings suggest parents' decision about allowing their children to walk or bike to school is not simply a reaction to environment conditions but a more conscious pursuit in accordance with their preference. Choosing residential location is an important process that parents have used to help them obtain the kind of environment congruent with their children's school travel preference. However, the distribution of housing opportunities surrounding schools could place a limit on the extent to which residential location choice follows school travel preference.

In "Safe Schools: Identifying Potential Threats to the Health and Safety of Schoolchildren in North Carolina," Salvesen and Zambito focus on a different set of consequences of school location decisions: exposure to environmental threats. Every school day, nearly fifty million children spend six hours or more at one of the nation's approximately 97,000 public schools. Most of these schools are located in safe, healthy environments. However, numerous school campuses are located on or dangerously close to an environmental threat such as an industrial facility, underground gasoline pipeline, former landfill, earthquake fault zone, waste disposal facility, railroad track, floodplain, or other hazards that threaten the health and safety of children as well as teachers, administrators, and others who work at schools.

Using North Carolina as a case study, Salvesen and Zambito investigate the extent to which public schools are located close to environmental hazards and whether state policies for siting schools adequately address the potential threats posed by such hazards. Their findings suggest that 1,445 public schools in North Carolina, nearly half of all schools in the state, are in close proximity to an environmental hazard, calling into question the adequacy of state policies guiding local school boards in selecting sites for schools. They also found that environmental hazards were disproportionately located near schools with a higher percentage of minority or poor students.

In "Engaging the Public in Comprehensive Planning and Design for Healthy Schools," Shoshkes develops a case study from planning practice. She tells the story of a highly innovative pair of national school design competitions in New Jersey: design competitions for a large new high school in the city of Perth Amboy and for renovation and expansion of the one-hundred-year-old Robbins Elementary School in a historic neighborhood of the city of Trenton. The overarching goal of these projects was to create a model process to engage the public in comprehensive planning and design for healthy schools that serve as centers of community life that could be replicated in New Jersey—where an $8 billion court-ordered school construction program was under way—as well as in other places undertaking school construction. Shoshkes describes the model process, the problems that arose during implementation, how those were addressed, and the lessons for both policy and practice.

REFERENCES

Ad Hoc Coalition for Healthy School Siting. 2008. Revising CDE school siting policy documents. Memo to State Superintendent of Public Instruction. California Department of Education, Sacramento, CA.

Agron, J. April 2009. 38th annual maintenance and operations cost study: Schools. *American School and University* 81(9): 20–23.

American Society of Civil Engineers (ASCE). 2009. Report card for America's infrastructure. http://www.asce.org/reportcard/2009/grades.cfm.

Appatova, A. S., P. H. Ryan, G. K. LeMasters, and S. A. Grinshpun. 2008. Proximal exposure of public schools and students to major roadways: A nationwide US survey. *Journal of Environmental Planning and Management* 51 (5): 631.

Bae, C., G. Sandlin, A. Bassok, and S. Kim. 2007. Settlement patterns in FAPS (Freeway Air Pollution Sheds): The case of central Seattle and the Portland region. *Environment and Planning B* 34(1): 154–70.

Baum, Howell S. 2004. Smart growth and school reform: What if we talked about race and took community seriously? *Journal of the American Planning Association* 70 (1): 14–26.

Beaumont, Constance E. 2003. *State policies and school facilities: How states can support or undermine neighborhood schools and community preservation.* Washington, DC: National Trust for Historic Preservation.

Beaumont, Constance E., and Elizabeth G. Pianca. 2000. *Historic neighborhood schools in the age of sprawl: Why Johnny can't walk to school.* Washington, DC: National Trust for Historic Preservation.

Clapper, Michael. 2006. School design, site selection, and the political geography of race in postwar Philadelphia. *Journal of Planning History* 5 (3): 241–63.

de Souza Briggs, X. 2005. More pluribus, less unum? In *The geography of opportunity: Race and housing choice in metropolitan America*, ed. X. de Souza Briggs. Washington, DC: Brookings Institution Press.

Dumbaugh, E., and Frank, L. D. 2007. Traffic safety and safe routes to schools: Synthesizing the empirical evidence. *Transportation Research Record: Journal of the Transportation Research Board* (2009): 89–97.

Eaton, D. K., Kann, L., Kinchen, S., Shanklin, S., Ross, J., Hawkins, J., et al. 2008. Youth risk behavior surveillance—United States, 2007. *MMWR Surveillance Summaries* 57 (4): 1–131.

Ewing, R., and W. Greene. 2003. Travel and environmental implications of school siting. EPA 231-R-03-004. Washington, DC: U.S. EPA. http://www.epa.gov/smartgrowth/pdf/school_travel.pdf.

Frankenberg, Erica, and Chungmei Lee. 2002. *Race in American public schools: Rapidly resegregating school districts.* Cambridge, MA: The Civil Rights Project, Harvard University.

Gurwitt, R. 2004. Edge-ucation: What compels communities to build schools in the middle of nowhere? *Governing* 17 (6): 22–26.

Hancock, T. 2000. Healthy communities must also be sustainable communities. *Public Health Reports* 115, 151–56.

Haskell, W. L., I.-M. Lee, R. R. Pate, K. E. Powell, S. N. Blair, B. A. Franklin, C. A. Macera, G. W. Heath, P. D. Thompson, and A. Bauman. 2007. Physical activity and public health: Updated recommendation for adults from the American College of Sports Medicine and the American Heart Association. *Med. Sci. Sports Exerc.*, 39 (8): 1423–434.

Kouri, Christopher. 1999. *Wait for the bus: How low country school site selection and design deter walking to school and contribute to urban sprawl.* Charleston: South Carolina Coastal Conservation League.

Kozol, J. 1991. *Savage inequalities: Children in America.* New York: Crown Publishers.

Lees, Emily, David Salvesen, and Elizabeth Shay. 2008. Collaborative school planning and active schools: A case study of Lee County, Florida. *Journal of Health Politics Policy and Law* 33 (3): 595–615.

Lewis, J. H. 2008. Race and regions. In *Urban and regional policies for metropolitan livability*, ed. D. K. Hamilton and P. S. Atkins. 126–66. Armonk, NY: M. E. Sharpe.

McDonald, Noreen C. 2007. Active transportation to school: Trends among U.S. schoolchildren, 1969–2001. *American Journal of Preventive Medicine* 32 (6): 509–16.

Norton, Richard K. 2007. Planning for school facilities: School board decision-making and local coordination in Michigan. *Journal of Planning Education and Research* 26 (4): 478.

Ogden, C. L., M. Carroll, L. Curtin, M. McDowell, C. Tabak, and K. Flegal. 2006. Prevalence of overweight and obesity in the United States, 1999–2004. *Journal of the American Medical Association* 295 (13): 1549–55.

Orfield, G., M. D. Bachmeier, D. R. James, and T. Eitle. 1997. *Deepening segregation in American public schools: A special report from the Harvard Project on School Desegregation. Excellence in Education* 30 (2): 5–24.

Papas, M. A., A. J. Alberg, R. Ewing, K. J. Helzlsouer, T. L. Gary, and A. C. Klassen. 2007. The built environment and obesity. *Epidemiologic Reviews*, 29, 1, 129–43.

Salvesen, David, and Philip Hervey. 2003. *Good schools, good neighborhoods: The impacts of state and local school board policies on the design and location of schools in North Carolina.* Chapel Hill, NC: Center for Urban and Regional Studies, University of North Carolina at Chapel Hill.

Samet, J., F. Dominici, F. Curriero, I. Coursac, and S. Zeger. 2000. Fine particulate air pollution and mortality in 20 U.S. cities, 1987–1994. *New England Journal of Medicine* 343: 1742–49.

U.S. Department of Health and Human Services (U.S. DHHS). 1996. *Physical activity and health: A report of the Surgeon General.* Atlanta, GA: U.S. Department of Health and Human Services, Centers for Disease Control and Prevention, National Center for Chronic Disease Prevention and Health Promotion.

U.S. Environmental Protection Agency (U.S. EPA). 2009. Siting of school facilities. http://www.epa.gov/schools/siting.html.

Walberg, H. 1992. On local control: Is bigger better? In *Source book on school and district size, cost, and quality*, 118–34. Minneapolis: Hubert H. Humphrey Institute of Public Affairs, University of Minnesota.

World Health Organization (WHO). 1948. Preamble to the constitution of the World Health Organization as adopted by the International Health Conference, New York, June 19–22, 1946.

Health Impacts of School Siting
An Analytical Framework

REBECCA MILES

EARLIER IN THE HISTORIES OF URBAN PLANNING AND PUBLIC HEALTH, THERE WAS A greater awareness of the links between the urban built environment and the health of populations. In fact, the emergence of urban planning as a profession and academic discipline had its basis in nineteenth-century public health initiatives, including tenement housing reforms, the construction of urban water supply and sewerage systems, and the design of parks and playgrounds. The work of professionals in the two fields diverged over much of the twentieth century, with public health focusing on the medical model and urban planning emphasizing land use and the physical environment.

Since the 1970s, however, it has been recognized that major improvements in health can result from improving our physical and social environments and changing our personal and collective lifestyles rather than simply investing further in the health care system which focuses on those who are already sick. A growing literature in planning reflects these concerns, focusing on population health and the built environment (see, for example, Miles-Doan and Thompson 1999; Saegert, Klitzman, and Freudenberg 2003; Frank, Andresen, and Schmid 2004; Forsyth et al. 2007; Miles and Jacobs 2008). The built environment includes all buildings (e.g., schools, workplaces), homes, roads and other components of transportation systems, utilities (i.e., electrical transmission lines, water, and waste disposal systems), parks and recreation areas, fixtures, and other spaces created or significantly modified by humans.

As part of the built environment, school facilities provide a compelling focus for concerns about the effect of environments and planning on population health. School buildings house a large number of Americans—one in five every day—and school users spend extended periods of time in them in very close quarters (Frumkin 2006, 3). There is growing recognition that where we invest in schools, and not just how much, has important consequences for health (particularly for children) that are rarely factored into public decision making about school facilities.

In practice, school siting involves a bundle of decisions and activities related to the location of investments in school facilities. Location-related decisions include whether to build new schools or to upgrade or expand existing schools, where to locate new schools, and whether and where to close or merge existing schools. Location-related decisions are also made about the design of school environments, such as the compactness of buildings, the location and quantity of student parking, the provision of sidewalks on main roadways linking schools and homes, and the proximity of tracks and playing fields to high-volume roadways or industrial sites.

As is true for public planning decisions in general, the consequences for human health of particular school siting decisions depend on a number of interconnected factors—building conditions, adjacent land uses, the mix of housing types, and transportation systems—that are in turn affected by the actions of different public agencies ranging from school districts to transportation departments. Decisions about school siting, however, often reflect "silo thinking," a metaphor suggesting that agencies are like silos that stand alone, not interacting with other stakeholders. Stakeholders in school siting decisions are all those who have an interest in, or may be affected by, where schools are located.

Decisions about where to locate new schools and other investments in school facilities are typically within the sole purview of school districts. State and local governments rarely work with school districts on decisions related to siting, building, and renovating schools. Likewise, although school districts use planners' population forecasts when deciding whether and where new schools are needed, they are rarely involved when state and local governments carry out the visioning that is incorporated into population forecasts and when planners develop land use, transportation, or housing plans.

This chapter discusses an analytical framework that can be used by school siting stakeholders interested in balancing the objective of producing the most up-to-date educational programs and facilities as possible with the desire to protect the health of school populations and surrounding communities. It includes two main tools: the web of associations, which portrays the interconnected factors that affect the health of school populations, and scenarios depicting typical school siting processes and the associated health impacts. The analytical framework is likely to be most effective when used in the early stages of planning for school capital investments, that is, at the time when a range of alternative strategies are identified and evaluated. These tools may be used in conjunction with a full health impact assessment (WHO 1999) that would result in evidence-based recommendations for selecting among alternatives or on their own to facilitate collaboration among stakeholders.

TOOL 1: A WEB OF ASSOCIATIONS

The web of associations tool (fig. 1) is based on the Social Determinants of Health framework developed by Schultz and Northridge (2004; see also Galea, Freudenberg, and Vlahov 2005).

It portrays how as part of the built and social environments of communities, the location and design of school facilities influence the environmental stressors and toxins school occupants and the school community as a whole are exposed to daily; their levels of safety and security; the extent to which physical activity, healthy eating, and other health behaviors are supported; and whether the school community (including students, teachers, staff, volunteers, and visitors) is surrounded by a "good" social environment—that is, one that provides access to good schools and public services, safe streets, and economic prospects (de Souza Briggs 2005, 8).

The location and design of school facilities ultimately contribute to population health through these interconnected pathways (fig. 1). Population health refers both to health outcomes—such as injuries, respiratory symptoms or infections, or weight status—and to the distribution of health outcomes across subpopulations. When applied in a specific context, the web of associations tool therefore can be used to examine whether certain subgroups—racial

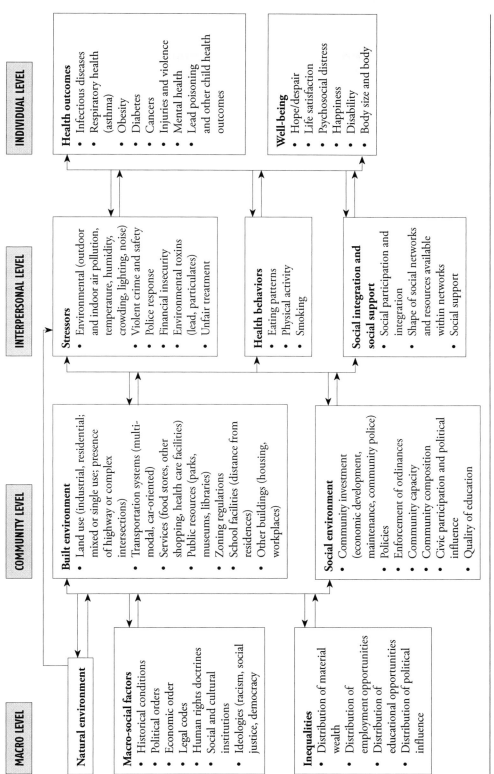

Figure 1. Tool 1: A Web of Associations
Source: Adapted from Schultz and Northridge (2004)

or ethnic minorities, low-income children—are likely to experience a disproportionate share of negative health effects associated with a particular proposed site. Tool users may also want to incorporate into their analysis the direction and strength of the association between characteristics of schools environments and population health. Because of a lack of scientific evidence specific to school populations, the level of risk associated with many of the links can only be assessed qualitatively.

Adjacent Land Uses

A school's location, and in particular the land uses of adjacent plots, affects the extent to which school occupants are exposed daily to a number of environmental stressors, including outdoor (ambient) air pollution and environmental toxins. There is now compelling scientific evidence that levels of ambient air pollution are higher near congested roadways or interstates and near polluting industrial facilities (summarized in Hricko 2006). And there is emerging evidence that a substantial proportion of school populations is affected. A recent study reports that "a large percentage of public schools and students (approximately ⅓ to ½, depending on the metropolitan area) were found in close proximity (≤400 m) to Interstate, US or state highways, the major arteries for diesel-powered vehicles and motor vehicle traffic" (Appatova et al. 2008, 9).

Children are especially vulnerable, as their lungs continue to grow until adulthood; they therefore breathe in more air relative to their size than adults and develop respiratory infections more often than adults (American Academy of Pediatrics 2004). Health impacts are likely to be greater when tracks or playing fields are located next to such pollution sources. Children breathe harder when they exercise. Those who play outdoor team sports and spend more time outside in high-ozone communities have been found to have a higher incidence of newly diagnosed asthma (McConnell et al. 2002). Ambient air may also enter buildings through open windows and doors or penetrate through cracks in walls, floors, or ceilings.

Services

The types of services located near schools can have an impact on population health. Convenience stores and fast-food eateries have been of particular interest because they tend to cluster around schools in the United States (Austin et al. 2005), and fast-food consumption is linked to poorer quality eating patterns: more total energy, more energy per gram of food, more total fat, more total carbohydrates, more added sugars, more sugar-sweetened beverages, less fiber, fewer fruits, and nonstarchy vegetables; links to weight status are found in some studies but not all (French et al. 2001; Bowman et al. 2004).

There are also potential health consequences associated with the absence of desirable destinations within walking distance of high schools. Although most high schools implement closed-campus policies, many students have the option of traveling to nearby eateries for lunch (Wechsler et al. 2001). Locating high schools far from commercial areas increases the distance students must drive in order to go out for lunch. This further increases traffic emissions and exposes students to the risk of injury due to a motor vehicle collision.

Transportation Systems

The design of campus and neighborhood transportation systems relates to school location and a number of health behaviors and outcomes, including the likelihood of traffic-related injury, levels of physical activity, and the number of respiratory symptoms and infections. Motor vehicle–related injuries are the leading cause of death for children in the United States (CDC 2007). However, the role of the built environment along the route to school in these injuries is unclear. One study finds that the presence of a driveway or turning bay at the school entrance decreases both crash occurrence and injury severity (Clifton and Kreamer-Fults 2007).

A recent synthesis of the literature on the effectiveness of safety countermeasures incorporated into Safe Routes to School programs suggested uneven results. Safe Routes to School is a program designed to address parents' concerns and encourage them to allow their children to walk or cycle to school (FHA 2009). It typically includes sidewalks, crosswalks, and applications to achieve slow speeds for motor vehicles, along with education and enforcement components (Dumbaugh and Frank 2007). Only sidewalks and raised medians showed clear evidence of reducing the incidence of pedestrian crashes in the general population and "only active police enforcement and speed reducing traffic calming applications were found to result in meaningful changes in behaviors that result in pedestrian crashes" (Dumbaugh and Frank 2007, 95). However, none of the safety countermeasures had been evaluated specifically for their effects among children.

The design of the campus and neighborhood transportation system is also likely to play a role in supporting or constraining school occupants' health behaviors, such as physical activity, and hence their health outcomes, such as obesity and diabetes. There is a large body of literature investigating the extent to which distance between homes and schools and the characteristics of the street environment near schools are associated with whether or not children walk or bike to school (see, among others, Ewing and Greene 2003; Ewing, Schroeer, and Greene 2004; Boarnet et al. 2005; McDonald 2006; Schlossberg et al. 2006; McMillan 2007). The distance between homes and schools, which determines the number of children who live within walking or cycling distance from school and therefore have the opportunity to walk or cycle to school, is the factor that has been found consistently to influence active travel to school. The distance between home and school also affects transit time for children, with implications for more or less time for sleep, homework, and physical activity. It also affects the commuting time for parents, and longer commutes are in turn associated with stress and less time for physical activity.

Finally, the design of the campus and neighborhood transportation system influences school occupants' exposure to environmental stressors and environmental toxins when children are dropped off and picked up near where school buses idle or when school buses idle near the entrance to the school where students congregate. The health effects of diesel exhaust from older school buses include eye and respiratory irritation, asthma exacerbation, and an increased risk of cancer (U.S. EPA 2002; Hricko 2006).

Community Composition

The mix of housing available near schools affects community composition (fig. 1)—that is, the mix of families that are able to live close enough for children to walk or bike to school. For example, zoning ordinances that only allow single-family residences near a school limit the number of children who can live near the school and exclude families with limited incomes. Zoning that allows multifamily housing increases both the number and potentially also the income diversity of children who have the opportunity to walk or bike to school.

Condition of School Buildings

The quality of the school buildings also affects exposure to environmental stressors. For example, school buildings with poor control of temperature and humidity levels are likely to have high levels of mold and mildew; occupants with allergies to mold can suffer adverse effects, which in turn are associated with respiratory health problems (Geller 2006).

Family- and Individual-Level Determinants of Health

One of the most robust findings in the social determinants of health literature is the important effect of socioeconomic status. It influences health outcomes by imposing constraints or creating opportunities that in turn help shape stressors, health behaviors, and health outcomes (fig. 1). For example, families' resources influence where students and their families live and therefore the place-based stressors they face on a day-to-day basis. Also important are individual-level characteristics such as age, race, educational achievement, family history, and genetic makeup. Family socioeconomic status and whether or not a family owns a vehicle are two of the most important determinants of active travel to school.

TOOL 2: SCHOOL SITING SCENARIOS

The scenarios developed here all represent typical school siting processes. They can be used to clarify the pathways by which school community environments in a particular context may affect population health and guide consideration of locally appropriate alternative strategies that better protect health. The first scenario examines the implications of locating a new high school far from existing residences. The second focuses on siting a new elementary school within a residential area. And the third scenario examines the potential health impacts of creating a magnet program in an existing urban school.

Scenario 1 (fig. 2) typically occurs because school districts must find plots large enough to meet existing regulations and the public's expectations regarding recreational and computing facilities; large sites in built-up areas are often only found at the edges of existing settlements.

The main potential health consequences of this school siting scenario are associated with the distance between homes and the school (a characteristic of the built environment). There are also potential effects of the built environment associated with adjacent land uses such as high-traffic roadways or industrial land uses (fig. 1). Distance determines what proportion of the student body has the opportunity to walk or bike to school and is also the factor most consistently found to influence whether or not children actually walk or bike to school (see, among others, Ewing and Greene 2003; Ewing, Schroeer and Greene 2004; Boarnet et

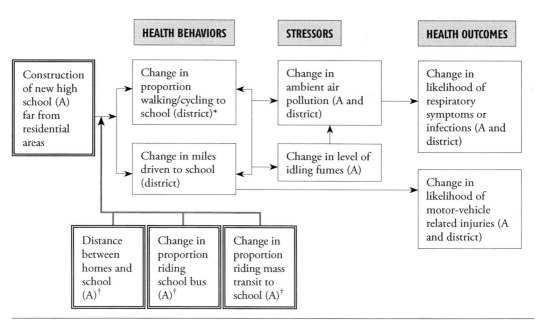

Figure 2. Scenario 1 Depicting Potential Health Impacts of Siting a New High School at a Distance from Residences

* Amount of change depends on proportion of transfers from within the district who walked or cycled to school previously
† Size of the effect on miles driven and proportion of students walking or cycling to school depends on this factor

al. 2005; McDonald 2006; Schlossberg et al. 2006; McMillan 2007). Schools built far from residences make it impossible for students to walk or cycle to school, thereby depriving them of an opportunity for physical activity as part of their daily routines. Physical activity plays an important role in controlling body weight, and a lack of physical activity is associated with obesity and diabetes.

Building a high school far from residences is also likely to contribute to increased miles driven to and from school in private vehicles during school opening and closing times and to increased idling fumes as students are dropped off or picked up at the school entrance. The size of this effect and the health impacts, depend on the proportion of students who ride school buses and whether or not mass transit is available and reasonably convenient. When students use the mass-transit system, they not only reduce their impact on ambient air pollution but also add a significant amount of physical activity to their daily routines and reduce their exposure to the risk of traffic-related injury. A recent study found that "Americans who use transit spend a median of 19 minutes daily walking to and from transit; 29 percent achieve 30 minutes of physical activity a day solely by walking to and from transit" (Besser and Dannenberg 2005).

The health impacts of increased idling fumes are particularly problematic when student drop-off and pickup occurs at the entrance to the main school building where some students are arriving by foot or bicycle and where students are walking from parked vehicles into the building. In some school environments, this is also where school buses are idling as they pick up or drop off students. Potential health consequences associated with this scenario include an increased incidence of respiratory symptoms and infections such as asthma.

At the district level, the health impact of siting a new high school far from residences depends on the extent to which it attracts current residents of the area whose children previously walked or cycled to school. School quality is one of the main factors that parents consider when choosing a neighborhood. If new schools with their updated equipment and facilities are perceived to provide a higher quality of education, they are likely to draw students from existing schools. If these students walked or cycled to their old school but are driven or drive themselves to their new school, they contribute to an overall reduction in school-related physical activity.

When locating a high school far from residences is the only financially feasible option for a district, decisions can be made at the school-siting phase that maximize opportunities for physical activity and minimize the effect on ambient air pollution. These decisions are not likely to be popular and will require widespread public education on the issues. Limiting the construction of parking spaces while making mass transit widely available is a strategy that has been effective in reducing motor vehicle commuting to many college and university campuses (Balsas 2003; Brown, Hess, and Shoup 2003; see also McDonald Librera, and Deakin 2004). This would require school districts to work with mass-transit agencies. Limiting student commuting to the new school also has implications for the design of any roadways associated with the school; decisions about capacity and design features would need to be coordinated with departments of transportation. If parking areas are to be built, they can be located at a distance from buildings; this removes a safety hazard near school entrances and introduces the opportunity for walking to and from the parking areas as part of daily routines.

Scenario 2 (fig. 3) illustrates the potential health impacts of siting an elementary school within walking distance of residences and designing or upgrading the surrounding environment to be supportive of active travel to school. Such a scenario typically occurs when an

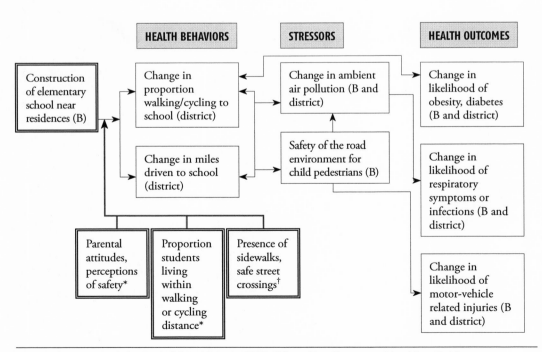

Figure 3. Scenario 2 Depicting Potential Health Impacts of Building a New Elementary School Near Residences

* Size of the effect on walking or cycling to schools also depends on these factors
† Size of the effect on safety of the road environment also depends on these factors

elementary school is built within a new development. In more recent years, there has been explicit attention paid to siting such schools and designing surrounding roadways to maximize the number of students who walk to school, thereby reducing the likelihood of high school–related traffic volume and congestion on local roads and at the same time making it safer for students who do walk or cycle to school. Such strategies may include allowing higher-density, affordable housing to be built immediately surrounding the school. In scenario 2, the school and nearby roadways become part of the public infrastructure that substantially increases property values in the new development (Vincent 2006).

As part of the built environment, schools are connected to transportation systems, land use patterns, and neighborhood social environments that may or may not support walking and cycling to school (fig. 1). The density and affordability of nearby residences influence what proportion of students live within walking or cycling distance. Transportation systems influence traffic speed on streets near the school and the safety of intersections and therefore influence both the likelihood of injury to pedestrians and the likelihood that parents will allow their children to walk or cycle to school. Sidewalks separate student walkers from traffic and may influence vehicle speeds, thereby affecting the likelihood both of active travel to school and of injury (fig. 3). Evidence for both links is mixed (McMahon et al. 1999; Ewing Zhang, and Greenwald, this volume).

Neighborhood social environments affect perceptions of safety, which in turn influence parents' decisions about their child's travel to school (McMillan 2007). Whether or not students actually walk or cycle to school also depends on family- and individual-level characteristics such as parental attitudes (McMillan 2007) and the age and sex of the student. Safe Routes to School is an increasingly popular program designed to address parents' concerns (FHA 2009) Another promising approach known as Crime Prevention through Environmental Design (CPTED) addresses both physical and affective (emotional and behavioral) components of an environment (Schneider 2006). Specific measures include, among others, replacing demeaning advertising or graffiti on the route to school with inspirational artwork or student-created posters, trimming street and campus greenery to levels that allow for natural surveillance while maintaining contact with nature, and providing consistent lighting throughout the school environment (Schneider 2006, 256).

There are additional health impacts associated with the failure to modernize and upgrade existing school facilities even as new schools are built in rapidly developing areas. Old buildings need to be modernized and existing facilities upgraded in order to support today's educational programs, such as early childhood education and technology and science education. Upgrading existing school facilities is also important for protecting the physical and mental health of school occupants. For example, aging buildings with poor control of temperature and humidity levels are associated with respiratory health problems and lower motivation among students. Poor ventilation can also boost asthma rates and respiratory illness (fig. 1).

Scenario 3 (fig. 4) illustrates the health impacts of a common strategy for improving existing urban schools: creating magnet programs. By increasing enrollment, magnet programs may allow an older school to remain open and available to the community. Magnet programs may also help schools with an increasingly low-income student population improve school quality by attracting students from higher-income families.

The main potential health impacts of creating magnet programs in existing urban schools, both positive and negative, arise from the fact that magnet programs are designed to attract students from outside school attendance boundaries. This in turn is likely to be associated

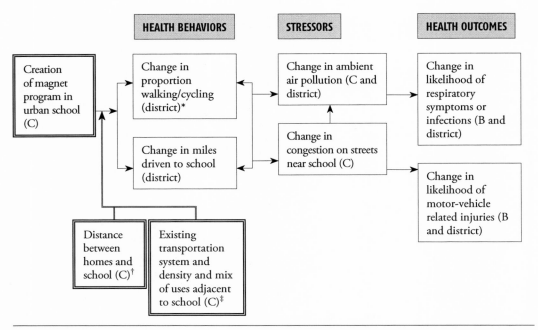

Figure 4. Scenario 3 Depicting Potential Health Impacts of Creating a Magnet Program in an Urban School

* Depends on proportion of transfers from within the district walking/biking to school previously
† Size of the effect on miles driven depends on this factor
‡ Size of the effect on congestion on streets near the new school depends on this factor

to varying degrees with greater distance between schools and residences and with changes in school quality; both are ultimately linked to health outcomes (fig. 1). As in figure 2, the distance between homes and schools is an important determinant of both the number of miles driven to school and the associated change in ambient air pollution; the size of the effect, however, depends in part on the proportion of students who travel to school by mass transit or by school bus (fig. 4).

In addition, because the magnet program in this scenario is in an urban school surrounded by a given set of neighborhood streets and land use patterns, there are substantial constraints to changing the school environment in order to promote population health. It is much more difficult and costly to retrofit school environments and surrounding local roadways to address potential conflicts between motor vehicles and student pedestrians and cyclists than to design and build new schools in fairly undeveloped areas or as part of new developments. Scenario 3 indicates that the extent of the problem depends to some extent on the density and land use mix of adjacent neighborhoods (fig. 4). The severity of the constraints also depends on the characteristics of the existing transportation system: speed limits; presence of sidewalks, crosswalks, and traffic-calming applications; intersections; and the location of mass-transit stops.

Whether or not there are other population health impacts associated with attracting students from outside school attendance boundaries depends largely on the extent to which school quality increases as a result. As part of the social environment, the quality of education is linked to levels of stressors, social integration, and social support and to health behaviors, which in turn influence health and well-being outcomes (fig. 1). Magnet programs can influence school quality by attracting more middle-class students to a school with a high proportion of low-income students or by opening up opportunities for low-income students to attend good schools outside their school attendance zone. A number of studies show that children from resource-poor families learn best when surrounded by middle-class classmates and that higher-achieving students do not suffer from being in economically diverse schools (Rusk 2008; Summers and Wolfe 1977). A number of school districts, in order to equalize educational opportunities, have implemented school economic integration programs including busing, controlled school choice, and housing programs (Rusk 2008). School choice programs include a wide array of options for allowing families to choose the school their children attend rather than being restricted to attending the school for which they are zoned.

DISCUSSION

The usefulness of the analytical framework developed here would be greater if there were more evidence specifically documenting the health effects of school community environments. There is a need to "grow" the evidence base by investigating the potential size and direction of population health impacts as a result of different combinations of policies and practices. The proliferation of programs with non-place-based eligibility for school attendance, such as magnet and charter schools, and school choice options of various kinds point to a rich area for future research (see, for example, Reback 2005). As discussed in scenario 3, school choice programs are likely to have negative health impacts due to the greater distances students must travel to attend their school of choice and the potential increase in ambient air pollution, traffic congestion, and the risk of motor vehicle–related collisions that results. At the same time, school choice programs may also yield important benefits. They are often developed to better utilize existing school capacity and therefore have important economic and environmental benefits. They may also contribute to reducing educational inequalities at the district level and therefore contribute to greater social equity, all of which indirectly influence population health.

As is the case with public planning strategies in general, however, more and better technical analyses of potential impacts, as important as they are, will not ensure "healthy" school siting processes alone. Most of the alternatives discussed here involve actions that are beyond the current authority of many school boards and therefore entail developing collaborations across government agencies and partnerships with a range of stakeholders. Furthermore, opportunities to transform school siting processes will vary from place to place since communities have differing levels of tolerance for change. Therefore, there is also a need for studies providing guidance as to *how* to integrate health considerations into the school site selection process in different political, economic, and social contexts. In the meantime, the precautionary principle would suggest that, given scientific uncertainty about the health risks posed by certain aspects of school environments, a critical criterion for deciding where to invest in school facilities should be to ensure at least basic safety for schoolchildren.

REFERENCES

American Academy of Pediatrics Committee on Environmental Health. 2004. Ambient air pollution: Health hazards to children. *Pediatrics* 114 (6): 1699–707.

Appatova, A. S., P. H. Ryan, G. K. LeMasters, and S. A. Grinshpun. 2008. Proximal exposure of public schools and students to major roadways: A nationwide US survey. *Journal of Environmental Planning and Management* 51 (5): 631.

Austin, S. B., S. J. Melly, B. N. Sanchez, A. Patel, S. Buka, and S. L. Gortmaker. 2005. Clustering of fast-food restaurants around schools: A novel application of spatial statistics to the study of food environments. *American Journal of Public Health* 95 (9): 1575–81.

Balsas, C. J. L. 2003. Sustainable transportation planning on college campuses. *Transport Policy* 10 (1): 35–49.

Besser, L. M., and A. L. Dannenberg. 2005. Walking to public transit steps to help meet physical activity recommendations. *American Journal of Preventive Medicine* 29 (4): 273–80.

Boarnet, Marlon G., Kristen Day, Craig Anderson, Tracy McMillan, and Mariela Alfonzo. 2005. California's *Safe Routes to School* program: Impacts on walking, bicycling, and pedestrian safety. *Journal of the American Planning Association* 71 (3): 301–17.

Bowman, S. A., S. L. Gortmaker, C. B. Ebbeling, M. A. Pereira, and D. S. Ludwig. 2004. Effects of fast-food consumption on energy intake and diet quality among children in a national household survey. *Pediatrics* 113 (1): 112–18.

Brown, J., D. B. Hess, and D. Shoup. 2003. Fare-free public transit at universities: An evaluation. *Journal of Planning Education and Research* 23 (1): 69–82.

Centers for Disease Control and Prevention (CDC). 1999-2007. Web-based Injury Statistics Query and Reporting System [online]. National Center for Injury Prevention and Control, Centers for Disease Control and Prevention (producer). www.cdc.gov/ncipc/wisqars.

Clifton, K. J., and K. Kreamer-Fults. 2007. An examination of the environmental attributes associated with pedestrian–vehicular crashes near public schools. *Accident Analysis and Prevention* 39 (4): 708–15.

de Souza Briggs, X. 2005. Introduction. In *The geography of opportunity: Race and housing choice in metropolitan America*, ed. X. de Souza Briggs, 1–16. Washington, DC: Brookings Institution Press.

Dumbaugh, E., and L. D. Frank. 2007. Traffic safety and *Safe Routes to Schools*: Synthesizing the empirical evidence. *Transportation Research Record: Journal of the Transportation Research Board* (2009): 89–97.

Ewing, R., and W. Greene. 2003. Travel and environmental implications of school siting. EPA 231-R-03-004. Washington, DC: U.S. EPA. http://www.epa.gov/smartgrowth/pdf/school_travel.pdf.

Ewing, R., W. Schroeer, and W. Greene. 2004. School location and student travel: Analysis of factors affecting mode choice. *Transportation Research Record* 1895 (1): 55–63.

Federal Highway Administration (FHA). 2009. Safe routes to school. http://safety.fhwa.dot.gov/saferoutes.

Forsyth, A. J., M. Oakes, K. H. Schmitz, and M. Hearst. 2007. Does residential density increase walking and other physical activity? *Urban Studies* 44 (4): 679–97.

Frank, L. D., M. A. Andresen, and T. L. Schmid. 2004. Obesity relationships with community design, physical activity, and time spent in cars. *American Journal of Preventive Medicine* 27 (2): 87–96.

French, S. A., M. Story, D. Neumark-Sztainer, J. A. Fulkerson, and P. Hannan. 2001. Fast food restaurant use among adolescents: Associations with nutrient intake, food choices and behavioral and psychosocial variables. *International Journal of Obesity* 25: 1823–33.

Frumkin, H. 2006. Introduction. In *Safe and healthy school environments*, ed. H. Frumkin, R. J. Geller, I. L. Rubin, and J. Nodvin. 3–10. New York: Oxford University Press.

Galea, S., N. Freudenberg, and D. Vlahov. 2005. Cities and population health. *Social Science and Medicine* 60 (5): 1017–33.

Geller, R. J. 2006. Mold. In *Safe and healthy school environments*, ed. H. Frumkin, R. J. Geller, and I. L. Rubin, 133–40. New York: Oxford University Press.

Hricko, A. 2006. Outdoor air pollution. In *Safe and healthy school environments*, ed. H. Frumkin, R. J. Geller, and I. L. Rubin, 141–152. New York: Oxford University Press.

McConnell, R., K. Berhane, F. Gilliland, S. J. London, T. Islam, W. J. Gauderman, E. Avol, H. G. Margolis, and J. M. Peters. 2002. Asthma in exercising children exposed to ozone: A cohort study. *The Lancet* 359 (9304): 386–91.

McDonald, N., S. Librera, and E. Deakin. 2004. Free transit for low-income youth: Experience in San Francisco Bay area, California. *Transportation Research Record* 1887 (1): 153–60.

McDonald, Noreen C. 2006. Exploratory analysis of children's travel patterns. *Transportation Research Record* (1977): 1–7.

McMahon, P. J., C. Duncan, J. R. Stewart, C. V. Zegeer, and A. J. Khattak. 1999. Analysis of factors contributing to "walking along roadway" crashes. *Transportation Research Record* 1674 (1): 41–48.

McMillan, T. E. 2007. The relative influence of urban form on a child's travel mode to school. *Transportation Research Part A* 41 (1): 69–79.

Miles, R., and D. E. Jacobs. 2008. Future directions in housing and public health: Findings from Europe with broader implications for planners. *Journal of the American Planning Association* 74 (1): 77–89.

Miles-Doan, R., and G. Thompson. 1999. The planning profession and pedestrian safety: Lessons from Orlando. *Journal of Planning Education and Research* 18: 211–20.

Reback, R. 2005. House prices and the provision of local public services: Capitalization under school choice programs. *Journal of Urban Economics* 57: 275–301.

Rusk, D. 2008. Housing policy *is* school policy. In *Urban and regional policies for metropolitan livability*, ed. D. K. Hamilton and P. S. Atkins, 204–31. New York: M. E. Sharpe.

Saegert, S., S. Klitzman, and N. Freudenberg. 2003. Healthy housing: A structured review of published evaluations of US interventions to improve health by modifying housing in the United States, 1990–2001. *American Journal of Public Health* 93 (9): 1552–59.

Schlossberg, M., J. Greene, P. P. Phillips, B. Johnson, and B. Parker. 2006. School trips: Effects of urban form and distance on travel mode. *Journal of the American Planning Association* 72 (3): 337–46.

Schneider, T. 2006. Violence and crime prevention through environmental design. In *Safe and healthy school environments*, ed. H. Frumkin, R. J. Geller, and I. L. Rubin, 251–69. New York: Oxford University Press.

Schultz, A., and M. Northridge. 2004. Social determinants of health: Implications of environmental health promotion. *Health Education & Behavior* 31 (4): 455–71.

Summers, A. A., and B. L. Wolfe. 1977. Do schools make a difference? *American Economic Review* 67 (4): 639–52.

U.S. Environmental Protection Agency. 2002. *Fact sheet: Diesel exhaust in the United States*. Washington, DC: EPA 420-F-02-048. U.S. EPA. http://www.epa.gov/OMS/retrofit/documents/420f03022.pdf.

U.S. Environmental Protection Agency (EPA). 2009. *EPA Schools Monitoring Initiative fact sheet*. http://www.epa.gov/schoolair/about.html.

Vincent, Jeffrey M. 2006. Public schools as public infrastructure: Roles for planning researchers. *Journal of Planning Education and Research* 25 (4): 433–37.

Wechsler, H., N. Brener, S. Kuester, and C. Miller. 2001. Foodservice and foods and beverages available at school: Results from the school health policies and programs study. *Journal of School Health* 71: 313–24.

World Health Organization (WHO). 1999. Health impact assessment: Main concepts and suggested approach. *Gothenburg consensus paper*. Brussels: WHO Regional Office for Europe. www.apho.org .uk/resource/view.aspx?RID=44163.

School Siting in Suburban Areas
A Case Study of Maryland and Northern Virginia

NOREEN C. MCDONALD

DECIDING WHERE TO LOCATE NEW SCHOOLS IS DIFFICULT. FACILITY PLANNERS MUST balance the educational and recreational needs of students with construction and operating costs. But school planners are also tasked with meeting community desires for the ideal school. While "ideal" may mean "walkable" to some or "lots of ball fields" to others, the resulting school location choices will influence the long-term spatial development of the community.

Understanding how decisions about school location are made is critical because the United States has embarked on an unprecedented era of school construction (Agron 2004). School construction averaged over $20 billion per year between 2000 and 2007 (Vincent 2008). For example, New Jersey has implemented over $9 billion in school construction (New Jersey Schools Construction Corporation 2005). Ohio began a four-year, $10.5 billion program (Gurwitt 2004). California has passed over $80 billion in new K-12 school facilities construction measures since 1996 (Coleman 2004, Vincent 2009). Given the large amounts that will be spent on school construction in the next decade, we have a huge opportunity to design schools that are connected to communities, minimize transportation costs, and promote educational objectives—but only if we understand how school planners decide where to locate new schools and how state and local land use policies affect the acquisition of school sites.

To improve this understanding, this study looks at the process and factors influencing school planning in the suburbs of Washington, DC. Through interviews with school facility and land use planners in northern Virginia and Maryland, insights were obtained on how state and local education and land use policies affect site acquisition in suburban areas. An overview of the history of school siting and more detail on the case studies is available from McDonald (2010). This chapter is organized as follows: the first section describes the study area and the policy environment, the next section discusses how the counties in the study area acquire school sites, and the final section considers how the research findings inform the debate over school size and connections between smart growth and schools.

STUDY AREA

The goal in this study was to isolate the effects of state and local policy regimes on how school facility planners acquire sites for school construction. To do this, the northern Virginia and

Maryland suburbs of the Washington, DC, metropolitan area were selected for study. This approach yields a quasi-experimental design because the two study areas are demographically and economically similar but subject to very different state policy regimes. Maryland allows counties to use Adequate Public Facilities Ordinances (APFOs), which tie development approvals directly to school planning. Virginia does not allow APFOs; instead, development approvals hinge on "voluntary" proffers of cash or land. Not only are there large differences in the state policy environment, but also each county implements its land use regulations in slightly different ways, allowing investigations of intrastate variation.

The counties in the study—Fairfax, Fauquier, Loudoun, Prince William, and Stafford in Virginia and Anne Arundel, Frederick, Howard, Montgomery, and Prince George's in Maryland—are physically proximate and relatively similar demographically. The study area is high income with a range in median household incomes between $65,000 in Prince George's County and $100,000 in Fairfax County in 2006—much above the U.S. median income of $48,000 (table 1). Most of the study area is very diverse with many counties having a higher proportion of minorities than the United States as a whole.

METHOD

The goal was to understand how the state and local policy environment affected the way school facility planners approached the task of acquiring land for schools. To do this, semistructured interviews were conducted with school facility planners in the ten counties of the study area. The director or staff member of the County School Construction or School Facility agency was interviewed. In general, these agencies were subunits of the county board of education. Transcriptions of the interviews were reviewed to identify key themes. To document the policy environment, information available on state and county websites was analyzed and interviews with state and local planners were conducted to confirm and clarify information.

POLICY ENVIRONMENT

School Size Policies

Maryland has no state acreage guidelines. However, the Maryland Inter Agency Committee for Public School Construction (IAC), which has members from the State Departments of Education, General Services, and Planning, must approve each school site. While there is no legal requirement that schools locate in Priority Funding Areas (PFA)—defined as places where the state concentrates new infrastructure—there has been unofficial encouragement from the Department of Planning for schools to develop sites within the PFAs. The governor also issued an executive order that schools should comply with the 1997 smart growth legislation as much as possible. In addition, Maryland regulations favor the renovation of existing schools rather than the construction of new ones (Beaumont 2003).

Virginia recommends, but does not require, four acres plus one acre for every 100 students at the elementary level and ten acres plus one acre for every 100 students at the middle and

Table 1. Study Area Demographics

2005–2007 data	Maryland counties				
	Anne Arundel	Frederick	Howard	Montgomery	Prince George's
Total population	510,824	222,034	270,651	925,719	833,862
Pop change since 2000	4.3	13.7	9.2	5.6	4.0
Persons per sq. mi., 2000	1,177.2	294.5	983.5	1,760.8	1,652.6
Median HH income ($)	79,294	76,920	97,837	89,284	68,410
% white	78.2	83.8	68.3	61.2	22.8
% black	14.5	8.1	16.3	16.2	64.1
% Asian	3.0	3.3	10.8	13.0	3.9
% Hispanic/ Latino	3.9	5.1	4.4	14.0	11.3
% bachelor's degree	34.2	33.6	56.7	56.5	30.1

2005–2007 data	Virginia* counties				
	Fairfax	Fauquier†	Loudoun	Prince William	Stafford
Total population	1,006,576	65,417	266,087	352,773	118,551
Pop change since 2000	3.8	18.6	56.9	25.6	28.2
Persons per sq. mi., 2000	2,455.1	84.9	326.2	831.3	342.4
Median HH Income ($)	102,460	80,549	104,612	85,538	85,793
% white	67.7	86.3	73.3	61.3	73.8
% black	9.3	7.7	7.8	19.1	16.1
% Asian	15.8	1.6	11.6	6.9	2.6
% Hispanic/ Latino	13.3	5.0	9.7	18.3	7.4
% bachelor's degree	58.4	28.7	55.2	36.5	33.6

*Does not include data for the independent cities
†Only 2000 data available
Note: The 2005–2007 estimates represent the average characteristics between January 2005 and December 2007 and are calculated from American Community Survey estimates.
Sources: U.S. Census Bureau State and County QuickFacts.

high school levels as a minimum site size. Under these guidelines a 300-person elementary school would need to be at least seven acres and a 1,500-student high school would need twenty-five acres. School districts may construct on smaller sites and adopt their own siting guidelines. However, the state unofficially recommends fifteen to twenty acres for an elementary school, twenty to thirty acres for a middle school, and thirty to forty or more acres for a high school.

Pupil Transportation Policies

Pupil transportation policies do not vary across the two states. Neither state requires free pupil transportation. However, all school districts in the study areas provided free transportation to students living outside the locally decided walk zone. Therefore, transportation costs should factor equally into all siting decisions and will not confound the analysis of the effects of state and local land use policies on school siting.

Land Use Policies

Virginia is often portrayed as a progrowth state. Under Virginia law, localities cannot require developers to pay fees to offset the cost of their projects. However, local planning commissions may consider voluntary conditions proffered by an applicant seeking a change to the existing zoning (i.e., a rezoning per Virginia Code 15.2-2303). These proffers typically address ways to mitigate the transportation and public facility impacts of a proposed development. As described by Fairfax County, "all rezoning applications for residential development are expected to offset their public facility impact . . . [through] . . . dedication of land, . . . construction of public facilities, contribution of . . . cash" (Fairfax County Department of Planning and Zoning 2002). So even though the proffers are technically voluntary, there is a clear quid pro quo. The proffer system is characterized by a high degree of negotiation. Local authorities can deny the rezoning, and developers can forgo the rezoning and develop at "by-right" densities, thereby not providing any mitigation to the local authority.

In general, Virginia planning commissions are able to consider proffers of land or cash during the development approval process but have been restricted from specifically requesting certain fees or exactions in order to approve a project. More recently, Virginia adopted legislation to allow high-growth counties to establish cash proffer guidelines that allow them to make the planning board's requirements for the (still-voluntary) cash proffers public (Virginia Code 15.2-2296 and 15.2-2298). In this study all counties except Fairfax had established cash proffer guidelines with costs ranging between $30,000 and $50,000 for every single-family unit in excess of what they are allowed "by-right." This money is divided among county agencies, including schools, to offset the cost of improvements in the area of the development.

While Fairfax County has no adopted proffer guidelines, they have developed a School Impact Methodology, which assesses the impact of new residential development on schools (Fairfax County Department of Planning and Zoning 2003). Under that assessment each student generated by a new development had a cost of $7,500 (changed to $11,630 in June 2006). For each rezoning the Fairfax County Public Schools provides an estimate of the number of new students generated by the proposed development and the estimated costs.

Maryland, the "smart growth" state, places land use control in the hands of county and municipality governments. However, the state regulatory environment allows localities in Maryland to use land use controls, such as APFOs, that are not allowed in Virginia. APFOs say that "if the roads are too congested, if the school classrooms are too crowded, if the water system cannot provide enough water, if the sewer pipes or treatment plant are full, or if there are not enough playing fields for recreational use, then development can not be approved until the problem is corrected" (Maryland Department of Planning n.d.). Each Maryland county in the study had adopted an APFO that considers the adequacy of public schools before new developments are approved (National Center for Smart Growth Research and Education 2006).

The APFOs in Maryland have been criticized because some analyses suggest they have acted as de facto no-growth measures by creating long-term building moratoria. One study (funded by the Home Builders Association) found that the APFOs have deflected growth into outlying areas and have actually worked against the smart growth framework enacted by the state (Bento 2006). Other studies have found similar effects from other growth control measures such as Florida's concurrency regulations (Steiner 2001; Nicholas and Steiner 2000; Downs 2003).

While each county has an APFO, there are important differences in the specifics of the regulations. The standard for closing an area to development varies. Some counties stop development approvals when school capacity matches projected student enrollment. Others allow expected enrollments to be up to 120 percent of capacity before stopping development.

There are also differences in what developers can do to have a building moratorium lifted. Some counties allow developers to build schools or pay a fee in lieu of construction to lift the building moratorium.

Comprehensive Plans

In both states, proposed developments must be consistent with local comprehensive plans. These plans establish the type, location, and timing of future land use in the community. Land use and school planners work together to put "floating symbols" on the map to indicate future schools needs. As developments come online, they must designate school sites if their development is near a future school. While this process is straightforward for large developments, there is much more negotiation for smaller developments. In Virginia, "by-right" developments—that is, at the limit allowed by zoning—are not generally required to provide mitigation. In Maryland school planners negotiate with smaller developers to see what they can provide. For projects that will not produce many students, they generally do not require developers to provide school sites. But the process depends on the overall subdivision approval process and whether a building moratoria is in place.

SCHOOL SITE ACQUISITION PROCESS

There are two methods of acquiring land for school sites: purchase land on the open market or negotiate with developers seeking approval for their subdivisions. Acquisition through the

development approval process is more common in counties where developers are constructing large planned unit developments. The strong nexus between the proposed development
and school infrastructure needs gives the government a strong negotiating position. This is
particularly true in Maryland, where developers may not be allowed to build anything until
they address school capacity problems. Counties purchase land when they are more developed
with few large developments planned—for example, Fairfax and Montgomery; previously
proffered sites fail to meet school needs; or, in the case of Virginia, they need to meet the needs
of by-right developments.

Effect of the APFO

Each of the Maryland school planners reported a close working relationship with county
planners. The presence of an APFO has required each organization to coordinate their planning and meet with each other regularly. For example, Maryland school planners stated the
following:

- "The county has a subdivision review process that causes a meeting to occur every week and
  there is [school] staff that attends that meeting every week so we have an ongoing review of any
  development that is occurring."
- "We jump in when the land use is undergoing revision, we collaborate with the county to identify the number of schools that are needed and where they should be located. And then later on
  when the preliminary plan is submitted by a developer we sit on the development review board
  to collaborate with other county agencies to figure out where exactly the schools should be
  located, whether or not it can be a donated site or if it would have to be a sale, a purchase, and
  then later on still we may be involved with the site plan."
- "Most of our sites are acquired through development approval process with the County, or with
  the City. . . . When a development is going through the approval process then we work with the
  County to identify sites within the proposed development for a future school site and we have
  that dedicated through that process."
- "The adequate public facilities ordinance . . . kind of organizes everyone into a system of relating
  to each other."

The strength of this relationship is important since it is ultimately the county planners that
negotiate with the developer and the planning commission that makes a recommendation on
whether the developer has accommodated enough of the school's needs. For example, there
was general agreement that developers would try to give the county planners the "crappiest
land"—a phrase repeated by several school planners. The effectiveness of these negotiations
hinged on the abilities of the individual planner and how much support the planning commission would give to the school's concerns. This was true across state lines. As a Maryland
school planner described it,

> We negotiate with the developers . . . I give them all my demands and they generally come back
> with a left over piece of property on the back of their development that has steep slopes, wetlands,
> a stream, where we have to wait for them to a build a road to be able to access the site. Then I say
> "that's not acceptable." Then they try to redraw it. Then they finally end up going to the Planning

Commission. And they say "this is what we are offering." And I say "that's not acceptable" to the Board and the Planning Commission. Depending on—sometimes we have a very strong Planning Commission that says go back and work it out and sometimes we have a weaker Planning Commission that says "okay you've done your best . . . that's the best you're going to get."

While an APFO is not required to build this strong relationship—Fairfax County has had a long-term collaboration between land use and school planners—it tends to create institutional arrangements that encourage close work between the two groups.

Acreage Guidelines for School Sites

Even though neither state imposes binding acreage requirements for school sites—all facility planners reported acreage guidelines that either had been officially adopted by their school board or were unofficial rules of thumb used to structure the siting process. Most planners looked for fifteen to twenty developable acres for an elementary school, twenty to forty for a middle school, and forty to eighty for a high school. However, the acreage guidelines, particularly at the high school level, do reflect the policy context and stage of development of the county. For example, school districts in Maryland generally have lower acreage guidelines for schools at each level than their counterparts in Virginia. In addition, the most built-out counties had lower acreage requirements for high schools than other counties in their state.

Across both states, planners were consistent in the factors they look for in potential school sites. These factors guide their negotiations with developers or their real estate search if they are purchasing land. As one of the Virginia school planners summarizes,

> We want to make sure that there is water and sewer available in the location and it has sufficient capacity and pressure; road access for our pupil transportation folks. We want natural drainage. We don't want schools in flood plains. Soils have to be checked out. To make sure the site is suitable for construction, that it's a balanced site. I don't want to have to haul tons and tons of material off of the site; or vice-versa, hauling it onto the site. We'd rather not have rock; obviously, not hazardous materials.

The desire to put schools in areas with services—sewer and water—often conflicts with the desire for large school sites. As Loudoun County supervisor Jim Burton described it, "'There are very few large parcels available. It's a problem.' . . . [This] makes it very difficult to follow the language in the county's Comprehensive Plan that requires schools to be located near existing infrastructure" (*Leesburg Today* 2008a). However as a Maryland school planner found, the cost of building outside the existing service areas can be substantial. This district constructed a school outside the service area and had to put in special wastewater treatment equipment to meet the standard for nitrogen in effluent. The equipment cost approximately $5 million to $6 million, about 10 percent of the cost of constructing a high school, and has high operating costs. This experience led the facility planners to emphasize the importance of acquiring sites in the service area in the future.

DISCUSSION

Why Large Sites?

Advocates for smart growth and healthy communities have identified state acreage guidelines as a primary cause of school sprawl and have worked with CEFPI to eliminate minimum standards and emphasize context-sensitive school siting (Beaumont and Pianca 2002). However, this study shows that state guidelines do not necessarily affect local school size guidelines. Neither Maryland nor Virginia had size standards, yet school planners in the study used relatively generous acreage guidelines in their work. Understanding the reasons why school planners choose large sites is critical to changing policy. This research shows that the rationale for acquiring large school sites is primarily a risk—there is generally little risk when acquiring extra land but potentially large risks when not acquiring enough. These risks come from a need to provide extra space for future growth, increasing land costs, construction contingencies, and public desire for large schools with ample sports fields. If advocates for smart growth truly want to change school siting practices, they need to develop policies that address these important concerns.

Additions to existing schools are a key way to add school capacity, particularly in more urban counties. As a Virginia school planner noted,

> The big push for us right now in adding capacity is trying to use our existing buildings and maximize that kind of space through additions. We have a program where we are actually using modular, prefabricated additions. . . . They can be put onto existing schools and it will cost us about half as much as permanent construction, actually less than half, and we can do it in half the time. So we've gone down that road with about 25 or 30 of our schools so far and will probably continue to do that route in the future.

Linked to these concerns about accommodating future growth is the sharp rise in land values that these counties experienced during the housing bubble. In residential markets, rising housing prices cause people to enter the market so that they do not miss out on the surge in land values experienced by their neighbors (Myers and Ryu 2008). A similar psychology appears to operate among school planners. In counties experiencing the most rapid recent growth, the response has been to acquire exceptionally large sites—even through use of eminent domain powers.

Larger sites also provide insurance for construction contingencies. Many planners recounted stories of land acquired through donation that had many challenges when they actually went to construct a school. As one Maryland planner noted, "We're building a high school right now for a lake development that's on steep slopes, has an old fire pond, and two streams. And so we have thirty-five-foot retaining walls, we have to terrace that site to get all the fields, the school—it's a very expensive site to develop."

Such experiences have taught school planners how hard it is to get developable acres and therefore create incentives to get larger parcels to ensure enough land will be available. While all planners had guidelines and site requirements meant to avoid getting an inadequate site, the cost of doing all due diligence work prior to accepting a donation makes it unrealistic to definitively establish the site quality. For example, a Virginia county has found that due diligence costs at least $500,000 for an elementary site and $750,000 for a secondary school site.

So particularly when districts are getting land from a developer, there is a strong incentive to negotiate for as much land as possible.

Finally, larger sites also provide insurance against public and school board displeasure. There was general consensus that the school must serve the recreational needs for the town and that this required a great deal of land. As a Maryland planner summarized, "The reason why we look for that much land is because there is a significant community use aspect to any school site. Ball fields have nothing to do with our curriculum. There is nothing in the gym curriculum that requires a softball diamond or a baseball diamond. There's no actual need for it but there's so much youth athletics and recreational leagues and so forth that we routinely put those in because of the demand and if we don't put it in that'll be a problem."

Potential for Smaller Sites

Many advocates have promoted the use of smaller school sites that could be better integrated into communities, thereby allowing youth to walk to school and creating opportunities to colocate community services. For example, some communities have made the school library and the town library one facility. Another option is placing schools near parks so that students can access recreational facilities. The interviews revealed that districts are considering changing their site acquisition process or seeing that in the future they will need to reduce their parcel size. As a school planner noted,

> One of the things that we have cautioned our Board on is that most of the low-hanging fruit is gone and we are going to be making some adjustments in having to do the same program on less land simply because you don't have those desirable properties out there and what is there is going to have its limitations and they're also getting squeezed by the price. In the end we're looking at now instead of more suburban model schools like one story school for elementary and middle schools we're now looking at two story designs to have a little more compact footprint to cut down on our acreage requirements. We are starting to adapt.

Planners seemed most optimistic about adapting elementary and middle schools to smaller sites. As the following quotes show, most planners reported that space needs for student parking and developer objections to having high schools near residential land make it difficult to change the footprint and location of secondary schools. For example, school planners reported, "Usually developers will be more inclined to offer elementary or middle school sites. They see those as more of a positive to their development—a piece that they can sell. Whereas a high school is more of a detractor, because of its size, because of its after school activities, because of the teenage driving, traffic, etc etc. It is our experience that it is harder to get proffers from high school sites than it is for elementary or middle."

POLICY OPTIONS

As discussed earlier, much of the policy effort in reducing school size has been aimed at changing the school acreage standards set by states. For example, the Environmental Protection

Agency (EPA) worked with the education facility planners' professional organization to elimi-nate minimum standards and emphasize context-sensitive design (Council of Educational Facility Planners International and Environmental Protection Agency 2004). However, this study shows that the elimination of state acreage requirements does not necessarily change local guidelines around size. If advocates want to see changes in the siting of suburban schools, they need to refocus their efforts on local school districts and county commissions—a rather daunting task—or work with states to develop regulatory or incentive strategies to encourage smaller site sizes.

One option is state acreage maximum site size standards. As opposed to the minimum school acreage guidelines that were common before, these standards would set sizes that school parcels could not exceed. This is similar to the evolution in parking standards (Shoup 1999). Many localities have moved away from minimum parking requirements to instead cap the provision of (often) free parking. However, such a command and control strategy is unlikely to garner political support, particularly from the education community.

A more incentive-based approach to changing siting decisions might be more successful. As discussed earlier, there are few incentives for school planners to acquire small school sites and many for them to acquire large ones. In fact, until an area comes close to build out, it is difficult to imagine communities creating smaller schools—especially wealthy communities in areas where developers can afford to provide school sites. If encouraging smaller schools that are better integrated into communities is a goal, then states need to change the incentive structure. One promising approach is Massachusetts's Smart Growth School Cost Reimburse-ment (2005). This program provides that "any city or town that has established 1 or more smart growth zoning districts shall receive smart growth school cost reimbursement from the commonwealth" (Massachusetts Smart Growth School Cost Reimbursement 2005). While this mechanism was developed to encourage localities to build more housing, it could also provide a mechanism to reimburse school districts for capital costs *if* the new school or reno-vation was integrated into the community.

Another option is to take advantage of the development approval process. In both states, a large portion of the school sites were acquired through negotiation with developers, par-ticularly for elementary schools. This offers obvious opportunities for locating schools within communities and optimizing their accessibility to residential properties. Education of county planning commissions—who must approve any proffered school sites—on the benefits of smaller, better integrated sites might make the choice of school site more of a priority in their discussions. Developers might also be open to options that allowed them to dedicate smaller school sites if they were more centrally located. This option is attractive because it takes advan-tage of existing processes, but the education and outreach required is substantial.

CONCLUSION

Interviews with school planners showed that APFOs give school districts a stronger negotiat-ing position when trying to acquire school sites to accommodate greenfield development. This can occur without an APFO as shown by the experience in Fairfax County, but it requires long-standing coordination of school and land use planning. The APFOs encour-age institutional practices where schools and planners coordinate. Under the current system in Maryland and Virginia, counties and school districts face pressure to get as much as they can—particularly in terms of acreage—because of the difficulties they will face in purchasing sites themselves. While obtaining school sites through the subdivision process is advantageous for the school district, it is not clear that it necessarily promotes schools that are centers of their communities. If the goal is to encourage growth in existing areas, it might be more effective for states to place more stringent requirements upon capital construction money they provide to districts. This could be done through maximum size requirements or construction cost reimbursement programs. They might also require communities to identify school sites long before the need is immediate and put them on official maps that are tied to local capital improvement programs, so they are purchased when the land is cheap.

REFERENCES

Agron, Joe. 2004. Growth spurt: 30th annual official education construction report. *American School & University Magazine*, May.

Beaumont, Constance E. 2003. *State policies and school facilities: How states can support or undermine neighborhood schools and community preservation.* Washington, DC: National Trust for Historic Preservation.

Beaumont, Constance E., and Elizabeth G. Pianca. 2002. *Historic neighborhood schools in the age of sprawl: Why Johnny can't walk to school.* Washington, DC: National Trust for Historic Preservation.

Bento, Antonio. 2006. The effects of moratoria on residential development: Evidence from Harford, Howard, and Montgomery county. National Center for Smart Growth, University of Maryland (online database). College Park, MD. http://www.smartgrowth.umd.edu/research/pdf/Bento _MoratoriaResidential_042606.pdf.

Cohen, James. 2005a. Adequate public facilities ordinances in Maryland: An analysis of their implementation and effects on residential development in the Baltimore metropolitan area. National Center for Smart Growth, University of Maryland (online database). College Park, MD. http:// www.smartgrowth.umd.edu/research/pdf/Cohen_APFOBaltimore_041906.pdf.

———. 2005b. Adequate public facilities ordinances in Maryland: An analysis of their implementation and effects on residential development in the Washington metropolitan area. National Center for Smart Growth, University of Maryland (online database). College Park, MD. http://www .smartgrowth.umd.edu/research/pdf/Cohen_APFOWashington_041906.pdf.

Coleman, J. 2004. Proposition 55's narrow win opens flow of money to schools. *Associated Press State & Local Wire.* March 4.

Council of Educational Facility Planners International (CEFPI) and Environmental Protection Agency (EPA). 2004. *Schools for successful communities: An element of smart growth planning.* Scottsdale, AZ: Council of Education Facility Planners International.

Downs, Anthony. 2003. Why Florida's concurrency principles (for controlling new development by regulating road construction) do not—and cannot—work effectively. *Transportation Quarterly* 57 (1): 13–18.

Fairfax County Department of Planning and Zoning. 2002. Residential development criteria. http:// www.fairfaxcounty.gov/dpz/zoning/resdevelop/criteria.htm.

———. 2003. Implementation motion: School impact methodology. http://www.fairfaxcounty.gov/ dpz/zoning/resdevelop/motion.pdf.

Gurwitt, Robert. 2004. Edge-ucation: What compels communities to build schools in the middle of nowhere? *Governing Magazine*, March.

Leesburg Today. 2008a. Buy land now, task force recommends. February 8.

———. 2008b. Deal reached on Leesburg high school site. February 13.

Maryland Department of Planning. n.d. *Managing Maryland's growth: Adequate public facilities ordinances (APFOs)*. http://www.mdp.state.md.us/PDF/OurProducts/Publications/ModelsGuidelines/mg24.pdf.

Massachusetts Smart Growth School Cost Reimbursement. 2005. Mass. Gen. Laws 40S, S2.

McDonald, Noreen C. 2010. School siting: Contested visions of the community school. *Journal of the American Planning Association* 76 (2): 184–98.

Myers, Dowell, and SungHo Ryu. 2008. Aging baby boomers and the generational housing bubble: Foresight and mitigation of an epic transition. *Journal of the American Planning Association* 74 (1): 17.

National Center for Smart Growth Research and Education. 2006. *Adequate public facilities ordinances in Maryland: Inappropriate use, inconsistent standards, unintended consequences*. College Park, MD: University of Maryland.

New Jersey Schools Construction Corporation. 2005. Overview. http://www.njscc.com/general_info/index.asp.

Nicholas, James C., and Ruth L. Steiner. 2000. Growth management and smart growth in Florida. *Wake Forest Law Review* 35: 645–70.

Shoup, Donald C. 1999. The trouble with minimum parking requirements. *Transportation Research Part A* 33 (7–8): 549–74.

Steiner, Ruth L. 2001. Florida's transportation concurrency: Are the current tools adequate to meet the need for coordinated land use and transportation planning? *University of Florida Journal of Law and Public Policy* 12 (2): 269–97.

Vincent, Jeffrey. 2008. *The complex and multi-faceted nature of school construction costs: Factors affecting California*. Berkeley, CA: Center for Cities and Schools, University of California, Berkeley. http://citiesandschools.berkeley.edu/reports/K-12_CA_Construction_Report.pdf.

———. 2009. *Schools as centers of sustainable communities: A vision for future school facility construction*. Testimony before the Joint Information Hearing Senate Committee on Housing and Transportation and Senate Select Committee on State School Facilities. http://citiesandschools.berkeley.edu/reports/Vincent-testimony-121509.pdf.

PART 2

School Sprawl in High- and Low-Growth States

School Construction Investments and Smart Growth in Two High-Growth States

Implications for Social Equity

JEFFREY M. VINCENT AND MARY W. FILARDO

There are about 100,000 public schools in the United States, all of which combined contains nearly 6.6 billion square feet of building space over 100,000 acres of land (Filardo 2008). Nearly $500 billion (in 2005 dollars) of capital outlay was spent on this—a long-lived and spatially fixed infrastructure—inventory over the period from 1995 to 2004, with virtually 100 percent of the money from public funds (Filardo et al. 2006). The management and decisions governing public education infrastructure investment are wholly the result of public policy and budget and spending decisions—almost entirely made at the state and local levels.

This chapter builds on the recent analysis of the scale, scope, and distribution of school facility spending by local public school districts nationally in *Growth and Disparity: A Decade of U.S. Public School Construction 1995–2004* (hereafter referred to as *Growth and Disparity*), published by the Building Educational Success Together (BEST) national collaborative (Filardo et al. 2006).[1] Here we expand on the previous analysis and explore how these findings may help explain how school siting, educational facility planning, and public school construction investment decisions are affecting neighborhoods, human health, the environment, and social equity.

In our *Growth and Disparity* analysis, we found an unprecedented rise in school construction spending (both new construction and renovation and repair of existing schools) as many states and localities made progress improving their public school buildings. However, we also found a significant disparity in the students and communities receiving these public investments; low-income students and communities received about half the investment per student of their wealthier counterparts. Considering that in the mid-1990s the U.S. General Accounting Office (U.S. GAO 1995, 1996) found that low-income students were much more likely to attend schools with poor or inadequate facilities, the spending patterns during the decade following this finding appear to have done little to alleviate the disparity in school conditions experienced by children from different socioeconomic backgrounds.

To provide a deeper analysis of the spatial and social equity dimensions of school construction spending patterns, we analyze school district facility spending patterns within the state policy and demographic contexts of two high-growth, high-spending states, California and Florida. Between 1995 and 2004, both states saw about 20 percent public school enrollment growth. Both have increasingly diverse racial and ethnic enrollment and have a mixture of place types, from large urban centers to rural areas. California led the nation in public school capital outlay (for construction, land and existing structures, equipment and interest) by spending more than $65 billion, while Florida spent more than $31 billion over the decade. However, while California led the nation in *total capital outlay* spending, it spent far less on a *per pupil* basis on school construction than Florida (Filardo et al. 2006). The differences between California and Florida are even greater because the cost of school construction in California is one of the highest in the nation (Vincent and McKoy 2008).

GROWTH IN U.S. PUBLIC SCHOOL CONSTRUCTION, 1995–2004: CALIFORNIA AND FLORIDA

Recent years have seen tremendous growth in public school construction in the United States. The U.S. Census of Governments data show that between the years of 1995 and 2004, annual school construction expenditures nearly doubled from $20 billion in 1995 to more than $37 billion in 2004.[2] Including construction, land, and equipment, school districts spent $504 billion (in 2005 dollars) on capital outlay during the decade as shown in figure 1.

Following the national trend, California and Florida public school construction expenditures have also been increasing, even when adjusted for inflation. However, Florida has had a more stable program for school construction than California's episodic state bond–driven program, as shown in figure 2. Such capital funding stability is an important element of a well-managed school construction program (Filardo 1999).

Looking at school construction expenditures per student between 1995 and 2004 across the nation, figure 3 shows tremendous disparity by state. California spent $4,919 per student,

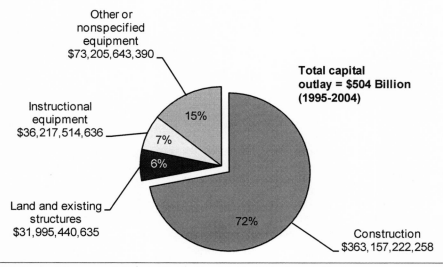

Figure 1. U.S. Census of Governments Reported Public School Capital Outlay (2005 Dollars)
Source: U.S. Census of Governments.

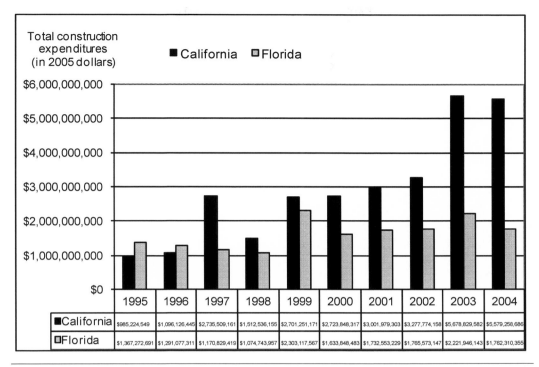

Figure 2. Comparison of Public School Construction Bid Starts in California and Florida, 1995–2004
Source: McGraw-Hill Construction.

The chart shows Total construction expenditures (in 2005 dollars) for California and Florida:

	1995	1996	1997	1998	1999	2000	2001	2002	2003	2004
California	$985,224,549	$1,096,126,445	$2,735,509,161	$1,512,536,155	$2,701,251,171	$2,723,848,317	$3,001,979,303	$3,277,774,158	$5,678,829,582	$5,579,258,686
Florida	$1,367,272,691	$1,291,077,311	$1,170,829,419	$1,074,743,957	$2,303,117,567	$1,633,848,483	$1,732,553,229	$1,765,573,147	$2,221,946,143	$1,762,310,355

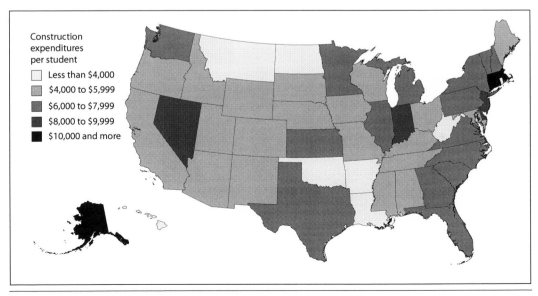

Figure 3. Public School Construction Expenditures per Student by State, 1995–2004
Sources: McGraw-Hill Construction; National Center for Education Statistics.

Construction expenditures per student
- Less than $4,000
- $4,000 to $5,999
- $6,000 to $7,999
- $8,000 to $9,999
- $10,000 and more

well below the national average of $6,519 per student, and Florida spent $6,915 per student, slightly more than the national average (Filardo et al. 2006).

These data are not adjusted for regional differences in the cost of labor and so mask differences in the "real" construction work these dollars buy. For example, the same dollar in Florida buys almost 30 percent more school construction than in California (Vincent and McKoy 2008).[3] Although California led the nation in *total* school construction spending, school districts in the state invested far less *per student* than the national average and due to the high cost of construction, procured fewer improvements for those investments.

SPENDING PRESSURES

The need for public school facilities investment across the country over the last decade—both for new construction and for renovating and expanding existing schools—has largely been driven by four factors: (1) enrollment growth, (2) aging buildings, (3) federal and state mandates, and (4) changes in education.

Enrollment Growth

California and Florida, along with other southwestern and southeastern states, have experienced tremendous public school enrollment growth since 1995, as shown in figure 4. Public school enrollment in California increased by 19 percent, while Florida enrollment increased by 23 percent. California and Florida's growth has been driven largely by national domestic migration patterns to south and western regions and by continued strong immigration rates.

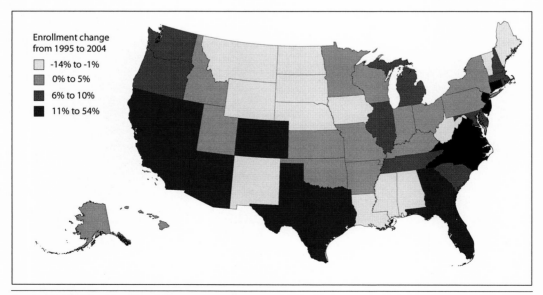

Figure 4. Public School Enrollment Change, 1995–2004
Source: National Center for Education Statistics.

California and Florida's growth, in part, has come at the expense of many midwestern, northern, and northeastern urban regions, particularly those in the "Rust Belt." Many of these communities have seen slow or declining population and economic growth and stagnating public investment in public infrastructure (Rubin 2006; Fox and Truehaft 2005). In these areas older cities are being abandoned, while suburban and exurban areas continue to grow, mainly as families seek employment, new housing choices they can afford, better schools, public safety, and other public services and infrastructures that local governments in declining cities are hard pressed to provide.

Like many other western and southeastern states, California and Florida both spent a large share of their school construction expenditures on new school construction (43 percent and 54 percent, respectively), as shown in figure 5. This is not surprising given the high enrollment growth and intense overcrowding California and Florida experienced since 1995 (Colmenar et al. 2005).

Aging Buildings

The average age of the nation's public schools is about forty years (NCES 1999). Without necessary ongoing maintenance and capital investment, conditions in existing school facilities deteriorate. Inadequate maintenance spending on school facilities is evident by the fact that American Society of Civil Engineers (ASCE 2005) gave public schools nationally one of the lowest ratings ("D") of all infrastructures. In its national study of the condition of the country's public school buildings, the GAO (1995, 1996) found that California had among the worst school facility conditions.[4] In California, 43 percent of schools reported having one or more inadequate building. In Florida, 31 percent of schools reported having one or more inadequate buildings. Florida was slightly better than the national average of 33 percent, with

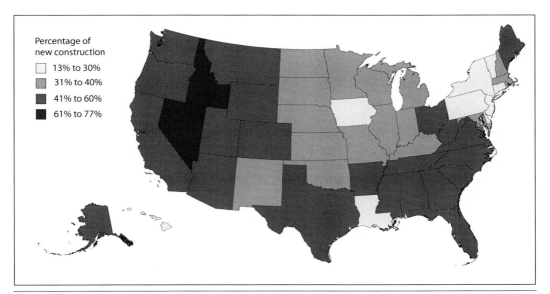

Figure 5. Share of New Construction Bid Starts by State, 1995–2004
Source: McGraw-Hill Construction.

California being significantly worse. However, in both states, the vast majority (87 percent and 85 percent, respectively) of schools reported the need to upgrade or repair on-site buildings to good overall condition. Thus while both states had condition disparities in school facilities in 1995, California was found to have worse conditions compared to Florida. Although California and Florida experienced comparable public school enrollment growth over the decade, their schools were not in the same condition in the mid-1990s. As a result, having more than twice as many students as Florida, California needs a far greater scale of investment in its existing schools.

Federal and State Mandates

There are a number of federal and state mandates that put pressure on school district construction costs and requirements. These mandates address issues of health, safety, and rights of access. Some requirements affect the actual design of a building, while others affect the methods or processes required during construction or renovation.

The key health and safety requirements mandated by federal law are related to asbestos and lead. The federal requirements associated with their management and abatement affect the cost, type, and scope of construction work undertaken by school districts. The Asbestos Hazard Emergency Response Act (AHERA), which promulgated the Asbestos-Containing Materials in Schools Rule and is managed by the Environmental Protection Agency (EPA), has had widespread impact. This rule requires all private and public nonprofit elementary and secondary schools to inspect their schools for asbestos-containing building materials (ACBM), develop a plan to manage the asbestos in each school building, notify parents and staff regarding the management plan availability, provide asbestos awareness training to school maintenance and custodial workers, and implement timely actions (repair, encapsulation, enclosure, removal) to deal with dangerous asbestos situations.

Another environmental hazard addressed by the EPA is lead. In any child-occupied facility, there must be inspections, risk assessments, and abatements of lead-based paint. Lead-based paint was commonly used on radiators, pipes, windows, and particularly exterior doors, baseboards, and boiler rooms up until the 1970s. It must be abated when it creates dust or is loose and when a building is renovated. Like asbestos, when working on existing buildings, contractors have special requirements for testing for lead-based material, working in areas with lead-based paint, and disposing of materials that contain lead-based paint that increase the cost of a project.

The federal mandates affecting access to public schools and education are the Americans with Disabilities Act (ADA), the Individuals with Disabilities Education Act (IDEA), and Title IX of the Elementary and Secondary Education Act. The most significant new federal requirement affecting facilities is Title II of the American with Disabilities Act, which extends the rights of individuals with disabilities. All public buildings must be accessible to persons with handicaps. Existing buildings should all be modified within a timeframe, and buildings undergoing a certain level of improvements must be modified to meet ADA requirements. While most people think of the ADA affecting mobility within a building, it also affects requirements for acoustics and signage associated with hearing- or sight-related disabilities.

With the passage of the first Individuals with Disabilities Education Act in 1972, school systems began a transformation to extend schooling to students who were often excluded from public school altogether. Now IDEA requires that any school receiving federal funds must provide a free appropriate public education (FAPE) to children with disabilities in the least restrictive setting with the appropriate instruction and services to advance them socially and academically. The regulations implementing these laws require that students with disabilities receive benefits and services comparable to those given to their nondisabled peers. In addition to changes that extend education by disability, Title IX has extended educational programs—particularly athletics and physical education—by gender. Title IX requires that no school receiving federal funds can exclude from participation, deny benefits, or discriminate by gender access to any education program or activity.

Finally, although not occurring at the federal level, as ADA, IDEA, and Title IX, some states are extending the age for which education is available by right. In many communities full-day kindergarten is still considered an innovation, but more and more school districts offer not just full-day kindergarten but also prekindergarten for four-year-olds, early childhood Head Start programs, and even locally funded preschool programs for three-year-olds. New Jersey in particular must provide preschool to all children from the lowest income school districts as a part of the settlement of the educational adequacy and equity challenge brought about by the *Abbott v. Burke* court case.[5] The expansion of early childhood education is changing schools dramatically, increasing enrollments and bringing significant modifications to building and ground design and construction.

There are other state-level mandates for school districts that impact the need for school construction and the school construction programs. In California, the Field Act is often identified as the most costly with which to comply. It requires schools to be constructed to meet heightened structural safety standards to withstand earthquakes. In Florida, designated public schools have hurricane-protection requirements for windows and roofs that ensure they are secure shelters for the public.

Changes in Education

The need for school construction spending has also been driven by demands on school facilities to support the changing needs of students, teachers, and communities. There are many new practices, programs, and services in public schools for which design changes are needed. There are a number of educational changes that put pressure on school facilities:

- The desire by parents and educators for small class size and small schools has significant effect on school facility design and is changing the size and amount of space needed for schools.
- Schools built in urban districts at the beginning of the twentieth century did not provide cafeterias since it was a common practice for students to return home for lunch. While this practice has long since been changed, with schools providing lunch and often breakfast daily to students, many of the oldest school buildings do not have adequate cafeteria or food service amenities.
- Technology in schools is changing school design and construction. There is wide and growing use of multimedia, "smart boards," online material, and computers in instruction at all levels. School administration and operations are also using more technology, particularly for security-related issues.
- Significant changes in our economy have transformed career and technical education in secondary schools.
- Many schools are also now being designed or reconfigured for use by members of the community outside of regular school hours.

These trends and others associated with curriculum and pedagogy are seen across the country, and the school design needed to support these educational programs, practices, and services are included in any high quality new school design and should be included in any school renovation.

METHODOLOGY

The U.S. Census of Governments database is the only national public record of school construction and related expenditures. However, it only includes *total* school district capital spending and lacks detailed information about the location and type of school construction. To overcome this data limitation, BEST developed a unique dataset on public school construction projects (new construction and modernization and renovation of existing schools) undertaken in all fifty states and the District of Columbia between 1995 and 2004. BEST researchers utilized raw data provided by McGraw-Hill Construction, a segment of McGraw-Hill Companies, which collects detailed project-level data on every building contract valued at more than $100,000 undertaken by the nation's school districts. These proprietary McGraw-Hill data represent the most robust information available on public school construction at the project level. They are collected in real time for the purpose of informing construction industry manufacturers, contractors, and subcontractors of projects that will be built so they can market their goods or services to the project owner and contractor. Daily, hundreds of McGraw-Hill reporters review construction contracts awarded by school districts all across the country. These data capture the value of hard construction costs of specific projects at the time a bid is awarded to a contractor along with other information relevant to prospective subcontract bidders such as the type of work, its location, and who has won the bid award. These "construction start" data therefore reflect the contract value, or accepted bid price, of each project and represent the construction hard costs: the basic labor and material expenses of the project. The soft costs, such as site acquisition, architecture, engineering, and project management, are not collected by McGraw-Hill. Other hard costs that are added to the construction start cost via change orders are also not part of the McGraw-Hill data. Hard costs typically account for about 70 percent of a project's total cost, although this can vary by project and locale.

In the research for *Growth and Disparity* (Filardo et al. 2006), the McGraw-Hill data was cleaned and organized so it could be used to analyze school construction spending at the school district and zip code levels. In the current study, we utilize this modified McGraw-Hill data set, which contained approximately 146,000 pre-K–12 public school projects totaling $304 billion of school construction spending (see appendix for a description of this data and method for analysis). Figure 6 shows what proportion of the total capital outlay of school districts is encompassed by the McGraw-Hill school hard construction bid start data.

The $304 billion is a subset of the $363 billion of capital construction outlay reported by the U.S. Census of Governments. For this study, we aggregated the McGraw-Hill project level construction data to the district level and aligned it with U.S. Census data and school district data from the National Center for Education Statistics.

We analyze the data by type, location, and against geographic measures of income, race, and place type to understand the scale, scope, and distribution of school construction spending. Because construction costs can rise during the course of a project, the "construction start"

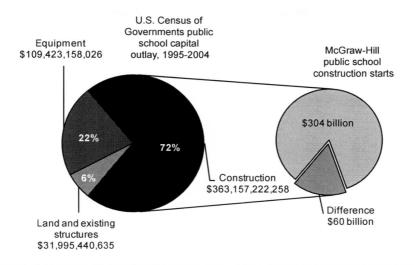

Figure 6. Comparison of Total Capital Outlay and Hard Construction Bid Start
Sources: U.S. Census of Governments; McGraw-Hill Construction.

McGraw-Hill data can be used as an estimated measure of actual final project costs. Therefore, it is important to note that in this study we analyze the hard construction costs for new schools as a measure of total capital investment.

PATTERNS OF SCHOOL CONSTRUCTION INVESTMENT IN CALIFORNIA AND FLORIDA

As we showed for the nation as a whole, the last decade has been a period of intense school construction spending in California and Florida (fig. 3). The dramatic increase in school construction spending in California in 2003 illustrated in figure 3 is largely the result of the heightened understanding of the substandard condition of public school facilities. This awareness was generated in large part by the landmark educational equity suit, *Eliezer Williams, et al., v. State of California, et al.*, which was finally settled in 2004. The suit was intended to improve the materials and physical conditions of the state's lowest-performing schools. Plaintiffs argued that the state agencies responsible for providing education to the state's children failed to provide students with equal access to instructional materials, safe and decent school facilities, and qualified teachers (California Department of Education 2006). Part of the argument was that overcrowded schools had moved from two-semester calendars to "multitrack year-round" schedules, so these students attended school far fewer days than students in traditional calendar schools. In its settlement, the state of California agreed to allocate $800 million for facility repairs to alleviate the facilities inequities. As a result of this court challenge, recent state bonds have had several equity-oriented elements, including that they are paid back through California's progressive state taxes, payment is spread over future populations, hardship grants from the state are meant to make up for the inability to raise local funds, and preliminary apportionment has replaced the first-come, first-serve approach that disadvantaged urban school districts use (Pastor and Reed 2005).

The more stable and higher level of per pupil school construction spending in Florida and the fact that school buildings were not in such poor condition to begin with in 1995 provide a rationale for why Florida has not had school facility conditions litigated in court. States that had successful challenges to their school funding formula, which included public school facilities, spent on average about 25 percent more on school construction than their counterparts (Filardo et al. 2006).

In this section, we ask, who has benefited by this enormous public infrastructure spending? What can we learn about how facility investment has affected communities?

Nationally, students from low-income families received about half the facility investment compared to their wealthier peers. Additionally, the poorest neighborhoods received less than half the school construction investment per student compared to wealthier neighborhoods (Filardo et al. 2006). Our analysis of the distribution of school facility spending in California and Florida by neighborhood income and racial composition reveals disparities that largely mirror the national trends found in the *Growth and Disparity* study. Further, our analysis of spending by geographic locale finds that existing areas received much less school construction investment per student compared to rural and suburban areas.

Investment by Neighborhood Income

Because school districts can cover hundreds of square miles and include many types of communities, an analysis of school construction spending at the school district level can mask important variations in spending, particularly in states with county school districts such as Florida. To understand what is happening at the neighborhood and project level in California and Florida, we analyze median household income and the McGraw-Hill data by project zip code. California is divided into 1,052 school districts and 2,490 five-digit zip codes. In Florida there are 67 county school districts and 1,832 five-digit zip codes.

Zip code areas were divided into five categories according to their 2000 U.S. Census median household income:

- Very low income (less than $20,000)
- Low income ($20,000 to $34,999)
- Moderate income ($35,000 to $59,999)
- Middle income ($60,000 to $99,999)
- High income ($100,000 and more)

According to the 2000 U.S. Census, just over half the preschool through twelfth grade children in public school in both California (52 percent) and Florida (54 percent) attended schools located in "moderate-income" neighborhoods. Very few students attended schools in "high-income" neighborhoods (2 percent in California and 0.1 percent in Florida). A quarter of California's students and 37 percent of Florida's students attend schools in "low-income" neighborhoods.

Figure 7 shows that, except for an unusual distribution in California, lower investments were made in the lower-income neighborhoods, while the highest investments were made in

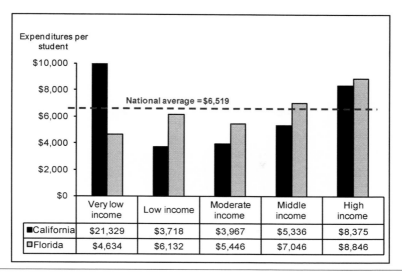

Figure 7. Public School Construction in California and Florida by Student and 2000 U.S. Census Median Household Income, 1995–2004[6]
Sources: McGraw-Hill Construction; U.S. Census 2000; analyzed by zip code.

the higher-income neighborhoods. The high expenditure per student in the "very low income" zip code in California can largely be explained by one very large and very expensive school— Los Angeles Unified School District's Belmont High School; it is being built in downtown Los Angeles in a zip code area that has very few residents. The project has been plagued by serious environmental- and site-related problems. Removing this more than $350 million school brings the investment per student below $4,000 per student.

In Florida, schools in "very low-income" neighborhoods received about half the expenditure per student ($4,634) as schools in "high-income" neighborhoods ($8,728). However, school construction expenditures in Florida, while still following the pattern of lower investment in the lowest-income communities, are less disparate than the expenditures in California. This may in part be explained by the school finance system in California and Florida. Because Florida has county school districts, and only sixty-seven of them, and has had a strong state construction program over an extended period of time, it appears to have done a better job of meeting its responsibilities to allocate construction funds by need. California, on the other hand, has over one thousand school districts, each of which must come forward with its school construction plan and priorities and compete with the others for state construction funding.

Still, overall, the more affluent a community, the more funds were spent per student on school construction in both California and Florida. This distribution is even more troublesome because most public school students in California (77 percent) and Florida (91 percent) attend schools in districts with "low-income" and "moderate-income" majorities.

Investment by Project Type

The McGraw-Hill data place each project in one of three project type categories: new construction, existing building, or addition and existing building. During the period from 1995 to 2004, California spent 43 percent of its hard construction funds on new construction. Florida spent 54 percent of its construction funds on new construction. In California, the high-income neighborhoods received nearly three times the investment per student in existing schools as both low-income and moderate-income neighborhoods, as shown in figure 8. The high expenditure in spending per student on existing schools in very low-income neighborhoods is largely the result of Los Angeles Unified School District's massive school renovation and modernization program and the impact of the *Williams* case that required maintenance and repair funds to the poorest schools. The high expenditure per student on new construction is again explained by Belmont High School in Los Angeles. Otherwise, spending per student on new construction in California neighborhoods was fairly even.

Patterns in Florida are somewhat more equitable than in California, at least in terms of spending on existing schools, as shown in figure 9. Very low-income and low-income neighborhoods—likely the places with the oldest school buildings—received the most spending per student. But spending on new construction in Florida was quite different; high-income neighborhoods received between two and four times more than nearly all other neighborhood types. However, very few students (3,676, or less than 1 percent) attend schools in high-income neighborhoods, and not much total money ($32 million, or less than 1 percent of the total) was spent, which explains the high per student spending.

Older existing schools represent over 80 percent of the public school facility inventory, but only about half of each state's school construction expenditures were used to upgrade, renovate, or expand these existing assets. The enrollment growth and overcrowding trends suggest there is a real problem with facility conditions in the existing schools, which have had very low investments relative to their number and need. Even the aggressive school construction spending of the 1995–2004 period left a tremendous backlog of deferred maintenance. Los Angeles Unified School District estimates a multibillion-dollar deferred maintenance accumulation spanning the district's eight hundred–plus schools.

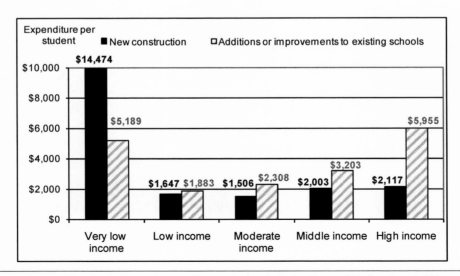

Figure 8. California Public School Construction Spending per Student by Project Type and Median Household Income, 1995–2004
Sources: McGraw-Hill Construction; U.S. Census 2000; analyzed by zip code.

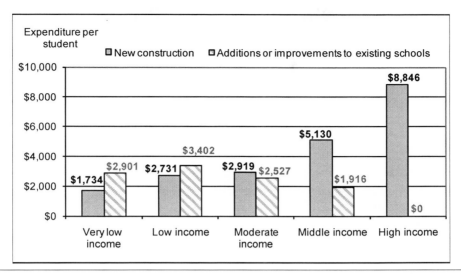

Figure 9. Florida Public School Construction Spending per Student by Project Type and Median Household Income, 1995–2004
Sources: McGraw-Hill Construction; U.S. Census 2000; analyzed by zip code.

To better understand the magnitude of the lack of investment in existing schools, consider the data in table 1. If the new construction funds are only allocated to the increased enrollment, there remains only $3,066 per student for existing facilities in California and $3,544 per student for existing facilities in Florida. This is only $306 and $354, respectively, per student per year for existing facility funding. These numbers are low, considering that existing facilities are under pressure to accommodate enrollment change, replace aging components and systems in existing buildings, meet federal and state mandates, and support new educational space requirements.

Table 1. Construction Spending Allocated by Student by Construction Project Type

State	*California*	*Florida*
New Students (Enrollment Increase, 1995 to 2004)	1,006,387	476,440
New Construction Expenditures, 1995 to 2004	$12.6 billion	$8.8 billion
New Construction Expenditure per New Student, 1995 to 2004	$12,632	$18,555
Enrollment, 1995	5,407,475	2,111,188
Expenditures on Existing Schools, 1995 to 2004	$16.7 billion	$7.5 billion
Expenditures on Existing Schools per 1995 Enrollment	$3,066	$3,544
Annual Average Expenditure on Existing Schools per 1995 Enrollment	$306	$354

Sources: McGraw-Hill Construction; National Center for Education Statistics.

Investment by Neighborhood Racial Composition

Enrollment in public schools across the country—and particularly in California and Florida—is changing, and minority enrollment is increasing. Many of our nation's school districts are racially diverse, a condition made possible by desegregation in the 1950s and immigration, which has accelerated since the 1970s. These enrollment trends mirror the fact that both city and suburban neighborhoods exhibit more diversity—along the lines of race, ethnicity, nativity, and income—than is commonly recognized (Turner and Fenderson 2006). But at the same time, a substantial share of neighborhoods remain either exclusive (occupied predominantly by affluent, native-born whites) or isolated (occupied predominantly by lower-income minorities and immigrants). However, many school districts and schools are resegregating at rapid rates across the country, generally reflecting greater segregation than local neighborhoods (Orfield and Lee 2004).

To further understand the types of communities benefiting from school construction investment, we analyzed the McGraw-Hill data by racial composition at the project zip code level using 2000 U.S. Census data. We utilized the typologies developed by Margery Austin Turner and Julie Fenderson (2006) to report neighborhood racial and ethnic diversity. Using this typology, zip code areas were divided into four categories according to their racial composition:

- Predominantly minority (population is less than 10 percent non-Hispanic white)
- Majority minority (population is 10 to 50 percent non-Hispanic white)
- Majority white (population is 50 to 90 percent non-Hispanic white)
- Predominantly white (population is more than 90 percent non-Hispanic white)

According to the 2000 U.S. Census, children attending public preschool through twelfth grades in California and Florida attend schools in a variety of neighborhood types. In California, 41 percent of students attend schools in "majority white" neighborhoods and 59 percent attend schools in "majority minority" neighborhoods. In Florida, 70 percent of students attend schools in "majority white" neighborhoods, while 30 percent attend schools in "majority minority" neighborhoods. Only 1 percent of students in California and 12 percent of students in Florida attend schools in neighborhoods that are "predominantly white."

As shown in figure 10, the highest average expenditures occurred in California and Florida neighborhoods that were "majority white" with per pupil spending at $4,383 and $6,142, respectively. The lowest spending was in "predominantly minority" neighborhoods with per pupil spending at $2,344 and $3,325, respectively. It is interesting to see that in both California and Florida, the zip code areas that were predominantly white were funded at lower levels than schools in majority white zip code areas—and in the case of Florida, they were also funded at lower levels than majority minority neighborhoods.

Interestingly, our analysis reveals that construction-spending disparity by race is less than the disparity by neighborhood income. This suggests that a substantial number of minority children are affluent enough or attend schools in neighborhoods with enough affluent children to benefit from a higher level of investment than would be likely in more economically isolated and poor neighborhoods. The drop in investment in the "predominantly white" zip codes most likely reflects a higher-than-average use of private schools among affluent whites, which may explain patterns of disinvestment even in very high-income communities. It also

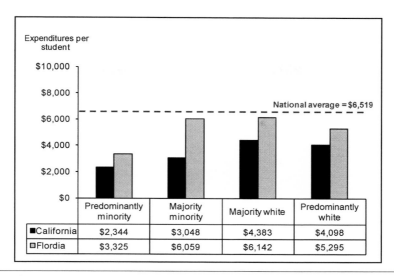

Figure 10. Public School Construction Spending per Student by Neighborhood Racial Composition, California and Florida, 1995–2004
Sources: McGraw-Hill Construction; 2000 U.S. Census; analyzed by zip code.

may reflect better ongoing maintenance and spending from operating budgets, which reduces the amount needed on expensive major maintenance projects.

Investment by Locale

As part of the original data analysis by the research team, the school construction projects were linked to school districts and the school districts were identified by their "urban-centric local" codes assigned by the National Center for Education Statistics (NCES). This analysis suggests that existing urban neighborhoods within metropolitan areas have received far less school construction investment per student than growing outer suburbs. To understand investment by geographic place type, school districts were divided into four categories according to the NCES local code typologies:

- City (territory inside an urbanized area and inside a principal city)
- Suburb (territory outside a principal city and inside an urbanized area)
- Town (territory inside an urban cluster but outside an urbanized area)
- Rural (rural territory outside an urbanized area and outside an urban cluster)

However, because the locale code is at the district level, it masks variations within school districts. This is problematic for Florida with its vast county school districts, where one district can encompass a large city, suburbs, small towns, and even rural areas. Still, we present the findings on a national level to illustrate that existing areas (cities and towns) received less school construction investment per student compared to rural and (presumably growing) suburban areas, as shown in figure 11.

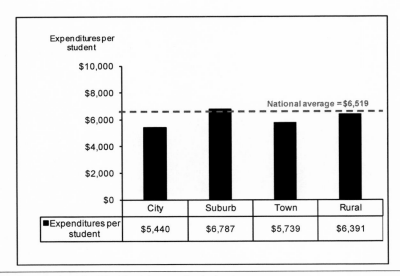

Figure 11. National Distribution of Public School Construction by Locale, 1995–2004
Sources: National Center for Education Statistics; McGraw-Hill Construction.

THE RELATIONSHIP AMONG SCHOOL CONSTRUCTION INVESTMENTS, SMART GROWTH, HEALTHY COMMUNITIES, AND SOCIAL EQUITY

Our analysis of school construction spending reveals a significant disinvestment in existing schools and their neighborhoods. This disinvestment in existing schools within established communities runs counter to smart growth, regional equity, and healthy communities goals of reinvesting in existing communities to make them more desirable places to live, work, and play. Due to limitations in the availability of data, our analysis is strongest with regard to school construction investment and social equity. However, given the growing linkages being made in the literature between equity issues and those of smart growth, environmental sustainability, and human health, we believe our findings have relevance beyond their immediate equity implications.

Most fundamentally, we use the analysis of California and Florida to posit that the disinvestment seen in school facilities in lower-income and minority urban areas is yet another factor continuing to drive families with children from—or discourage them to remain in—core cities and older suburbs. These families are seeking better schools for their children and the public investment that helps support them. Families largely choose to live in communities that offer the services, amenities, and qualities they desire (Tiebout 1956). School construction spending is an important and historically overlooked input that has a multitude of influences on school quality, residential patterns, segregation, and land use (Vincent 2006). Researchers and advocates in the education, smart growth, social equity, and public health fields are increasingly finding overlapping agendas and common ground related to educational improvement, sustainable transportation, social inclusion, human health, and efficient and environmentally responsible land use and development (see PACE and CC&S 2009; McKoy, Vincent, and Makarewicz 2008; Glover-Blackwell and Truehaft 2008; Bell and Rubin 2007; Fox and Glover-Blackwell 2004; Proscio 2003). From these perspectives, the school construction trends of inequitable spending and the disinvestment in existing schools and communities are troubling because, we argue, the significantly reduced spending in existing schools, particularly in low-income communities, is also a disinvestment in existing neighborhoods. In turn, these actions have likely helped increase neighborhood decline and segregation in older urban areas and helped fuel suburban growth on the fringes.

Looking at neighborhood income in both California and Florida, lower-income neighborhoods received the least investment per student, while the wealthier neighborhoods received the most. The income and racial categories we utilized in the earlier disparity analysis serve as proxy measures for geographic location—with lower-income and higher-minority neighborhoods tending to be concentrated in urban areas and older suburbs. The failure to modernize and adapt existing public school infrastructures to meet current educational space or health and safety requirements or to revitalize the basic physical conditions in schools is yet another factor that drives families with children away from core cities and older suburbs and towns. These families are seeking better schools for their children and the public investment that helps support them. The flight of middle- and working-class families from cities, particularly the older cities, has left low-income families, who are likely to be politically weak constituents, with school facilities in the worst condition.

There are two key reasons why the inequities in public school construction investment are so important. The first is that a growing body of empirical evidence finds that poor physical condition and design of school facilities contribute to poorer performance by students and teachers (Schneider 2002; Higgins et al. 2005; Uline and Tschannen-Moran 2008). Thus low-income students are further disadvantaged when they are in substandard school buildings. In 1995, low-income students were much more likely to attend schools with poor conditions (U.S. GAO 1995, 1996), and as we have shown, the schools these students attend received very low investments for maintenance, renovation, and modernization to "catch up" to their more advantaged peers in wealthier zip code areas. Coupled with the other very significant socioeconomic-related disadvantages that low-income students already face in performing well in school (Rothstein 2004), the inequity in their school building conditions—which is a function of public investment policy—is an inequity that erects yet another barrier these students must overcome. Still, much more research is needed to understand the relationships between school building conditions and student and teacher performance.

The second reason is that while these spending patterns create barriers to teaching and learning for low-income minority children, they also have important impacts on neighborhoods, cities, and metropolitan regions, as they affect residential patterns, segregation, economic development, and land use development. Evidence suggests that the condition and quality of school buildings contribute to neighborhood vitality or decline; poor school building conditions send signals that educational quality is also poor, which in turn decreases neighborhood desirability (Weiss 2004). In other words, the physical quality of a school—which is largely a function of the capital dollars spent on design, maintenance, and renovation—is seen as one factor among many that determine perceptions of overall school quality. Parents' perceptions of the quality of a given school have tremendous push–pull effects on families within metropolitan regions (Orfield 2002); survey research frequently finds perception of local school quality as a top reason people choose where to live (APA and AICP 2000; Baldassare 2002; Landis and Hood 2005), and access to better schools typically results in increased home prices (Black 1999; Bogart and Cromwell 2000). Furthermore, perceptions of poor quality educational opportunities for their children drive families from urban centers and first-ring suburbs, a pattern that helps fuel suburban fringe growth (McKoy and Vincent 2008). Again, more research into these relationships is needed; much of the work in this area is anecdotal or loosely connected to the physical quality of school buildings. The typical measures of school quality have to do with test scores and racial composition.

While the disinvestment in existing school infrastructure is one side of the story of how school construction investment patterns impact neighborhoods, cities, and metropolitan regions, the outcomes of enormous spending on building new schools is the other side. The tremendous investment in new school construction has largely funded suburban schools typically surrounded by low-density suburban development. In part, new schools are mimicking their surrounding development patterns, but state and local school planning, siting, and design policies are also typically mandating or incentivizing these practices (Beaumont 2003). Since World War II, school enrollments are growing and schools are occupying larger sites. While the number of schools has declined by nearly 70 percent, their average size has grown fivefold (Local Government Commission 2002). It is not uncommon for new suburban high schools to enroll two to three thousand students and be on fifty- to seventy-five-acre sites. Typically, sites this large can only be found on undeveloped suburban greenfields located some distance from existing suburban fringes, where land is cheaper and more plentiful.

As some have argued, the design and location choices of new suburban schools are encouraging inefficient low-density suburban growth patterns because new suburban school site choices are not adjacent to existing urban infrastructure (PACE and CC&S 2009; CEFPI and U.S. EPA 2004; McClelland and Schneider 2004; U.S. EPA 2003; Salvesen and Hervey 2003; Passmore 2002). In many instances new suburban school sites have leapfrogged out to undeveloped locations and made automobile access the only option—a practice known as "school sprawl" (Beaumont with Pianca 2002; McMahon 2000; Steward 1999). These site decisions have been criticized as undermining smart growth goals of efficient use of land, infill development, open space preservation, and reducing automobile reliance. Studies have documented these patterns in Maine (Maine State Planning Office 1997), South Carolina (Kouri 1999), and Michigan (McClelland and Schneider 2004). Conventional suburban environments (and the large schools serving them) are characterized by inefficiently using land and increasing automobile reliance, which means that more students are traveling in buses or being driven to school by parents; walking or bicycling to school is now the exception not the rule, which is linked to lower rates of physical activity and higher rates of sedentary living among children (Ewing et al. 2003; U.S. EPA 2003; Schlossberg et al. 2006; McDonald 2007; McMillan 2007).

Historically, public schools were located within neighborhoods and in the heart of communities. In rural communities, one-room schoolhouses dotted the countryside, so they would be accessible to families living in isolated rural areas. One-room schoolhouses were consolidated at a rapid pace when children could be bused to schools beginning in the 1940s. We believe the relatively high level of expenditure in the rural areas seen in our analysis represents a second wave of consolidation as the schools from the 1950s and 1960s needed upgrading. Rural school consolidations typically mean even greater distances between home and school because there are fewer schools serving the area's children.

In cities, public schools were historically located in neighborhoods and on transportation corridors so students could walk or take public transportation to schools. Advances in transportation changed urban growth patterns, including the relationship of the school to community. Families moved out of cities to rapidly growing suburbs in droves—first white families, then, once fair housing laws were put in place and enforced, African American and Hispanic families, too, began leaving cities as soon as they were able. In 1950 there were about

212,000 public schools in the United States and about twenty-five million students. By 2006 to 2007 there were nearly 100,000 public schools and about forty-eight million students. This means the average school enrollment size between 1950 and 2006 more than tripled from about 120 students to about 400 students.

Our analysis reveals that the distribution of a historic decade of public school construction and renovation has disproportionately benefited newer, wealthier neighborhoods, contributing to disinvestment in existing community infrastructure. Many of these existing schools are in the kind of neighborhoods that display the urban form characteristics promoted by smart growth and healthy community principles—relatively higher densities, access to transit options, and pedestrian infrastructure, which, among other things, make walking and bicycling to school more likely.

Families moving to the suburbs are both forcing and following public investment in the services, amenities, and conditions they desire in their public schools. While we do not mean to suggest that school construction investment is the most important driver of family residential choice by any means, it is an important and too-often overlooked piece of the "pie" of overall school quality. Our analysis has found this pattern as a national trend, not just in California and Florida. The findings suggest that the higher investment in suburban communities creates incentives for families to live in the new suburbs, not in core cities and older neighborhoods. The disparity in spending and the disinvestment in existing neighborhoods—in cities and towns—works to erode both school and neighborhood quality in many older neighborhoods, triggering the flight of families that can afford to leave and hampering opportunities for those who stay.

RECOMMENDATIONS AND CONCLUSION

From a smart growth, regional equity, and healthy communities perspective, the trends in inequitable spending and the disinvestment in existing schools and communities documented here have likely helped increase neighborhood decline and segregation in older urban areas and helped fuel the rapid, lower-density growth seen on the fringes of most metropolitan areas in the country.

Based on our analysis, we make the following policy-oriented research recommendations:

1. Track and monitor public school construction spending. As we have noted, a significant barrier to research and accountability for investing equitably in school facilities is a lack of publicly accessible information on the physical conditions, qualities, and facility spending of their schools. Few states track or report these data with the level of detail required to analyze the relationships between this spending and other community or regional measures. The same is true for most school districts across the country. What is needed is the political will to direct funding and create data collection guidelines on school construction investment. From there, researchers should expand on the analysis we have conducted to better understand how school construction investment coincides with, and impacts, school, neighborhood, city, and regional change.

Our two case states, California and Florida, offer insights into the effect that better data may have. California, like the vast majority of states, does not collect this information and so has no system in place for assessing existing facilities and prioritizing schools with the greatest need—a troubling fact given the low school facility condition ratings found by both the GAO in the mid-1990s and the ASCE in 2005. In contrast, Florida may have among the best state-level facility data systems in the country for monitoring and measuring school facility conditions and spending with the Florida Inventory of School Housing, where data are reported by local school districts and available publicly online. Our evidence that Florida has had more equitable school construction spending per student than California suggests that these data may support policies and spending that reduces disparities. A basic information system on facilities also enables intergovernmental planning, as is required by the Florida requirement for interlocal agreements and the stepped-up mandate for "concurrency." Florida's concurrency provision requires facilities and services to be available concurrent with the impacts of development; in essence, approving land use development only after there is sufficient funding to pay for the necessary public infrastructure such as schools. A second reason that may help explain Florida's greater equity in school construction spending is the fact that the state has sixty-seven school districts compared to California's more than one thousand, which greatly vary in size. Fewer, larger districts may be better able to prioritize funding to meet need across heterogeneous schools and regions. Still, data-driven decision making appears to have benefits.

2. Conduct research on the effect school facilities have on student performance, neighborhood quality, and land use patterns. While a variety of linkages between school facilities, school quality, and communities have been posited by us in this chapter and others, little empirical work has been done to test and understand the relationships and the mechanisms at play. Establishing more proven and quantifiable relationships (or disproving them) will give decision makers in school districts and other local government entities the footing to better coordinate and complement their respective investment efforts in schools and neighborhoods. For example, how can school renovation funds be best utilized to maximize enhancements in student performance? Are there design or condition improvements that yield more return than others? Do these then, in turn, translate into increased neighborhood desirability or investment in the case of older, existing neighborhoods? Often, local leaders and media sources make claims that new or modernized schools will help revitalize targeted neighborhoods, yet the mechanisms by which this may happen are unclear. Likewise, the school sprawl debate needs better analysis. Many of the claims are based on anecdotal evidence; while research has looked at the impacts associated with large fringe schools (e.g., increased automobile trips, high land consumption, and less walking or bicycling to school), little research has looked at whether these school sites are chosen before or after surrounding land development approvals. In other words, are the so-called sprawl schools driving growth or simply responding to it?

3. Conduct research on school district–level decision making on capital spending, including new school siting. School districts prioritize their limited school capital funds based on a variety of criteria, from growing or shrinking enrollment across schools and meeting base health and safety minimums to upgrading to incorporate new technologies. These decisions determine when new schools are built and when older schools receive upgrades or expansions or get shuttered altogether. As we argue in this chapter, these decisions have impacts on neighborhoods, human health, the environment, and social equity. Research should investigate the processes by which school districts make capital investment decisions and the criteria used. From this research, best practices in school district asset management should be developed—ones that support school district fiscal responsibility and principles of smart growth, healthy communities, and social equity.

4. Conduct research on how school buildings and sites are utilized by entities other than school districts. School buildings and grounds are often utilized for a variety of purposes by a variety of users, which in many cases, may be an unmeasured amenity or asset in many communities. We do not address the asset and land management of school districts in this chapter, largely because there is so little data on this issue. Documentation and analysis of the way school buildings and grounds are used by other agencies, as recreation, green space buffers, or transitional zoning, as well as locations for school-based social services or other community-based programs, will better enable understanding of the value of existing schools in existing communities. Such research will aid in crafting school facility investment and use policies that support this wide variety of uses.

While much has been written about the role of public policies in the creation of inequality (e.g., see Carr and Kutty 2008), public school construction spending has had little such investigation. A main reason is that it is overlooked as having the multitude of impacts on students, neighborhoods, and regions that growing evidence suggests it does. The issue of school facility planning and investment has traditionally flown under everyone's radar, from educators to researchers, even though the total sums tens of billions of dollars annually. Researchers have argued that the smart growth movement must look toward improving urban school quality (Baum 2004)—and we would add, joining with the social equity and healthy communities movements, which means strategically aligning school capital investments to support the broader local or regional goals of improving existing communities, ensuring sustainable regional growth, promoting healthier communities, and increasing social equity. In part, this requires adequately investing capital dollars to maintain and upgrade older schools in existing neighborhoods as well as making well-informed decisions when planning and siting entirely new schools. In general, regions across the country need investment in existing infrastructure to advance the goals of smart growth, regional equity, and healthy communities. Public school construction is one important and strategic infrastructure investment all communities make and should be done in accordance with the principles of these increasingly interrelated movements.

NOTES

1. BEST is a national community of practice with nine partner organizations nationally—working toward a vision where all children learn in school buildings that are safe and educationally adequate and that serve as community anchors in vibrant, healthy neighborhoods. BEST partners engage in and conduct research on school facility policy, spending, design, condition, and planning; http://www.bestschoolfacilities.org.
2. Each year the U.S. Census of Governments collects data on capital outlay for each state and school district. Capital outlay expenditures by school districts are reported in the Public Elementary-Secondary Education Finance Data and include construction of fixed assets (construction services), purchasing fixed assets (including land and existing buildings and grounds), and equipment (instructional and other or nonspecific). For more information, see http://census.gov/govs/cog.
3. Florida labor costs are 81 percent of the national average and California is 108 percent of the national average, according to Engineering News Record construction indices, 2003.
4. Nationally, the GAO found that one-third of all public school buildings in the country—about 25,000 serving nearly fourteen million children—were found to be in a serious state of disrepair.

Twenty-five million children attend schools in buildings with at least one unsatisfactory condition. These decrepit schools serve primarily minority and low-income students.

5. In the landmark *Abbott IV* (1997) and *Abbott V* (1998) rulings, the New Jersey Supreme Court ordered a set of education programs and reforms widely recognized to be the most fair and just in the nation. For more on the *Abbott* "education adequacy" framework, see http://www.edlaw center.org/ELCPublic/AbbottvBurke/AboutAbbott.htm.

6. The figures are derived by taking the total hard cost start bid amounts for projects awarded between 1995 and 2004 from the McGraw-Hill data set and analyzing them by 2000 U.S. Census median household income by zip codes, then dividing the total expenditure within a zip code by the number of public school-age children in preschool through twelfth grade living within the zip code where the project is located.

REFERENCES

American Planning Association (APA) and American Institute of Certified Planners (AICP). 2000. The millennium survey: A national poll of American voters' view on land use. Washington, DC: APA and AICP.

American Society of Civil Engineers (ASCE). 2005. Report card for America's infrastructure. http:// www.asce.org/files/pdf/reportcard/methodologyandgrades.pdf.

Baldassare, Mark. 2002. Public Policy Institute of California statewide survey: Special survey on land use. San Francisco: Public Policy Institute of California.

Baum, Howell S. 2004. Smart growth and school reform: What if we talked about race and took community seriously? *Journal of the American Planning Association* 70 (1): 14–26.

Beaumont, Constance E. 2003. *State policies and school facilities: How states can support or undermine neighborhood schools and community preservation.* Washington, DC: National Trust for Historic Preservation.

Beaumont, Constance E., and Elizabeth G. Pianca. 2002. *Historic neighborhood schools in the age of sprawl: Why Johnny can't walk to school.* Washington, DC: National Trust for Historic Preservation.

Bell, Judith, and Victor Rubin. 2007. *Why place matters: Building a movement for healthy communities.* Oakland, CA: PolicyLink.

Black, Sandra E. 1999. Do better schools matter? Parental valuation of elementary education. *Quarterly Journal of Economics* 114 (2): 577–99.

Bogart, William T., and Brian A. Cromwell. 2000. How much is a neighborhood school worth? *Journal of Urban Economics* 47 (2): 280–305.

Brunner, Eric J. 2006. *Financing school facilities in California.* Palo Alto, CA: Stanford University.

California Department of Education. 2006. *Williams* case history. http://www.cde.ca.gov/eo/ce/wc/ wmslawsuit.asp.

Carr, James H, and Nandinee K. Kutty. 2008. *Segregation: The rising costs for America.* London: Routledge.

Colmenar, Raymond A., Francisco Estrada, Theresa Lo, and Richard Raya. 2005. *Ending school overcrowding in California: Building quality schools for all children.* Oakland, CA: PolicyLink and the Mexican American Legal Defense Fund.

Council of Educational Facility Planners International (CEFPI) and U.S. Environmental Protection Agency (EPA). 2004. *Schools for successful communities: An element of smart growth planning.* Scottsdale, AZ: Council of Education Facility Planners International.

Ewing, Reid, T. Schmid, R. Killingsworth, A. Zlot, and S. Raudenbush. 2003. Relationship between urban sprawl and physical activity, obesity and morbidity. *American Journal of Health Promotion* 18(1): 47–57.

Filardo, Mary. 1999. Elements of a well managed school construction program. Report to the World Bank. Washington, DC: 21st Century School Fund.

———. 2008. Good buildings, better schools: An economic stimulus opportunity with long-term benefits. Economic Policy Institute, Briefing Paper #216. Washington, DC: EPI.

Filardo, Mary, Jeffrey M. Vincent, Ping Sung, and Travis Stein. 2006. *Growth and disparity: A decade of U.S. public school construction.* Washington, DC: Building Educational Success Together.

Fox, Radhika, and Angela Glover-Blackwell. 2004. *Regional equity and smart growth: Opportunities for advancing social and economic justice in America.* Funders' Network for Smart Growth and Livable Communities Translation Paper. Coral Gables, FL: Funders' Network for Smart Growth and Livable Communities Translation Paper.

Fox, Radhika, and Sarah Truehaft. 2005. *Shared prosperity, stronger regions: An agenda for rebuilding America's core cities.* Oakland, CA: PolicyLink.

Glover-Blackwell, Angela, and Sarah Truehaft. 2008. *Regional equity and the quest for full inclusion.* Oakland, CA: PolicyLink.

Higgins Steve, Elaine Hall, Kate Wall, Pam Woolner, and Caroline McCaughey. 2005. The Impact of School Environments: A literature review. Report for The Design Council by Centre for Learning and Teaching School of Education, Communication and Language Science, University of Newcastle.

Kouri, Christopher. 1999. *Wait for the bus: How low country school site selection and design deter walking to school and contribute to urban sprawl.* Charleston: South Carolina Coastal Conservation League.

Landis, John, and Heather Hood. 2005. *California state infill housing study report.* Berkeley, CA: Institute of Urban and Regional Development, University of California.

Local Government Commission. 2002. *New schools for older neighborhoods: Strategies for building our communities' most important assets.* Sacramento, CA: Local Government Commission and National Association of Realtors.

Maine State Planning Office. 1997. *The costs of sprawl.* Augusta: Executive Department, Maine State Planning Office.

McClelland, Mac, and Keith Schneider. 2004. *Hard lessons: Causes and consequences of Michigan's school construction boom.* Beulah, MI: Michigan Land Use Institute.

McDonald, Noreen C. 2007. Active transportation to school: Trends among U.S. schoolchildren, 1969–2001. *American Journal of Preventive Medicine* 32 (6): 509–16.

McKoy, Deborah L., and Jeffrey M. Vincent. 2008. Housing and Education: The Inextricable Link. In *Segregation: The Rising Costs for America*, ed. James H. Carr and Nandinee K. Kutty. New York: Routledge.

McKoy, Deborah, Jeffrey M. Vincent, and Carrie Makarewicz. 2008. Integrating infrastructure planning: The role of schools. *ACCESS* 33: 18–26.

McMahon, Edward T. 2000. School sprawl. *Planning Commissioners Journal* 39: 16–18.

McMillan, Tracy. 2007. The relative influence of urban form on a child's travel mode to school. *Transportation Research Part A* 41 (1): 69–79.

National Center for Education Statistics (NCES). 1999. *How Old are America's Public Schools?* Issue Brief, NCES 1999–048.

Orfield, Gary, and Chungmei Lee. 2004. *Brown at 50: King's dream or Plessy's nightmare?* Cambridge, MA: Civil Rights Project, Harvard University.

Orfield, Myron. 2002. *American metropolitics: The new suburban reality*. Washington, DC: Brookings Institution.

Passmore, Sam. 2002. *Education and smart growth: Reversing school sprawl for better schools and communities*. Washington DC: Charles Stewart Mott Foundation in collaboration with the Funders Network for Smart Growth and Livable Communities and Grantmakers in Aging.

Pastor, Manuel, Jr., and Deborah Reed. 2005. Understanding equitable infrastructure investment for California. The California 2025 Project, Public Policy Institute of California.

Policy Analysis for California Education (PACE) and Center for Cities & Schools (CC&S). 2009. *Smart growth, smart schools: Investing in education facilities and stronger communities*. Berkeley, CA: PACE and CC&S.

Proscio, Tony. 2003. *Community development and smart growth: Stopping sprawl at its source*. Washington DC: Funders Network for Smart Growth and Livable Communities.

Rothstein, Richard. 2004. *Class and schools: Using social, economic, and educational reform to close the black-white achievement gap*. Washington DC: Economic Policy Institute and Teachers College, Columbia University.

Rubin, Victor. 2006. *Safety, growth, and equity: Infrastructure policies that promote opportunity and inclusion*. Oakland, CA: PolicyLink.

Salvesen, David, and Philip Hervey. 2003. *Good schools, good neighborhoods: The impacts of state and local school board policies on the design and location of schools in North Carolina*. Chapel Hill, NC: Center for Urban and Regional Studies, University of North Carolina at Chapel Hill.

Schlossberg, Marc, J. Green, Paige Paulson, Bethany Johnson, and Robert Parker. 2006. School trips: Effects of urban form and distance on travel mode. *Journal of the American Planning Association* 72 (3): 337–46.

Schneider, Mark. 2002. *Do school facilities affect academic outcomes?* Washington, DC: National Clearinghouse for Educational Facilities.

Steward, W. Cecil. 1999. Lincoln, Nebraska, public school systems: The advance scouts for urban sprawl. In *Under the blade: The conversion of agricultural landscapes*, ed. Richard K. Olson and Thomas A. Lyson. 370–73. Boulder, CO: Westview Press.

Tiebout, Charles. 1956. A pure theory of local expenditures. *Journal of Political Economy* 64 (5): 416–24.

Turner, Margery Austin, and Julie Fenderson. 2006. *Understanding diverse neighborhoods in an era of demographic change*. Washington, DC: Urban Institute.

U.S. Environmental Protection Agency (EPA). 2003. Travel and environmental implications of school siting. EPA 231-R-03-004. Washington, DC: U.S. EPA. http://www.epa.gov/smartgrowth/pdf/school_travel.pdf.

U.S. General Accounting Office (GAO). 1995. School facilities: Condition of America's schools. Washington, DC: U.S. GAO.

———. 1996. School facilities: Profiles of school conditions by state. Washington DC: U.S. GAO.

Uline, Cynthia, and Megan Tschannen-Moran. 2008. The walls speak: The interplay of school facilities, school climate, and student achievement. *Journal of Educational Administration* 46: 55–73.

Vincent, Jeffrey M. 2006. Public schools as public infrastructure: Roles for planning researchers. *Journal of Planning and Education Research* 25 (4): 433–37.

Vincent, Jeffrey M., and Deborah L. McKoy. 2008. *The complex and multi-faceted nature of school construction costs: Factors affecting California*. Berkeley, CA: Center for Cities and Schools.

Weiss, Jonathan D. 2004. *Public schools and economic development: What the research shows*. Cincinnati, OH: Knowledgeworks Foundation.

The Implications of School Location Change for Healthy Communities in a Slow-Growth State
A Case Study of Michigan

MARK A. WYCKOFF, ADESOJI ADELAJA,
AND MELISSA A. GIBSON

MICHIGAN, LIKE MANY OTHER NORTH CENTRAL U.S. STATES, HAS HAD SLOW POPULA-tion growth for three decades. The slow growth has not been uniform, as many communities experienced slow to moderate population growth while others experienced population decline. Most of the growth in Michigan was due to a combination of intraregional population shifts and more births than deaths, with very little foreign or domestic migration. In contrast, central city areas experienced population decline largely due to out-migration to nearby suburban communities. In rural parts of the state, population decline was often the result of migration to (or near to) other small rural town centers. The largest net population shifts have been in the metro areas.

Figure 1 illustrates the general movement of population out of a central city into suburbs, movement within suburbs, and movement out of suburbs into nearby rural areas. This process

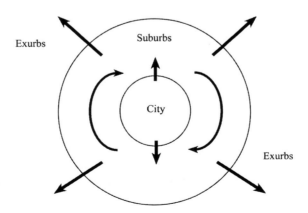

Figure 1. Principal Demographic Shifts in Urban Areas in Michigan

is easily observed from available census information over the past forty years. However, the degree of movement has varied significantly from one urban core city and associated metropolitan area to another.

School enrollment changes usually reflect general population changes, and Michigan is no exception. However, school openings and closures are not nearly as elastic as population and demographic changes for obvious economic and political reasons.[1] Nevertheless, the decisions to open or close schools can have a profound effect on community growth or decline, community stature and sense of place.

For various unique institutional reasons, school location decisions are often intertwined with other decisions. However, such decisions are often made without due consideration of other basic issues and impacts, including child health and community well-being. In order to improve understanding of these more complex interrelationships, the Michigan State University (MSU) Land Policy Institute (LPI) embarked on a comprehensive long-term study focused on school location geography, demography, and economics. The first phase of this initiative is to understand recent trends in demographic change, school openings, and school closings and the fundamental structure within which new school location and closure decisions are made. Such an analysis is a necessary preliminary step to understanding the complex interrelationships involved in the school geography issue and to identifying more effective policies to improve public benefits of school location decisions.

This chapter is one of several related projects and atlases that report on the results of the first phase of research by the MSU LPI into school location in Michigan from 1970 to the present.[2] The chapter focuses on providing answers to the following five questions:

- What has historically occurred with regard to school location?
- What are some of the recent trends and the land use implications of such trends?
- What are the differences in school location decisions between areas with enrollment growth and areas with declining enrollments?
- What is the institutional structure for making school location decisions?
- What opportunities exist for improving public policy on school location?

The very complex sets of interrelated parameters that exist in school location decisions likely vary from state to state. While this research is focused on Michigan, the observations are likely to be of value to other states facing population decline, economic decline, or both, many of which are in the North Central region of the United States. This research may also be of value to large older urban areas and very rural areas across the nation.

This chapter and other LPI research on schools complement research completed by faculty at Michigan State University, the University of Michigan, and Wayne State University on related aspects of the institutional structure for school location decisions in Michigan.[3]

The remainder of this chapter is organized as follows:

- Schools and healthy communities
- Historical school siting in Michigan
- Institutional structure for school siting
- Demographic change in Michigan
- School change in Michigan
- Summary of key observations

SCHOOLS AND HEALTHY COMMUNITIES

A community with a balanced set of land uses is comprised of residential, commercial, office, industrial, and governmental land uses, often surrounded by farm and/or forest lands. These land uses create the demand for specialized services, including roads, water, sewer, drainage, waste disposal, recreation, education, and library services. Some of these services are provided by the public sector, while others are provided by the private sector. Our focus in this chapter is the provision of public K–12 education facilities in the context of their role in healthy communities.

For the last decade, the Healthy Communities Movement has been active around the world, encompassing about a half-dozen major national and international initiatives and hundreds of local initiatives, organized loosely around the concept of "healthy communities."[4] As explained earlier in the "Introduction and Problem Context," a healthy community is defined as one in which all these needs of citizens are equitably and sustainably met within the context of community prosperity. Given the important role that K–12 schools play not only in student education but also in social interaction and building a sense of community and place, as well as serving as a source of community pride, K–12 schools must be carefully located if the educational and social functions of schools are to contribute to a healthy community (Bingler, Quinn, and Sullivan 2003).

A considerable number of papers, reports, and case studies have been published on the relationship of schools to a healthy community in the last decade (Jackson and Kochtitzky 2002). Several major reports have focused on developing principles of building better learning environments. At the U.S. Department of Education's National Symposium on School Design in October 1998, six principles were endorsed by the American Institute of Architects, the American Association of School Administrators, the Council of Educational Facility Planners International, and the Construction Managers Association of America. The six principles of building better learning environments they established are as follows (Bingler, Quinn, and Sullivan 2003):

- Enhance teaching and learning and accommodate the needs of all learners
- Serve as the center of the community
- Result from a planning and design process that involves all community interests
- Provide for health, safety, and security
- Make effective use of all available resources
- Be flexible and adaptable.

School location is a critical dimension in each of these principles, but it is not the central focus. The health dimension is prominent not only for its role in quality-of-life movements but more fundamentally because of rapidly rising childhood obesity. In Michigan, childhood obesity has risen from 4 percent in 1963 to 12 percent in 2005 (with another 13 percent at risk of being overweight). This is just below the nation as a whole (Michigan Department of Community Health 2006b; Boyse 2007; CDC 2007). Experts say that obesity is common enough among children that we should consider it an epidemic (U.S. National Institute of Environmental Health Sciences 2005).

There are many reasons for rising obesity, but one is that "walking and biking trips to school have dropped 40 percent over the past 20 years in Michigan," according to the State's

Surgeon General (Michigan Surgeon General's Health Status Report 2004). The National Trust for Historic Preservation (NTHP) published an influential report on reasons "Why Johnny Can't Walk to School," such as new schools being sited farther away from the school population served (Beaumont and Pianca 2002).

One response to concerns over growing childhood and adult obesity in Michigan has been a series of health initiatives. The Michigan Governor's Council on Physical Fitness, Health & Sports provides several programs and tools oriented around healthy communities and schools (Michigan Fitness Foundation 2008). The Safe Routes to School Program partners with the Michigan Department of Transportation to "facilitate the planning, development, and implementation of projects and activities that will improve safety and reduce traffic, fuel consumption and air pollution in the vicinity of elementary schools" (Wilkerson and Kokinakis 2006; Eberlein 2006). Michigan Health Tools is a suite of community assessments focused on evaluating and improving community health (Michigan Department of Community Health 2006). The Promoting Active Communities Program seeks to integrate school planning and community health. It has received a high degree of recognition by communities in Michigan. The program includes an online assessment focused on improving walkability and recognizing communities that make active living improvements with an award.[5] The governor also proposed a new state $300 million bond initiative to fund new smaller high schools in communities with underperforming students.[6] In short, these initiatives are based in part on the belief that if schools are located close to the school-age population they serve, then the potential for walking and biking goes up. Some evidence reveals this to be true (U.S. EPA 2003).

But for children to walk or bike to school, the infrastructure must be in place. If in place, adults are more prone to use it, and the community becomes more attractive to knowledge workers who place a premium on healthy living and walking and biking options.[7] Thus communities that meet the walking and biking needs of children are places that attract others who share those objectives. Meeting basic health needs also serves to improve local quality of life for everyone on many different levels: health, education, and economy in particular. This is part of the reason there is so much growing attention on placemaking in the new economy and one of the reasons why school siting is important in a state like Michigan, which is struggling to adapt itself to the new economy.

HISTORICAL SCHOOL SITING IN MICHIGAN

Ironically, in both rural and urban areas in Michigan, schools used to be located in ways that contributed to healthy children while also meeting other design considerations that have once again become important—such as small school size and neighborhood orientation. Urban schools naturally were located in areas with a high concentration of residents, served as the anchor for a number of community activities, and were easily accessible to a large number of school-age children. Rural schools used to be small, relatively close (at least one in each township), and in a location that put them no more than three miles from any home. Most were one-room schools serving grades one through six or one through eight, with not more than thirty children in most schools.

Schools used to be the centerpiece of small towns and urban neighborhoods and still are in some places today. Their importance to neighborhood development was well established in the nation as a whole by the 1920s. Some developers left space for school buildings as a part of the development plan in order to attract the target market—parents with children. Some well-known national examples include Radburn in New Jersey and Forest Hill Gardens on Long Island in New York (Klaus 2002; Lee and Stabin-Nesmith 2001). This practice was formalized as a part of city planning by Clarence Perry, who developed the Perry Neighborhood Unit Theory (Perry 1929). Perry's neighborhood plan attempted to separate vehicular and pedestrian traffic and develop community life around the neighborhood school (Keating and Krumholz 1998; see fig. 2).

Perry viewed neighborhoods as a "cellular unit" that was critical for the efficient functioning of a city and a safe environment for families and school children to live in. An elementary school was the usual center of the neighborhood, and it was connected to green space or nearby play areas. Other central facilities could include a community building like a library or meeting hall or a church. Most traffic passed on thoroughfares along the perimeter of the neighborhood while only vehicles coming and going from homes would traverse the center of the neighborhood. An interconnected system of sidewalks linked all parts of the neighborhood and it was a very pedestrian-friendly place. Commercial development was in a few key locations along the perimeter to permit easy pedestrian access from the neighborhood while also serving passing motorists.

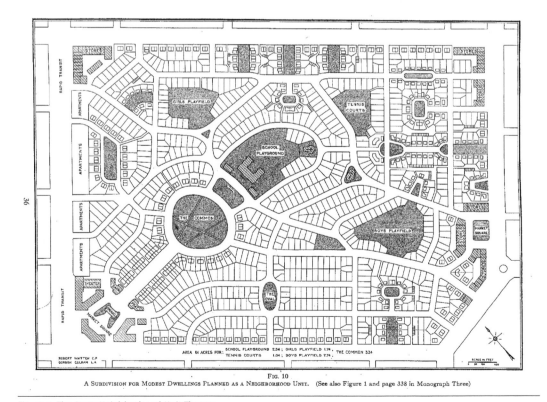

Fig. 10
A Subdivision for Modest Dwellings Planned as a Neighborhood Unit. (See also Figure 1 and page 338 in Monograph Three)

Figure 2. The Perry Neighborhood Unit Theory
Source: Clarence Arthur Perry, 1929, *The neighborhood unit*, Regional Survey of New York and Its Environs. Neighborhood and Community Planning, Regional Plan Association, vol. 7, pg. 36. Reproduced with permission of Bob Yaro, Regional Plan Association, New York.

Perry developed the neighborhood unit to be applied in a wide range of situations, including suburbs, dense urban areas, areas surrounded by light industry, and even areas integrated into redevelopment schemes. In his best known writing on the subject, Perry applied his neighborhood unit principles to three different settings and found the following parameters to be appropriate:

- A neighborhood size that served from 6,000 (in modest, medium density single family homes) to 10,000 persons (in high density apartments)
- A centrally located elementary school of about 1,000 to 1,600 students
- Scattered parks and recreation areas of at least 10 percent of the neighborhood area
- Commercial development (local shops) at about fifty feet per one hundred residents around the perimeter of the neighborhood (Perry 1929).

Perry advocated locating elementary schools in the middle of residential neighborhoods with a service area of one-quarter of a mile walking distance (five-minute walking distance). Many neighborhoods and city plans throughout Michigan reflected Perry's approach (albeit at much lower densities) well into the 1960s. The leading New Urbanist firm of Duany Plater Zyberk & Co. has resurrected Perry's original graphic depicting his idea and slightly updated it in 2002 to help promote the idea again nationwide (Walters 2007).

Perry's Neighborhood Unit Theory nicely complements the objectives of the healthy communities movement. Smart growth, perhaps the most prominent of the contemporary quality-of-life movements, has four (of ten) tenets that are especially pertinent (Smart Growth Network 2008):

- Create walkable neighborhoods or communities
- Foster distinctive, attractive communities with a strong sense of place
- Take advantage of compact development design
- Strengthen and direct development toward existing communities.

Similarly, the Congress for the New Urbanism,[8] the American Institute of Architects Communities by Design Initiative,[9] and the new Leadership in Energy & Environmental Design for Neighborhood Development (LEED ND) standards[10] all emphasize walkability and the location of key public facilities (including schools) within walking distance of the population served. However, while this return to what some describe as traditional or neotraditional neighborhood design, as Clarence Perry popularized it, is contemporary practice for some developers, architects, planners, and landscape architects, it is not consistent with existing school siting standards in many states, including Michigan.

More recently, as population has shifted away from cities and first-ring suburbs toward outer suburbs and rural communities, the school siting framework has changed considerably. Current school siting standards are also quite different. They promote schools that are neither close to the bulk of students served nor integrated with other land uses at the center of the service area. Instead, they are land consumptive (in part to accommodate extensive athletic facilities), and that makes it difficult to locate them near dense residential areas. They usually intensify automobile dependence, and several studies have linked them to unhealthy community designs (Beaumont and Pianca 2002).

In Michigan, school siting has taken on a new and special significance, given the depressed economy it has experienced for the last seven years. Slowly, communities are beginning to learn that a key secret to successfully competing in the new economy is to build places that are attractive to knowledge workers. This has led to an emergent focus on placemaking (Adelaja 2008). Walkability is a key component of all contemporary placemaking strategies—in part because of its health benefits, but also because of the focus on creating a critical mass of places that knowledge workers want to go within a short distance and without automobiles. Attention to walkability, of course, also focuses more attention on the location of new schools (e.g., are they easy to walk to by the students and families that use them). Neighborhoods with centrally located schools have not been such an important placemaking strategy since Clarence Perry. The added benefit is that effective placemaking improves quality-of-life not only for children ages five to eighteen but also for all other age cohorts.

We expect to see more and more focus on placemaking as economic troubles mount in states experiencing serious recession or depression. This suggests the time is ripe for new land use policy on school siting as part of aggressive placemaking strategies.

INSTITUTIONAL STRUCTURE FOR SCHOOL SITING

The institutional structure within which K–12 education operates in Michigan is complex, though it is not much different from some other North Central states. Ironically, many of these states have been the hardest hit by declines in manufacturing caused by global competition. The huge challenges they face in adapting to the new economy are complicated by the downsizing of population and the complex institutional structure of decision making for government services.

Public schools provide education to about 90 percent of the school-age children in Michigan. Public schools are further divided into three subcategories, while there are two categories of private schools. Table 1 presents the number and enrollments of each type of school in 2006 as reflected in the database of the Center for Educational Performance and Information (CEPI), maintained by the Office of the State Budget.

The white lines on map 1 show the geography of the existing traditional public school districts in the state. The black lines indicate the boundaries of the intermediate school districts

Table 1. K–12 Schools in Michigan, 2006

	Traditional public school districts*	Traditional public schools	Alternative schools in traditional public school districts	Public charter schools	Private schools**
Number	551	3,095	672	248	896
Enrollment	1,589,083	1,549,351	39,732	90,254	148,765

*Does not include prekindergarten or ungraded students.
**Private Schools, 2005–2006, CEPI; in addition, there were 1,009 home schools with 1,636 children enrolled.

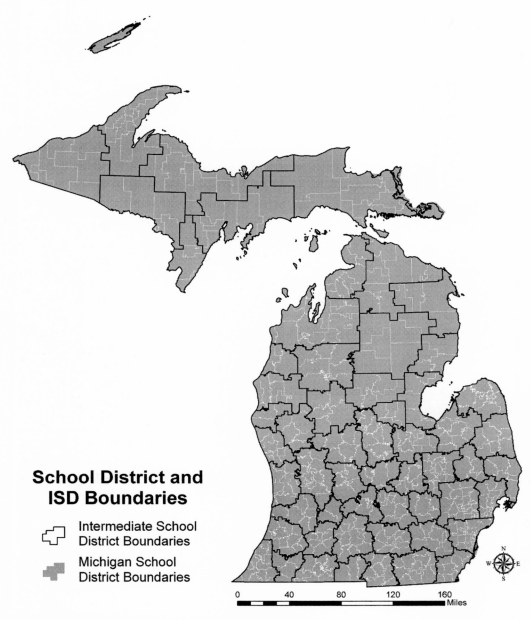

School District and ISD Boundaries

Intermediate School District Boundaries

Michigan School District Boundaries

0   40   80   120   160
Miles

Sources: Base map - Michigan Center for Geographic Information; Demographic- U.S. Census Bureau.
Prepared by Land Policy Research at the Land Policy Institute, Michigan State University. 2008.

Map 1. School District and ISD Boundaries

(ISDs). This structure and arrangement has changed little since a massive consolidation of small (often one-room school) districts in the 1950s. Charter schools first emerged as an option in 1994.[11] Twenty-seven state universities, community colleges, and ISDs are authorized to grant charters and monitor progress.[12]

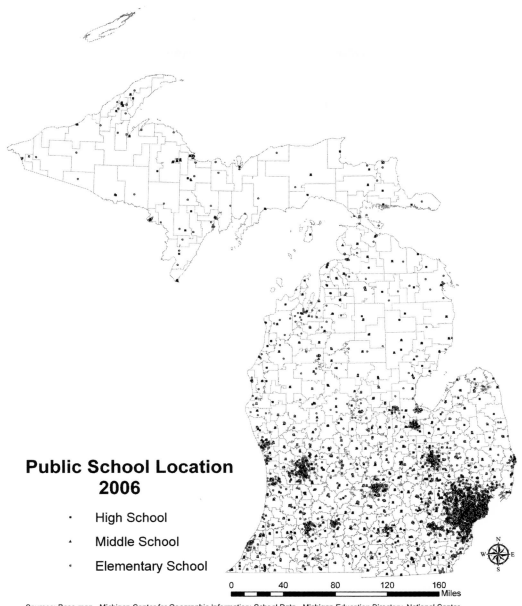

Public School Location 2006

- · High School
- ▲ Middle School
- · Elementary School

Sources: Base map - Michigan Center for Geographic Information; School Data - Michigan Education Directory, National Center for Education Statistics Common Core of Data, Center for Educational Performance & Information, LPI Survey of School Districts. Prepared by Land Policy Research at the Land Policy Institute, Michigan State University. 2008.

Map 2. Public School Location, 2006

Map 2 shows the location of all public schools by type, including charter schools in 2006. The overwhelming bulk of charter schools have been established in large cities and have attracted 90,254 students from the traditional public school districts (see table 1). Parents are often attracted to charter schools by having a choice in pursuit of a free, public education for their children. However, so far, there is little evidence that the charter schools in Michigan are providing a better education than traditional public schools. One observable outcome to date has been more creativity by traditional public school districts to try to attract students back, such as the creation of magnet schools and improved alternative education options for special needs children (MDE 2006; Horn and Miron 2000).

School districts are aggregated into fifty-seven ISDs, much like municipalities are also part of counties. ISDs provide a number of specialized administrative and instructional services that are not cost effective for every district to provide, including some special needs education and bulk purchasing. They also do auditing of student numbers for each district and provide career technical education and career preparatory programs. They are separate taxing units (MER 2000).

School districts are independent local governments with elected boards who have near complete autonomy in decisions about land acquisition and school facility location and design. Only recently were public schools required to be built to state construction code standards, whereas all other buildings have been subject to a state building code since the early 1970s.[13]

Unlike some states, public school district boundaries in Michigan have no relationship to municipal boundaries. Compare map 3, which shows the location of all counties (83), cities (274), and townships (1242) in Michigan to map 1 (259 villages are not depicted). Many public school districts overlap the boundaries of five to fifteen municipalities and many fall in more than one county. This creates numerous coordination problems and dissuades schools from cooperating with local governments on siting issues.

Table 2 lists the number of local units of government in Michigan by type. All cities, villages, and townships have the authority to plan and zone, but not all jurisdictions do so. Many townships are under county zoning in one of the two dozen rural counties, which have adopted zoning. Table 2 also shows the status of local planning and zoning in 1994 based on responses by all local governments to a state survey as well as the status in 2003, but 7 percent of local units of government did not respond in 2003, so the results are not directly comparable.

Table 2. Michigan Municipalities Engaged in Planning and Zoning in 1994 and 2003

Municipalities	Cities	Villages	Townships	Counties
Total municipalities (as of 1994)*	274	259	1,242	83
Number with plans, 1994[†]	224	115	499	47
Number with zoning, 1994[†]	261	174	583	26
Number with plans, 2003[‡]	254	155	756	61
Number with zoning, 2003[†]	256	186	797	25

Sources: *Michigan Municipal League and Michigan Townships Association, 2008; [†]Michigan Department of Management and Budget based on a 100 percent survey return in 1994, as published in Michigan Society of Planning Officials, 1995, Trend Future Project—Institutional structure working paper; and [‡]Institute for Public Policy Research, 2004, *To plan or not to plan*, Policy Brief, vol. 8. Not a 100 percent survey. http://www.ippsr.msu.edu/Publications/PBPlanZone .pdf. Data from the 2003 IPPSR Michigan Local Planning and Zoning Survey.

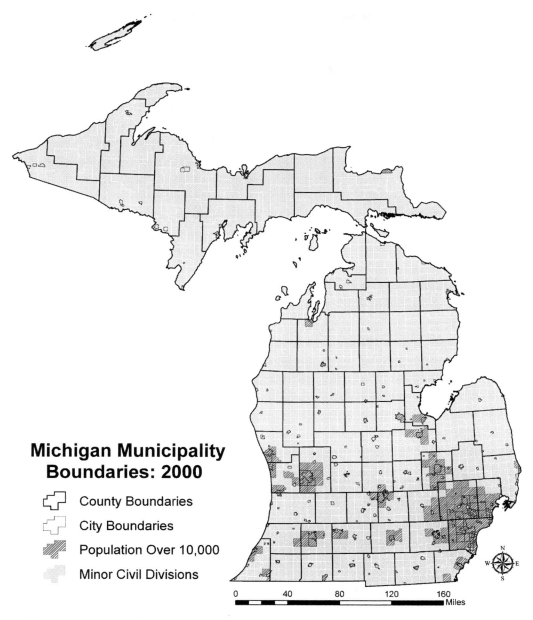

Michigan Municipality Boundaries: 2000

County Boundaries

City Boundaries

Population Over 10,000

Minor Civil Divisions

0   40   80   120   160
Miles

Sources: Base map - Michigan Center for Geographic Information; Demographic- U.S. Census Bureau.
Prepared by Land Policy Research at the Land Policy Institute, Michigan State University. 2008.

Map 3. Michigan Municipality Boundaries, 2000

Michigan is considered a modified home rule state, where home rule cities and villages have the greatest autonomy in local governance and townships and counties the least. For example, counties can only adopt ordinances specifically authorized by state law, whereas a home rule city can adopt any ordinance not precluded by state law. General law villages and general law townships fall somewhere in between. The hierarchy is complicated, as there are three types of cities and villages (home rule, fourth class, and general law), two types of townships (charter and general law), and three types of counties (general law, charter, and county executive), each with different powers and authority. However, they all can exercise planning and zoning, except counties cannot zone cities or villages or townships that have adopted zoning. Because of this, few counties zone in the densest part of Michigan (the lower half of the Lower Peninsula), where most townships have adopted zoning.

Traditional public school districts and charter schools currently have near autonomy in siting decisions due to a 2003 Michigan Supreme Court ruling stating that public schools were not subject to local zoning (Michigan Supreme Court 2003), but this has not always been the case. The issue of schools and the relationship to local zoning has been a significant legal issue in Michigan since 1982 when an appellate court ruled that public schools were subject to local zoning for the first time (Michigan Court of Appeals, 1983). Various statutory changes have tinkered with this relationship by partially taking away local zoning authority, but not to the satisfaction of either school districts or local governments. Local concerns usually focus on poor design for accommodating school traffic and buffers around both athletic facilities and abutting residences (Wyckoff 1998; Wyckoff and Cherry 1998). A 2006 statutory amendment to the State School Code made new high schools in townships subject to a coordinated site plan review process (Public Act 276 of 2006). However, this review occurs after the school has selected a site and prepared plans and ignores whether the land is zoned to permit a school in the first place. The state superintendent of public instruction has final authority to approve new school construction, but to our knowledge, no proposed school has ever been disapproved for any reason other than inadequate financing.

Private schools are and have always been subject to local zoning in Michigan. Most parochial schools are on the same site as or contiguous to a church, synagogue, or mosque. Other private schools are sometimes sited in old public school facilities.

Public traditional schools and charter schools receive operational funds from the state on a per pupil basis. Urban districts receive a little more than rural districts (Arsen and Plank 2003). However, unlike Great Lakes states like Ohio and Pennsylvania, where the state funds and oversees local school facility needs and construction (in order to ensure fiscal efficiency, equity, and uniformity in educational facilities), public school facilities in Michigan are funded locally. School districts usually bond for these facilities and local taxpayers must vote to approve the taxes associated with these facilities. School districts are not permitted to vote additional millage for operation of public schools.

Michigan has a low-interest bond fund available for use by poor school districts to build new schools. The state requirements for acceptance of bond applications do not include siting considerations tied to healthy community concepts, conformance with local plans and zoning, or any state siting standards.[14]

The Michigan Department of Education has been downsized over the past thirty years. A separately elected board oversees its operation and selects the state superintendent. It is a multifunction department with a focus on establishing and maintaining state testing of students and overseeing progress under the federal No Child Left Behind program. Other responsibilities include grant oversight, auditing, design, and delivery of various programs and provision of legal guidance to parents and districts.

The state superintendent of public instruction has exclusive jurisdiction to approve or deny requests for new school facilities proposed by local school districts and charter schools. In the mid-1960s, Bulletin 412 was created to guide siting decisions. While Bulletin 412 is no longer considered useful by the Department of Education, it is still on the website of the office of the State Construction Code Commission and is cited by local school districts in defense of large site sizes. There is no differentiation between rural or urban settings in the guidelines. A high school is suggested to be sited on thirty-plus acres. There are very few urban high schools on half that acreage or in a city with that much land available. These guidelines are nearly identical to those of the Center for Educational Facilities Planning International, which have been the subject of considerable criticism for years because of their sprawl-inducing and health-limiting effects.[15] There are no considerations related to creating or maintaining a healthy community or even healthy neighborhoods in Bulletin 412.

While states that directly provide the funding for local public school facilities obviously have a strong ability to require school designs and locations that promote healthy community principles, states like Michigan have similar potential if the state superintendent substituted contemporary standards that are suitable for the geographic setting and incorporated healthy community principles for Bulletin 412. This obvious fact has not gone unnoticed by the Michigan chapter of the American Planning Association, which has adopted a policy platform advocating the creation of a coordinated public school and municipal siting process with proposed standards to guide the siting of new schools so as to promote smart growth principles (MAP 2007). Other states have gone further, such as proposing reconstruction on the site of the existing school as the first option to always be considered (Pennsylvania) or providing financial incentives to rebuild on the same site as in Vermont, Maryland, Massachusetts, Maine, and Washington (Beaumont and Pianca 2002).

In a state, such as Michigan, where the state has not assumed responsibility for the provision of local public school facilities, the lack of data makes the evaluation of school location change over time very difficult. It appears that states with available data about individual school facilities tend to be states that are responsible for the provision of local schools. Where local taxpayers pay for local schools, individual facility data are hard to come by before 1986 when the federal government began releasing some data as part of the National Center for Education Statistics (NCES) program (Speicher and Goldstein 2002).

The federal NCES data, however, have three major problems for use in Michigan. First, address data are not necessarily location specific as many of the schools are listed with PO boxes, making it impossible to locate them geographically without contacting the school directly. Second, federal definitions for classifying school location in proximity to urban or rural communities have changed multiple times since 1987. Third, information contained in the NCES data are provided by the states, which have different standards and operating practices. Although the NCES is trying to ensure consistency, the Michigan data do not always match information from other private sources that is also reported by school districts.

The complexity of the number of players and potential relationships and authorities in the Michigan institutional structure creates a climate of independent decision making that may not meet broader public interests with any consistency and leads to inequity in facility characteristics. It also fails to advance contemporary or neotraditional healthy community principles. When economic and demographic tumult is added on top of this structure, fair and predictable outcomes are even more unlikely as districts struggle to meet payroll and maintain facilities in the face of the following:

- Rapidly growing employee health care costs
- Declining enrollment (from continued declines in population per household, out-migration, and the associated loss of students and their per pupil revenues, as charter schools and private schools offer alternative choices, and urban students continue to score lower on standardized tests than their suburban counterparts)
- Declining average incomes of local residents (due to reduced employment)
- Reduced property values (which undermine the ability to gain approval for new taxes to upgrade, replace, or build new school facilities).

Some of the other disparate factors affecting traditional public school facility decisions include the following:

- Rate of enrollment growth or decline
- Competition for students from charters or open/closed enrollment policies (schools of choice, where parents are permitted to send their children to a school in another district if that district has chosen for one or more of its schools to be open as "schools of choice")[16]
- Unwillingness of traditional public schools to allow charter schools to buy or lease unused facilities because of the competition that charter schools would bring to the district
- Ability to attract new students based on the quality of education offered as reflected in standardized tests or contemporary concepts like magnet schools
- Impacts on school site size created by accommodating sport facilities and the subsequent reduced location options unless the land considered is farther away from existing residential areas
- Desire of parents for a growing number of school amenities that add to the base size of the facility
- Willingness or unwillingness of taxpayers to support school facility bond proposals, especially as the population of a district ages
- The influence and effect of consultants and architects on school facility design (Norton 2007)

To this set of variables are more traditional siting considerations such as the following:

- Size and efficiency
- Student performance relative to size and efficiency (especially in light of contemporary ideas about school size, such as the movement to smaller schools for improved quality of education; Stevenson 2002; Abramson 2007)
- Equity considerations
- Taxpayer attitude about perceived value of the investment and capacity to be taxed.

DEMOGRAPHIC CHANGE IN MICHIGAN

All new school siting and closure decisions are driven by changes in student population, which in turn are driven by larger demographic shifts. Following is a summary of the bigger demographic changes taking place in Michigan that relate to school enrollment and hence school opening and closing decisions. This analysis is informed by examination of approximately seventy variables as mapped on 275 geographic information system (GIS)–prepared maps depicting key U.S. Census data at the county, ISD, school district, and minor civil division

(MCD) level for the years 1990 and 2000. However, only the most basic demographic variables are described below.

Figure 3 depicts Michigan's total population from 1810 to 2000 and projections until 2030 (U.S. Census Bureau 1975, 2005). The rapid growth curve until 1970 is evident; after 1970, population growth drops off noticeably. The projections indicate this diminishing trend will continue through 2025 with the population growing only 7.6 percent to reach a total of 10,694,172 persons in 2025. After 2025, the total population is projected to decline as the baby boomers die.

While total population growth slowed somewhat in the 1970s, it slowed dramatically from 1980 to 1990 to 0.4 percent. During this period Michigan experienced a four-year "double-dip recession" while the nation had a much shorter and less severe recession. From 1980 to 1984, Michigan lost nearly 250,000 persons to net out-migration while it battled the largest automobile industry downturn since World War II. Yet the out-migration trend had been under way for some time. In fact, from the early 1970s to the early 1990s there were no years with net positive in-migration. While Michigan's population grew 6.9 percent from 1990 to 2000 (automobile sales boomed, riding a strong national economy and raising per capita income), it still trailed the nation in growth (13.2 percent; U.S. Census Bureau 1980, 1990, 2000).

Of the fifteen counties in the Upper Peninsula (all predominantly rural), only four had slightly positive net migration from 1960 to 2000; the rest experienced negative net migration. In Michigan's three Thumb counties: Huron, Sanilac, and Tuscola, all very agricultural, had negative net migration from 1960 to 1990 and only one had a positive net migration from 1990 to 2000. Of the thirteen urban counties, only four had positive net migration from 1960 to 1990, with only three of those positive from 1990 to 2000. Those three (Oakland,

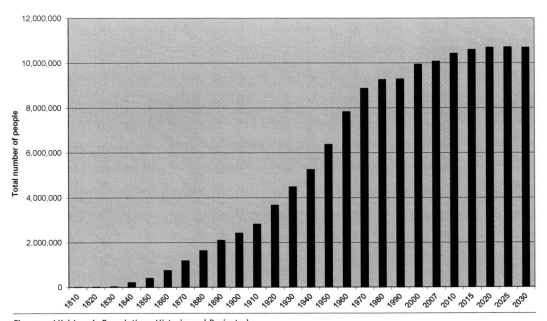

Figure 3. Michigan's Population: Historic and Projected
Source: U.S. Bureau of the Census.

Macomb, and Washtenaw) are all considered suburban to Wayne County, where Detroit is located (U.S. Census Bureau 1960, 1970, 1980, 1990, 2000).

The combined population of Michigan's ten largest cities is shown in figure 4. This includes a mix of old urban core cities and large suburban cities. The downward trend is evident.

Michigan's demographic prime, after which its population growth rate began to slow, probably occurred sometime between 1960 and 1970 when the baby boomers were graduating from high school. From 1900 to 1960, there had been six straight decades of population growth of 15 to 30 percent or more. In 1960, Michigan was the seventh largest state in the United States, and Detroit was ranked fifth among the largest cities in the nation (U.S. Census Bureau 1960). Detroit actually hit its population peak about 1955, when its population was estimated at 1.85 million. At that point, Detroit had infrastructure in place designed to accommodate a build-out population of about 2.2 million. However, since 1955, Detroit's population has fallen steadily (U.S. Census Bureau 1950, 1960, 1970, 2000). By 2000 it had fallen to 951,270 persons, a 48.6 percent decline. Detroit's population was estimated at 871,121 persons in 2006 (U.S. Census Bureau 2006). Six other large cities in Michigan also lost 20 to 35 percent of their population from 1950 to 2000: Flint (–38,200), Saginaw (–31,119), Bay City (–15,706), Jackson (–14,772), Royal Oak (–20,550, from 1960), and St. Clair Shores (–24,997, from 1970; U.S. Census Bureau 1950, 2000).

The projections illustrated on figure 3 were released in April 2005 based on 2000 U.S. Census data. Economic circumstances since then suggest that Michigan's population will not grow as much and will begin to fall much sooner than what is projected unless Michigan's

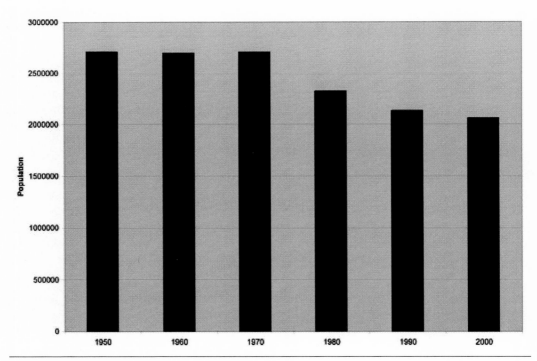

Figure 4. Population of Ten Largest Cities in Michigan, 1950–2000
Source: U.S. Bureau of the Census.

economy rebounds much faster than expected. From 2000 to 2006, Michigan lost about 240,000 manufacturing jobs. Most of these jobs were relatively high paying. Unemployment in Michigan has been the highest in the nation for most of the 2000s. Mortgage foreclosures remain near the top in the nation. The situation is described as a one-state recession (although many feel it is a depression). Michigan has faced serious state budget deficits every year since 2001 due to a declining revenue stream. A recent rewrite of business taxes was intended to spread the tax burden more equally across businesses instead of being shouldered largely by the suffering automotive sector, but because the recession has hit nearly all businesses, revenue stagnation is expected for several more years. Recent job losses have accelerated out-migration to the point that an estimated 75,000 persons left the state in 2006.[17]

The post-1950 out-migration and overall population decline has not been uniform. The populations of central cities, older "first-tier" suburbs, and most rural parts of the state have declined the most. The populations of the newest suburbs around the largest cities have increased. For example, the populations of the following large suburban cities all went up from 1950 to 2000: Warren (+240 percent), Livonia (+473 percent), and Sterling Heights (+1,812 percent). Several large cities that serve as the core of a small metropolitan area also rose in population over this period: Grand Rapids (+12 percent), Lansing (+29 percent), Kalamazoo (+33 percent), and Ann Arbor (+136 percent). However, according to U.S. Census Bureau estimates, these cities have all had a decrease in their population since 2000 (U.S. Census Bureau 2007). In short, except for the population that has migrated out of state, much of the rest of the population has merely moved around, out of the most rural areas and the oldest urban areas to small towns and suburban and suburbanizing areas. Since many of the suburbs are under the township form of government, politics has also shifted so that in 2000 slightly more than 50 percent of the population resided in townships rather than in cities or villages. Many of the new and larger schools have been built in townships where the new residents have higher average incomes and are families with children. They appear to be more willing than urban residents to support new taxes for new school buildings.

Map 4 illustrates total population by local unit of government in 2000. Map 5 shows changes in population by county from 1990 to 2000, while map 6 shows the same information by school district. The counties with the largest growth are suburban counties surrounding the largest cities. Most of the other growing counties are bisected by the interstate freeway system. Rural areas nearer to major metropolitan areas have experienced modest population increases over this period.

While the overall population of the state rose 11.9 percent (1,056,661 persons) between 1970 and 2000, the change has not been uniform over all age cohorts. As indicated in table 3, the total population of school-age children (five to seventeen) fell by 522,727 between 1970 and 2000, a drop of 21.4 percent. Similarly, the population under age five fell by 132,822, a decline of 16.5 percent. At the same time, the population over age sixty-five increased by 468,345 persons or 62 percent. As the baby boomers age, this number will go up substantially. The school-age population has moved as families moved. Map 7 illustrates the shift in school-age cohorts (five to eighteen years of age). These changes mirror the largest demographic patterns with growth in suburbs, declines in central cities, declines in lowest density rural areas, and flat to modest growth in the rest of the state.[18] These major patterns of demographic change are next examined in light of school change.

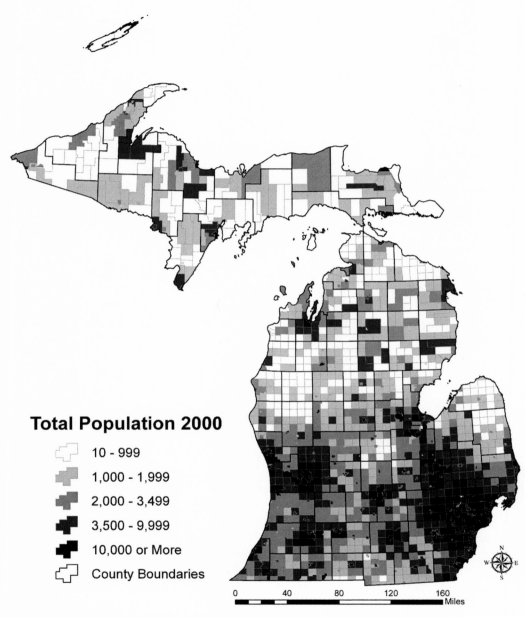

Total Population 2000

⬜	10 - 999
	1,000 - 1,999
	2,000 - 3,499
	3,500 - 9,999
⬛	10,000 or More
⬚	County Boundaries

0   40   80   120   160
Miles

Sources: Base map - Michigan Center for Geographic Information; School Data - Demographic - US Census Bureau.
Prepared by Land Policy Research at the Land Policy Institute, Michigan State University. 2008.

Map 4. Total Population, 2000

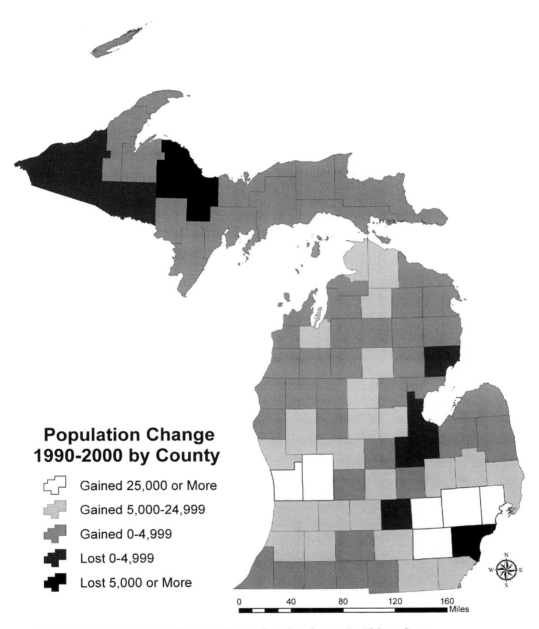

Population Change
1990-2000 by County

- Gained 25,000 or More
- Gained 5,000-24,999
- Gained 0-4,999
- Lost 0-4,999
- Lost 5,000 or More

0   40   80   120   160
Miles

Sources: Base map - Michigan Center for Geographic Information; School Data - Demographic - US Census Bureau.
Prepared by Land Policy Research at the Land Policy Institute, Michigan State University. 2008.

Map 5. Population Change by County, 1990–2000

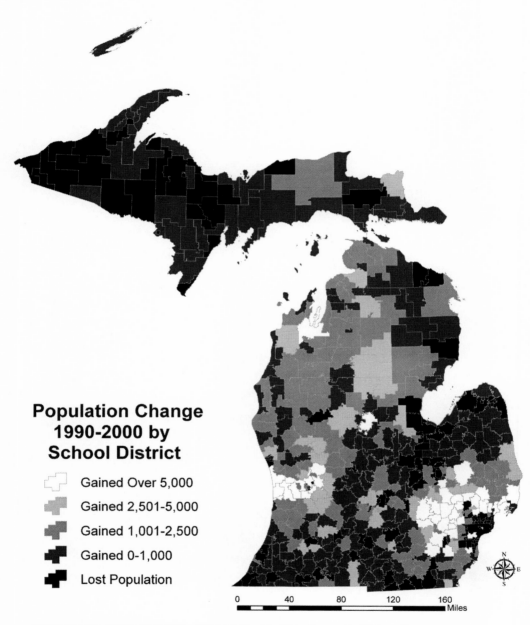

Population Change 1990-2000 by School District

- Gained Over 5,000
- Gained 2,501-5,000
- Gained 1,001-2,500
- Gained 0-1,000
- Lost Population

0   40   80   120   160
Miles

Sources: Base map - Michigan Center for Geographic Information; School Data - Demographic - US Census Bureau.
Prepared by Land Policy Research at the Land Policy Institute, Michigan State University. 2008.

Map 6. Population Change by School District, 1990–2000

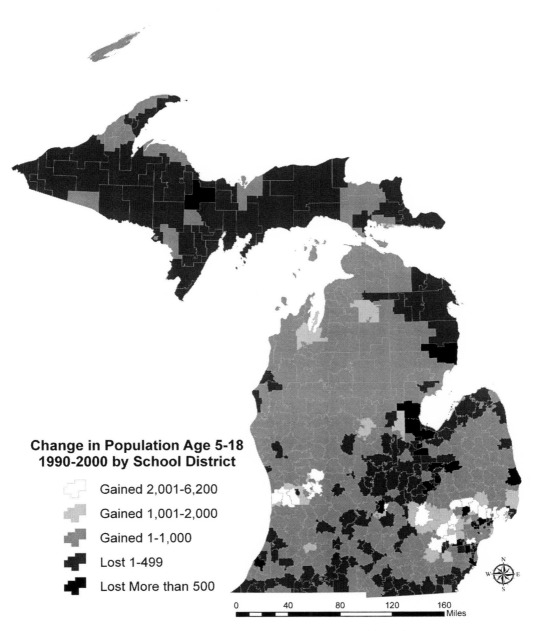

**Change in Population Age 5-18
1990-2000 by School District**

Gained 2,001-6,200

Gained 1,001-2,000

Gained 1-1,000

Lost 1-499

Lost More than 500

0   40   80   120   160
Miles

Sources: Base map - Michigan Center for Geographic Information; School Data - Demographic - US Census Bureau.
Prepared by Land Policy Research at the Land Policy Institute, Michigan State University. 2008.

Map 7. Change in Population Ages Five to Eighteen by School District, 1990–2000

Table 3. Age Cohort Change in Michigan from 1970 to 2000

Age cohort	1970	1980	1990	2000	Change 1970–2000	Change 1970–80 (%)	Change 1980–90 (%)	Change 1990–2000 (%)	Change 1970–2000 (%)
Under 5	804,463	685,113	702,554	672,005	–132,458	–14.84	2.55	–4.35	–16.47
5–17	2,446,907	2,066,873	1,756,211	1,923,762	–523,145	–15.53	–15.03	9.54	–21.38
18–24	1,031,542	1,257,828	1,004,527	932,137	–99,405	21.94	–20.14	–7.21	–9.64
25–44	2,084,685	2,544,286	2,980,702	2,960,544	875,859	22.05	17.15	–0.68	42.01
45–64	1,754,531	1,795,720	1,742,842	2,230,978	476,447	2.35	–2.94	28.01	27.16
65+	752,955	912,258	1,108,461	1,219,018	466,063	21.16	21.51	9.97	61.90
Total	8,875,083	9,262,078	9,295,297	9,938,444	1,063,361	4.36	0.36	6.92	11.98

Source: U.S. Census Bureau, 1970, 1980, 1990, and 2000 censuses.

SCHOOL CHANGE IN MICHIGAN

Due to varying definitions of school classifications, we utilized individual grade enrollment numbers from K–12, to establish K–5, 6–8, and 9–12 ranges. Prekindergarten, ungraded, and alternative education students were not included in this analysis. Table 4 shows the number and type of schools from 1970 to 2006. The net change from 1970 to 2006 is a decline of 686 schools or 18.14 percent. However, the data are from three different sources, so only the general trend can be identified.[19] Note that despite large enrollment drops (described later), the total number of middle and high schools has not varied much. The big drop has been in the number of elementary schools (27.4 percent).

Table 5 examines the data from 1990 to 2006 in more detail. Slight increases from 1990 to 2000 (when the economy in Michigan was very good) were followed by flat to falling facility numbers from 2000 to 2006. The total change over the sixteen-year period was a net loss of sixty schools. It is easy to see that schools are opening and closing in a geographic pattern very similar to demographic changes described earlier. Recall that map 2 shows the location of all traditional public schools in Michigan in 2000. Map 8 shows the change in school facilities from 1990 to 2006. New schools are largely being constructed in the suburbs where the population is growing the most, while most of the schools being closed are in the central cities and the most rural parts of the state.

Total enrollment in public schools from 1990 to 2006 is shown in table 6. In general, school enrollment in Michigan went up about 10 percent from 1990 to 2002 but went steadily down for the next four years. Map 9 shows how enrollment is distributed by school district. While total enrollment went up by nearly sixty thousand over this period, it fell by more than that in the elementary enrollment category and also had a slight fall in the middle school enrollment from 2000 to 2006. This appears to be the result of the demographic echo representing an increase in births from 1988 to 1990 and soon will result in enrollment declines unless the population of women of childbearing age begins to rise again and/or the average birthrate goes up. Figure 5 shows public school enrollment from 1986 to 2005. Total public school students went from 1,585,894 in 1986 to a peak of 1,772,123 in 2002 and fell to 1,711,544 in 2005.

The total enrollment trend is expected to continue to fall with declining births and the poor economic conditions of the state. Part of this is the result of the aging of the baby

Table 4. Total Number of Traditional Public School Facilities in Michigan by Type

	1970	*1980*	*1990*	*2000*	*2006*
Number total traditional facilities	3781	3602	3155	3258	3095
Number elementary (K–5)	2622	2333	2031	2072	1904
Number middle (6–8)	564	643	543	599	607
Number high (9–12)	595	626	581	587	584

Note: Charter schools and alternative schools are not considered "traditional" schools and are not included in this count. Also, 1970 and 1980 classifications were established by individual school districts and may not match the grade ranges of the remaining data exactly.

Table 5. Traditional Public School Type and Change, 1990–2006

School type	Count 1990	% of total	Count 2000	% of total	Count 2006	% of total	Change 1990–2000	% change	Change 2000–2006	% change	Change 1990–2006	% change
Elementary	2031	64.37	2072	63.6	1904	61.52	41	2.02	–168	–8.11	–127	–6.25
Middle	543	17.21	599	18.39	607	19.61	56	10.31	8	1.34	64	11.79
High	581	18.41	587	18.02	584	18.87	6	1.03	–3	–0.51	3	0.52
Total	3155		3258		3095		103	3.26	–163	–5.00	–60	–1.90

Source: National Center for Education Statistics Common Core of Data; Center for Educational Performance and Information, 1990, 2000 and CEPI for 2006.

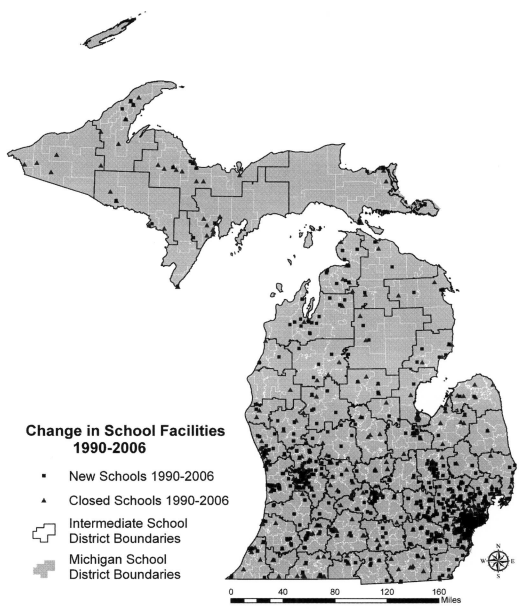

Change in School Facilities
1990-2006

- ■ New Schools 1990-2006

- ▲ Closed Schools 1990-2006

- Intermediate School
  District Boundaries

- Michigan School
  District Boundaries

```
0        40        80        120       160
                                      Miles
```

Sources: Base map - Michigan Center for Geographic Information; School Data - Michigan Education Directory, National Center for Education Statistics Common Core of Data, Center for Educational Performance & Information, LPI Survey of School Districts. Prepared by Land Policy Research at the Land Policy Institute, Michigan State University. 2008.

Map 8. Change in School Facilities, 1990–2006

Table 6. Traditional Public School Enrollment and Change, 1990–2006

School type	Enroll- ment 1990	% of total	Enroll- ment 2000	% of total	Enroll- ment 2006	% of total	Change	% change	Change	% change	Change	% change
Elementary	774,567	52.04	789,176	49.37	711,075	45.90	14,609	1.89	−78,101	−9.90	−63,492	−8.20
Middle	285,466	19.17	340,044	21.27	338,373	21.84	54,578	19.12	−1,671	−0.49	52,907	18.53
High	428,512	28.79	469,285	29.36	499,903	32.27	40,773	9.52	30,618	6.52	71,391	16.66
Total	1,488,545		1,598,505		1,549,351		109,960	7.39	−49,154	−3.07	60,806	4.08

Source: National Center for Education Statistics Common Core of Data; Center for Educational Performance and Information, 1990, 2000 and CEPI for 2006.

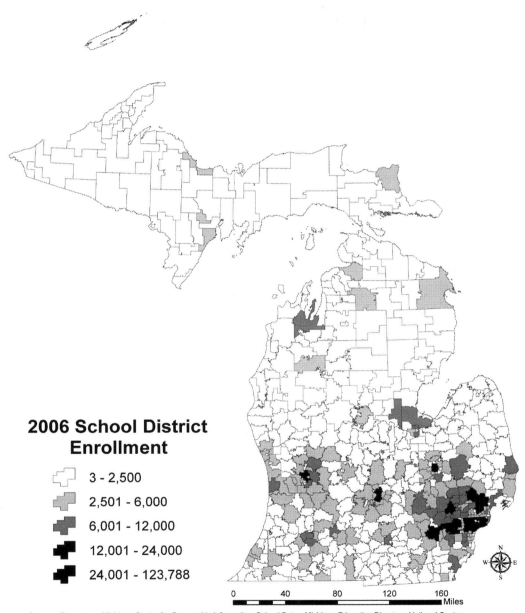

2006 School District Enrollment

- ⬜ 3 - 2,500
- 🟦 2,501 - 6,000
- 🟫 6,001 - 12,000
- ⬛ 12,001 - 24,000
- ⬛ 24,001 - 123,788

0   40   80   120   160
Miles

Sources: Base map - Michigan Center for Geographic Information; School Data - Michigan Education Directory, National Center for Education Statistics Common Core of Data, Center for Educational Performance & Information, LPI Survey of School Districts. Prepared by Land Policy Research at the Land Policy Institute, Michigan State University. 2008.

Map 9. School District Enrollment, 2006

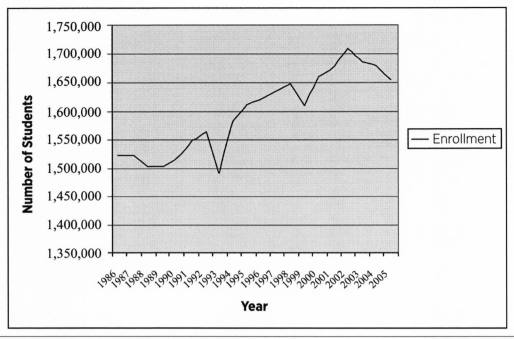

Figure 5. Total Public School Enrollment in Michigan
Source: NCES (National Center for Education Statistics), CCD (Common Core Data) for 1986–2005. This is the total number of students, minus enrollment in prekindergarten and ungraded, as compiled at the schools level for each year. It does not directly correspond to our total student enrollment for our target years, which was built upon individual grade enrollment at the school level (e.g., in 1999, total public schools enrollment is 1,609,793, and our total enrollment based on sums of K–12 for each school is 1,613,048, a difference of 3,255 students). Total enrollments compiled at the state and district level (as opposed to the school level) also result in slight differences in total enrollment.

boomers and subsequent generations being significantly smaller. Part of it is a general decline in birth rates and in the number of childbearing-age women, and much of it is reflected in the broader demographic shifts previously discussed.

While charter schools are public schools, they are not a part of existing public school districts. They are individual schools chartered in specific locations. The first charter school opened in Michigan in 1994. By 2000 there were 172 charter schools, and by 2006 there were 248. Enrollment rose from 46,078 in 2000 to 90,254 in 2006.[20] Table 7 shows the number of charter schools in Michigan by type, and table 8 shows enrollment by type from 2000 to 2006. Charter school enrollment has largely come at the expense of enrollment in traditional public school districts (rather than attracting children from private schools). Map 10 shows the change in total enrollment in traditional public schools from 1990 to 2006 (not including alternative schools or charter schools). Again, the suburban districts are growing and the densest urban and least dense rural districts are falling.

Statewide there were 103 more traditional public school buildings in 2000 than in 1990, but by 2006, there were 163 fewer schools in use. From 2000 to 2006, charter school enrollment nearly doubled with an increase of 44,176, a 96 percent increase. Additionally, 76 new charter schools were opened during this period. Of the new charter schools, 51 are elementary schools, 19 are high schools, and 6 are middle schools. Similarly the greatest increase in

Table 7. Charter School Type and Change, 2000–2006

School type	Count 2000	% of total	Count 2006	% of total	Change 2000–2006	% change
Elementary	128	74.42	179	72.18	51	39.84
Middle	11	6.40	17	6.85	6	54.55
High	33	19.19	52	20.97	19	57.58
Total	172	100.00	248	100.00	76	44.19

Source: CEPI, State of Michigan.

Table 8. Charter School Enrollment and Change, 2000–2006

School type	Enrollment 2000	% of total	Enrollment 2006	% of total	Change 2000–2006	% change
Elementary	37,958	82.38	70,766	78.41	32,808	86.43
Middle	2,670	5.79	4,983	5.52	2,313	86.63
High	5,450	11.83	14,505	16.07	9,055	166.15
Total	46,078	100.00	90,254	100.00	44,176	95.87

Source: CEPI, State of Michigan.

enrollment among charter schools was 32,808 new elementary students (86 percent), while middle schools increased by 2,313 (87 percent) and high schools by 9,055 (166 percent). The average enrollment per charter facility also increased substantially from 268 students to 362 students.

In contrast, total enrollment per district in traditional public schools rose from 1990 to 2006 by 60,806 students, or approximately 4 percent. However the rise was not uniform. From 1990 to 2000, enrollment rose by 109,960 students (about 7 percent), but from 2000 to 2006 it decreased by 49,154 students (about 3 percent). This drop is largely the result of increasing enrollment in charter schools. Together, total public school enrollment (traditional plus charter) rose by 104,982 students or 7 percent from 1990 to 2006.

Average enrollment per facility for traditional public school districts rose by eighteen students from 1990 to 2000 and by another ten students from 2000 to 2006 for an increase of twenty-eight students per facility over sixteen years (a 5.8 percent increase).

Analysis of the more detailed grade range data reveals some more startling changes. School districts are making a large number of changes to grade combinations. This is likely in response to the opposite challenges in shrinking and increasing districts. Shrinking districts, as well as those with budgetary issues, must close and consolidate schools, and uneven numbers of students per grade or facility limitations can "force" combinations of schools with elementary and middle school children or middle and high school children that were not previously in place. Similarly, as a growing school district builds new schools (especially high schools), they may turn over the existing high school for middle school use and increase the number of grades in middle school because of the larger facility.

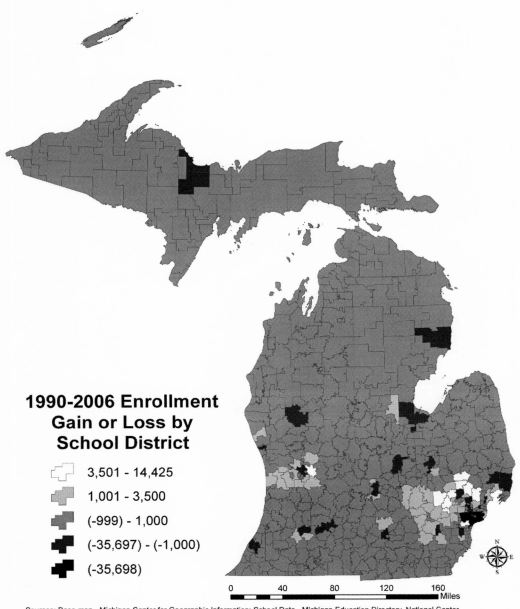

1990-2006 Enrollment Gain or Loss by School District

- 3,501 - 14,425
- 1,001 - 3,500
- (-999) - 1,000
- (-35,697) - (-1,000)
- (-35,698)

0   40   80   120   160
Miles

Sources: Base map - Michigan Center for Geographic Information; School Data - Michigan Education Directory, National Center for Education Statistics Common Core of Data, Center for Educational Performance & Information, LPI Survey of School Districts. Prepared by Land Policy Research at the Land Policy Institute, Michigan State University. 2008.

Map 10. Enrollment Gain or Loss by School District, 1990–2006

The biggest of these trends is a sharp decrease in the number of elementary schools with one or more middle school years (a decline of 460 from 1990 to 2006, 56 percent) and an increase by 218 of elementary only schools (K–5). Similarly there has been a decline in the number of high schools with one or more middle school years (70 or 52 percent). Likewise, the number of middle schools with one or more years of high school has also declined (by

44 or 76 percent) and the total number of middle schools went up by 121 (46 percent). This suggests that on a statewide basis, there is a shift back to more traditional grade groupings of K–5, 6–8, and 9–12. However, the shift is occurring by means of larger schools with a higher average enrollment than in the past.

Aggregation of the eight location characteristics of the NCES data for 1990 and 2000 and the CEPI data for 2006 into three categories (urban, suburb, and rural) is displayed on table 9 and enrollment information is presented in table 10. The following observations are pertinent:

Urban

- From 1990 to 2000, the number of schools classified as being in an urban location decreased by eight (–1.23 percent).
  - In 1990 urban schools composed 21 percent of all facilities and 24 percent of state enrollment.
  - In 2000 they composed approximately 20 percent of total facilities and 21 percent of total state enrollment.
- From 2000 to 2006, the number of schools classified as urban increased by forty-seven, a 7.3 percent change.
  - In 2006 there were 689 urban schools, which accounted for 22.3 percent of the state's facilities.
  - Enrollment in urban schools in 2006 was 374,313 or 24 percent.

Suburban

- From 1990 to 2000, there was an increase of 363 schools classified as suburban, a 39 percent increase in ten years.
  - In 1990 suburban schools accounted for 30 percent of all facilities and 32 percent of total enrollment.
  - In 2000 suburban schools accounted for 40 percent of all facilities and 44 percent of state enrollment.
- From 2000 to 2006, there were 116 fewer schools classified as suburban, a 9 percent decrease.
  - In 2006 there were 1,179 facilities classified as suburban, roughly 38 percent of the state's facilities.
  - In 2006 enrollment in suburban schools totaled 679,109, approximately 44 percent of state enrollment.

Rural

- From 1990 to 2000, there were 252 fewer schools classified as rural, a 16 percent decrease.
  - In 1990 rural schools composed 50 percent of all facilities and 44 percent of state enrollment.
  - In 2000 they accounted for approximately 41 percent of the state's school facilities and roughly 35 percent of the state's enrollment.
- Finally, from 2000 to 2006, there were 94 fewer rural schools, a 7 percent decline.
  - In 2006 1,227 schools were classified as rural—40 percent of the state's facilities.
  - Enrollment in rural schools in 2006 was 495,929, or 32 percent of the state enrollment.

Table 9. Traditional Public School Change by Location Category*

Location	1990		2000		1990–2000		2006		2000–2006		1990–2006	
	Count	% of total	Count	% of total	Change	% change	Count	% of total	Change	% change	Change	% change
Urban	650	20.60	642	19.71	–8	–1.23	689	22.26	47	7.32	39	6.00
Suburb	932	29.54	1,295	39.75	363	38.95	1,179	38.09	–116	–8.96	247	26.50
Rural	1,573	49.86	1,321	40.55	–252	–16.02	1,227	39.64	–94	–7.12	–346	–22.00
Total	3,155	100.00	3,258	100.00	103	3.26	3,095	100.00	–163	–5.00	–60	–1.90

Table 10. Traditional Public School Enrollment Change by Location Category*

Location	1990		2000		1990–2000		2006		2000–2006		1990–2006	
	Enrollment	% of total	Enrollment	% of total	Change	% change	Enrollment	% of total	Change	% change	Change	% change
Urban	355,143	23.86	340,400	21.30	–14,743	–4.15	374,313	24.16	33,913	9.96	19,170	5.40
Suburb	479,272	32.20	706,599	44.20	227,327	47.43	679,109	43.83	–27,490	–3.89	199,837	41.70
Rural	654,130	43.94	551,466	34.50	–102,664	–15.69	495,929	32.01	–55,537	–10.07	–158,201	–24.18
Total	1,488,545	100.00	1,598,465	100.00	109,920	7.38	1,549,351	100.00	–49,114	–3.07	60,806	4.08

* Notes to tables 9 and 10: These location categories were determined by the LPI. Of the 8 categories from NCES-defined locales, each was combined into a smaller category. Locales 1 and 2 = Urban; 3 and 4 = Suburb; 5 and 6 = Town; 7 and 8 = Rural. Additionally, Town was combined with Rural due to the NCES redefining its methodology for classifying school locales (see U.S. Department of Education, National Center for Education Statistics. *School Locale Codes 1987–2000, NCES 2002–02*, by Nancy Speicher. Arnold A. Goldstein, project officer. Washington, DC: 2002). Locale variables are not available from the CEPI as they are from the NCES CCD. Thus these variables were pulled from the most recent year of data available from CCD (2005–2006) and matched to schools in 2006 using the State School Identification Code, also known as a building code. This allowed a comparison of 2006 schools to 2000 and 1990. The eight possible locale codes were then converted to the three location categories, as defined by the LPI.

Examination of data from the 551 school districts in Michigan for 2006 provides some additional insights at the top and bottom of the ranked data. Table 11 shows the number of school buildings in the top five districts by enrollment in 2006. The Detroit School District in Wayne County is about four times larger than the next largest district in terms of number of school buildings (Grand Rapids, the state's second largest city) and five times larger than the third largest (Utica, which is a suburban district in Macomb County). At the bottom with the fewest number of school buildings are sixty rural school districts with only one building each (with a combined enrollment of 10,918 students).

As is to be expected, the school districts with the largest number of schools have the largest enrollment. Table 12 shows the top and bottom five school districts ranked by enrollment in 2006. Detroit, with the greatest number of buildings, also has the most enrollment. Note that two suburban districts occupy second and third place, while Grand Rapids falls to fourth on this list compared to second on table 11. The bottom five school districts are very rural with less than ten students in each district (one-room schools).

Table 11. Top Five Traditional School Districts by Number of School Buildings in 2006

Rank	School district	Number of buildings
1	Detroit public schools	204
2	Grand Rapids public schools	47
3	Utica community schools	40
4	Flint community schools	33
4	Lansing school district	33

Source: CEPI.

Table 12. Top and Bottom Five Traditional School Districts by Enrollment in 2006

Rank	School district	Enrollment
1	Detroit public schools	124,079
2	Utica community schools	29,288
3	Plymouth-Canton community schools	18,195
4	Grand Rapids public schools	17,788
5	Livonia public schools	17,294
1	Autrain-Onota public schools	33
2	Church school district	32
3	Big Jackson school district	31
4	Easton Township school district 6	29
5	Berlin Township school district 3	26

Source: CEPI.

Table 13 shows the top and bottom five school districts ranked by net change in the number of school buildings from 1990 to 2006. All the top five are suburban or suburbanizing school districts that are building the most new school facilities, while urban schools and small rural town districts are closing the most. In contrast, fifteen of the bottom twenty schools in terms of closing schools are urban school districts and most of the rest are first-tier (oldest) suburbs adjacent to central cities. In Detroit, thirty-six schools were closed during this period, while Grand Rapids closed the second largest number at ten schools.

Table 14 shows the top and bottom five school districts ranked by change in the enrollment from 1990 to 2006. Total state enrollment increased by 60,806 students over this period. Suburban school districts dominate the enrollment increases, while urban and very rural school districts lead with enrollment decreases. All the top five districts are suburbs or next-tier suburbanizing districts. All the bottom five districts with the highest enrollment decreases are urban core or first-tier suburbs. Detroit lost 35,433 students during this period while Flint lost over 9,646 students.

As startling as the loss of pupils in the urban school districts is over this sixteen-year period, it fails to pick up the even greater losses occurring in some of the largest urban school districts when looked at over a longer period of time. The following are examples:[21]

- At its peak enrollment in the mid-1960s, the Detroit School District had between 250,000 and 270,000 students compared to 104,975 (without preschool) in 2008. This is a loss of about 145,000 to 165,000 students (about 60 percent).
- At its peak in 1967, the Flint School District had 46,557 students compared to 15,629 in 2008. This is a loss of 30,928 students (66.4 percent).
- At its peak in 1971, the Lansing School District had 34,061 students compared to 14,860 in 2008. This is a loss of 19,201 students (56.4 percent).

Table 13. Top and Bottom Five Traditional Public School Districts Ranked by Change in Number of School Buildings

Rank	District	Net change
1	Forest Hills public schools	8
2	Walled Lake consolidated schools	6
3	Rochester community schools	5
3	Zeeland public schools	5
3	Chippewa Valley schools	5
3	Huron Valley schools	5
3	Kentwood public schools	5
1	Detroit public schools	−36
2	Grand Rapids public schools	−10
3	Flint Community schools	−9
4	Battle Creek school district	−7
4	Lansing school district	−7

Source: CEPI.

Table 14. Top and Bottom Five School Districts by Enrollment Gain/Loss

Rank	District	1990–2006
1	Utica community schools	6,293
2	Walled Lake consolidated schools	6,266
3	Chippewa Valley schools	5,682
4	Forest Hills public schools	4,510
5	Dearborn public schools	4,188
1	Detroit public schools	−35,433
2	Flint community schools	−9,646
3	Lansing school district	−5,115
4	Pontiac school district	−4,124
5	Grand Rapids public schools	−3,817

Source: CEPI.

- At its peak in the early 1980s, the Grand Rapids School District had just over 30,000 students compared to 19,885 in 2008. This is a loss of 10,115 students (33.7 percent).

The loss of students from urban schools began with the suburbanization of abutting jurisdictions (some would say the loss of students was created by suburbanization and new residential living options), and while it had begun before the Detroit riots in 1967, it accelerated rapidly in all urban areas that suffered population losses after that. Court-ordered busing in many of these urban school districts probably contributed to population movement as neighborhood schools no longer served neighborhood residents (Darden et.al. 1987).

Thus many urban school districts in Michigan have been dealing with contraction for three to four decades. Each time a neighborhood school closes though, the average distance from home to school goes up and not all students have equal access to a wide range of transportation options for getting to school. While public school busing is a staple service, even in urban districts (however, it is rare to charter schools), it is an expensive service. While large older urban school districts have seen the most school closures, very rural areas have also experienced many school closures. When a school closes in a rural area though, the average distance students must travel to school goes up much more than for those affected by an urban school closure. In the case of an urban district, a school closure may eliminate the healthy opportunity to bike or walk to school. In contrast, in a rural district, most students were likely being bused to begin with—however, their riding time could go up dramatically. Figure 6 illustrates the effect of school closure on proximity to students.

Travel implications of school closures in Michigan's urban school districts

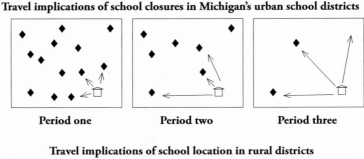

Period one   Period two   Period three

Travel implications of school location in rural districts

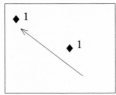

Figure 6. Travel Implications of School Closure in Urban and Rural Districts

SUMMARY OF KEY OBSERVATIONS

Clearly population, school facilities, and enrollments are linked in Michigan. If current population and economic trends continue, overall population growth in the state will be modest (at best), and population will continue to move around. Continued population growth in suburbs and decline in large urban core cities and first-tier suburbs as well as in very rural areas will likely continue for several decades. Efforts to reinvigorate central cities to better compete in the new economy will help attract new knowledge workers, but the lag before new school-age population results will likely prevent much improvement to urban school districts any time soon. Suburban districts will be building more new schools, and this is the principal opportunity to improve the health relationship between schools and the school-age population they serve. However, first-tier suburbs will likely see more school closures than new schools and that will mean longer, not shorter, distances between home and school for many students. In many rural areas, the distance between home and school will likely increase leading to longer bus rides as rural schools close.

Following are some observations based on Michigan's situation from the context of linking school location and health that may hold some interest to those in Michigan and other states, especially North Central states facing similar trends.

Historical Relationship

Schools used to be smaller and sited closer to the population served, and that was healthier as more students walked or biked to school. For all our contemporary focus on measuring the effectiveness of public education, we have largely ignored land use issues related to demography and geography. School siting issues should be an instrumental part of the decision about whether, where, and in what form to build a new school or renovate or retain an existing school. The contemporary push to more small schools will help, but only if they are closer to the school-age population served than they have been in suburban school districts. It may be time to return to the Clarence Perry Neighborhood Unit Theory.

Demographic Relationship

School location issues are quite different when considering districts facing enrollment expansion compared to districts facing decline.

- *Expansion.* New facilities in a new location will have a better health relationship to the school-age population only if siting standards reflect that relationship. A comparatively healthy location could be adopted as a standard if the state, local school district, and local unit of government want it to be, but it is not presently a standard in Michigan, and many other issues appear to be in the way of it becoming one.
- *Contraction.* Issues of cost, efficiency, age of structure, and facility condition or obsolescence are likely more important than school location and health to school administrators dealing with declines in school-age populations. Safe routes to school become very important for those who can walk or bike to school.

State Institutional Structure

The following key elements of the state institutional structure for school location decisions are very important.

- *Decision body.* Which body or bodies make the siting decision? Does the state or the school district decide, or does the local unit of government or some combination decide? The degree of autonomy or interdependence in final decision making can be critical to the outcome.
- *Decision process.* What process is followed? What process should be followed?
- *Standards.* What standards are used? State or local and in what combination and at what stage, the planning stage or the siting stage or both?
- *State control.* Obviously in those states where school buildings are financed by the state, the process is likely to be much simpler, but without good siting standards, perhaps not any better.

Local Competition

Competition for students changes the dynamic for new school decisions. While it enables parents to exercise choice, it also pits urban districts against suburban districts and both against charter schools.

Current System Is Very Complicated

The decision on where to locate a new school need not be as complicated as it is. There could be a clearer and more specific structure that leads to a more certain outcome for everyone.

However, that would require clear standards that permitted all the relevant stakeholders to have meaningful input at appropriate times in the planning, final design, and siting processes. However, changing the local institutional decision-making structure does not change factors leading to competition unless the state also changes the institutional decision-making structure that contributes to competition in the first place.

Lessons for Other States

Michigan is not unlike many other North Central "Rust Belt States," nor are many older urban areas in more rapidly growing states much different than Michigan's older urban areas, although the scale of the contraction may be less than in Michigan. If true, now may be the time for serious interventions to prevent having to deal with the problems that exist once 20 percent or more of the school-age population has disappeared.

- The demographic and school change data in contracting districts presents a parallel track with ominous implications for the future if current trends continue. Even if these trends stabilize, large urban school districts will continue to suffer for some time. If student performance does not improve, then radical measures are likely to be proposed. Many urban school districts are already at or near the tipping point. No one really knows what widespread failure of the public education system will mean in those cities.
- Quality schools are critical to attracting and retaining population, especially knowledge workers who are often free to move anywhere and take their children with them. Michigan (and other North Central states experiencing population and economic decline) must address this situation soon. It does not take the movement of a million residents before institutions suffer and fail, then the path back to prosperity is covered with major new impediments.
- If a severe recession of any length of time descends on the United States, then weak states will likely experience a depression and the disparity between growing and declining states will increase, and there will be more declining states than ever before. New development will focus more and more on the successful places rather than those facing myriad negative economic and social challenges.

NOTES

1. School creation and closure decisions require time. New school construction is often preceded by needs assessment, residents' commitment to funding and higher taxes, and site selection and design. Decommissioning a school often requires extensive school district discourse with representatives of neighborhoods affected.
2. Other products that have resulted from the first phase of MSU Land Policy Institute research include the following: First, a three hundred-page atlas of demographic maps of Michigan, depicting nearly seventy U.S. Census variables. This is available for 1990 and 2000 at each of the following political geographies: county, MCD (city, village, and township), intermediate school district (ISD), and school district levels. A second atlas presents location data on all schools in Michigan from 1970 to 2006. Both products are principally targeted to local units of government,

schools, and interested state agencies. Second, a companion research paper that examines the spatial distribution of schools on the landscape; how this distribution relates to the concentration of people, families, and types of communities; and the differential structure of schools between growing areas and contracting areas. The paper uses Gini coefficients and enrollment decomposition analysis via ordinary least squares regression to estimate the effects of demographic factors on school size–related factors such as enrollment. Third, a long table listing the core elements of all the major quality-of-life movements currently underway in the United States. It is titled *Comparison of Various Quality of Life Movements/Initiatives.* Fourth, an annotated bibliography of school siting and related materials. Fifth, a documentation of school location data the LPI has assembled on every public school in Michigan at ten year intervals from 1970 to 2000, as well as for 2006. It is titled *School Location Data Methodology: LPI Internal Documentation,* February 2008. Please visit http://www.landpolicy.msu.edu for more full reports and more information as it becomes available.

3. See Addonizio, Michael F. 2004. *Michigan School Finance: Running on Empty* (Detroit, MI: Wayne State University), http://web.ku.edu/~bdbaker/fipefsos/mi04.pdf; David Arsen and Thomas Davis, "Taj Mahals or Decaying Shacks: Patterns in Local School Capital Stock and Unmet Capital Need," *Peabody Journal of Education* 81, no. 4 (2006): 1–22; David Arsen and David Plank, *Michigan School Finance Under Proposal A: State Control, Local Consequences* (East Lansing: The Education Policy Center at Michigan State, 2003), http://www.epc.msu.edu; David Arsen, et al., "School Choice Policies: How They Have Affected Michigan's Education System," Working Paper No. 10, The Education Policy Center at Michigan State University, 2002, http://www.epc.msu.edu/publications/workpapers/choicepolicy.pdf; David Arsen, et al., *School Choice Policies in Michigan: The Rules Matter,* Education Policy Center at Michigan State University, http://www.epc.msu.edu/publications/rules/summary.pdf; Richard K. Norton, "Planning for School Facilities: School Board Decision-Making and Local Coordination in Michigan," *Journal of Planning Education and Research* 26, no. 4 (2007): 478–96; and Richard K. Norton, "Planning for Schools in Michigan: Local School Board Decision-Making on School Renovation, New School Construction, and School Siting," Policy Report Number 4, Center for Local, State, and Urban Policy, 2006, University of Michigan, http://closup.umich.edu/research/reports/pr-4-schools-sprawl.pdf.

4. Examples include the International Healthy Cities Foundation which supports the International Healthy Cities Movement, the Healthy Communities Initiative of the National Civic League, the Livable Communities Initiative of the Center for Livable Communities, the Association for Community Health Improvement, the Sustainable Communities Network, the Active Living Network, and the Smart Growth Network. In addition, many aspects of neotraditional town planning and New Urbanism incorporate healthy living into new development designs. A summary of many of these initiatives and website links can be found in Mark Wyckoff and Jason Ball, "Using Best Practice Principles to Guide Development of the Master Plan and Creation of Better Communities," *Planning & Zoning News* 27, no. 1 (November 2008): 7–19.

5. For more information, visit the Promoting Active Communities Program website, http://www.mihealthtools.org/communities.

6. For the full proposal, visit http://www.michigan.gov/documents/gov/Education_223203_7.pdf.

7. "In a 1998 report, Collaborative Economics, a Silicon Valley think tank, profiled the connections between the physical design of communities and dynamic elements of the new knowledge-driven, service-oriented economy. The contemporary economy—with its smaller, decentralized firms—thrives on land use patterns that harken back to the towns of early industrial years, with city centers,

corner stores and street car suburbs. Walkable downtowns with a mix of restaurants, offices and housing promote interaction. Interaction is key since the new economy thrives on accessibility, networking and creativity." The Economics of Livable Communities by the Local Government Commission, http://www.lgc.org/freepub/PDF/Land_Use/focus/walk_to_money.pdf.).

8. Congress for the New Urbanism, http://www.cnu.org.

9. The American Institute of Architects, Principles for Livable Communities, http://www.aia.org/liv_principles.

10. USGBC, LEED ND, http://www .usgbc.org/DisplayPage.aspx?CMSPageID=148.

11. "Charter schools are state-supported public schools. In Michigan three kinds are allowed: (1) Public School Academies (PSAs) chartered under Part 6A of the revised school code, (2) Urban High School Academies (UHSAs) chartered under part 6C of the revised school code to operate within Detroit, and (3) Strict Discipline Academies (SDAs) chartered under Public Act 23 of 1999 to serve suspended, expelled or incarcerated young people. Charter schools may include grades K–12 or any combination of those grades. They may not charge tuition, and must serve anyone who applies to attend; that is they may not screen out students based on race, religion, sex, or test scores. Students are selected randomly for admission if the number of students applying exceeds the school's enrollment capacity. Charter teachers must be certified and highly qualified; charter students are assessed annually as part of the Michigan Education Assessment Program (MEAP). Charter schools cannot be religiously affiliated." Michigan Department of Education, Charter Public Schools, http://www.michigan.gov/mde/0,1607,7-140-6530_30334_40088---,00.html.

12. Sec. 380.502 Revised School Code. Charter School authorizing entities. Michigan Department of Education, Charter Public Schools, http://www.michigan.gov/mde/0,1607,7-140-6530_30334_40088---,00.html.

13. On December 23, 2002, *Act 628 of the Public Acts of 2002 (1937 PA 306)* was signed into law, requiring the inspection of all school buildings, as well as the review of construction documents under the *Stille-DeRossett-Hale Single State Construction Code Act, 1972 PA 230* and the *State Fire Prevention Code, 1941 PA 207.*

14. The School Bond Qualification and Loan program was established by the *Michigan Constitution of 1963* and amended by *Public Act 92 of 2005* to provide a state credit enhancement and loan mechanism for school district bond issues. The bonds must be qualified by the state treasurer and the bond proceeds must be used for capital expenditure purposes. A separate fund, the Qualified Zone Academy Bond, is available only to public schools located in an empowerment zone.

15. Bulletin 412 was originally adopted in the 1960s and later updated in 1975. Originally it was an informational bulletin that was required to be supplied under statute—but apparently, that is no longer the case. Bulletin 412 is an "obsolete, out-of-date" document according to Carol Easlik of the Michigan Department of Education. Bulletin 412 is identical to recommended school construction guidelines established by Center for Educational Facilities Planning International. See http://www .cefpi.org/pdf/state_guidelines.pdf—see comments and readings on page 4. These standards have been widely criticized. See, for example, Constance E. Beaumont and Elizabeth G. Pianca, *Why Johnny Can't Walk to School: Historic Neighborhood Schools in the Age of Sprawl,* 2nd ed. (Washington, DC: National Trust for Historic Preservation, 2002), 10–16. See also Stacy Mitchell, "Jack and the Giant School," *Journal of the New Rules Project,* Institute for Local Self Reliance 2, no. 1 (Summer 2000), http://www.newrules.org/journal/nrsum00schools.htm, which has a lot of excellent information and statistics. David Salvesen and Philip Hervey, *Good Schools, Good Neighborhoods: The Impacts of State and Local School Board Policies on the Design and Location of Schools in North*

Carolina (Chapel Hill, NC: Center for Urban and Regional Studies, University of North Carolina at Chapel Hill), 2, http://www.mrsc.org/ArtDocMisc/goodschoolsreport2.pdf.

16. "The schools of choice provisions in Section 105 and 105c of the State School Aid Act are designed to allow local school districts to enroll nonresident students and count them in membership without having to obtain approval from the district of residence. Each school district decides whether or not it will participate in schools of choice under Section 105 and/or 105c." It can limit the schools and the number of students by school, which it makes open under the schools of choice option. State School Aid Act, PA 94 of 1979, http://www.michigan.gov/mde/0,1607,7-140-6530_30334-106922--,00.html. See also http://www.buildingchoice.org.

17. See http://www.michigan.gov/documents/hal_lm_census_state_rankings_of_projected_population_00_30_122923_7.xls, http://www.michigan.gov/hal/0,1607,7-160-17451_28388_28392-116118--,00.html; http://www.bea.gov/regional/spi/action.cfm, http://www.census.gov/popest/states/tables/NST-EST2007-05.xls.

18. The two large population losses in the northeastern part of the Lower Peninsula and the center of the Upper Peninsula are associated with Air Force Base closures.

19. 1970 and 1980 data was derived from school registry listings in a published school directory. 1990 and 2000 data is from the National Center for Educational Statistics (NCES) Common Core Data (CCD) Build-a-Table (BAT) function. Data for 2006 was obtained from the Michigan Center for Educational Performance and Information (CEPI). For more information, see *School Location Data Methodology: LPI Internal Documentation*, February 2008.

20. Information from the Michigan Department of Education, the schools and charter authorizers puts current enrollment in 2008 at 100,146 students, http://www.charterschools.org/pages/pressreleases.cfm?object=250&method=displayNewsItem&newsID=2375.

21. Data based on telephone calls to school district facility managers in each of the urban school districts in February 2008.

REFERENCES

Abramson, Paul. 2007. *2007 construction report.* Dayton, OH: College of Planning and Management, Peter Li Education Group.

Adelaja, Soji. 2008. Strategic growth: The new economy paradigm. *Planning and Zoning News* 26, no. 3 (January): 2–14.

Arsen, David, and David Plank. 2003. *Michigan school finance under proposal A: State control, local consequences.* East Lansing: The Education Policy Center at Michigan State University. http://www.epc.msu.edu.

Beaumont, Constance E., and Elizabeth G. Pianca. 2002. *Why Johnny can't walk to school: Historic neighborhood schools in the age of sprawl.* 2nd ed. Washington, DC: National Trust for Historic Preservation.

Bingler, Steven, Linda Quinn, and Kevin Sullivan. 2003. *Schools as centers of community: A citizen's guide for planning and design.* 2nd ed. Washington, DC: National Clearinghouse for Educational Facilities.

Boyse, Kyla. 2007. Your child topics: Obesity and overweight. University of Michigan Health Systems. http://www.med.umich.edu/1libr/yourchild/obesity.htm.

Centers for Disease Control and Prevention (CDC). 2007. Facts about obesity in the United States. http://www.cdc.gov/PDF/Facts_About_Obesity_in_the_United_States.pdf.

Darden, Joe T., Richard C. Hill, June Thomas, and Richard Thomas. 1987. *Detroit: Race and uneven development.* Philadelphia: Temple University Press.

Eberlein, Michael D. 2006. Federal funding for safe routes to school. *Planning & Zoning News,* February, 10–14.

Horn, Jerry, and Gary Miron. 2000. *An evaluation of Michigan charter school initiative: Performance, accountability and impact.* Kalamazoo: The Evaluation Center, Western Michigan University.

Jackson, Richard J., and Chris Kochtitzky. 2002. *Creating a healthy environment: The impact of the built environment on public health.* Washington DC: Centers for Disease Control and Prevention, National Center for Environmental Health, *Planning & Zoning News* 20, no. 3 (January 2002): 6–14; first published by the Sprawl Watch Clearinghouse in Nov. 2001.

Keating, Dennis, and Norm Krumholz. 1998. State of the art in planning education. Cleveland State University. http://www.planning.org/casey/academia.htm.

Klaus, Susan L. 2002. *Modern arcadia: Fredrick Law Olmsted Jr. and the plan for Forest Hill Gardens.* Amherst: University of Massachusetts Press.

Lee, Chang-Moo, and Barbara Stabin-Nesmith. 2001. The continuing value of a planned community: Radburn in the evolution of suburban development. *Journal of Urban Design* 6 (2): 151–84.

Michigan Association of Planning (MAP). 2007. *Schools and local government policy.* Board of Directors, Michigan Association of Planning.

Michigan Department of Community Health. 2006a. Healthy communities tool kit: How you can work toward creating healthy communities. Michigan Department of Community Healthy. http://www.mihealthtools.org/documents/HealthyCommunitiesToolkit_web.pdf.

———. 2006b. A statewide scan of childhood obesity programs, policies and resources in Michigan: Executive summary. Healthy Kids, Healthy Michigan. http://www.michigan.gov/documents/mdch/EnvironmentalScanExecutiveSummaryReduced_244924_7.pdf.

Michigan Department of Education (MDE). 2006. *Public school academies: Report to the legislature.* Lansing: Michigan Department of Education.

Michigan Education Report (MER). 2000. *What are intermediate school districts?* Education Report, Mackinac Center for Public Policy, February 10.

Michigan Fitness Foundation. 2008. Get Michigan moving. Governor's Council on Physical Fitness, Health & Sports and the Michigan Fitness Foundation. http://www.michiganfitness.org.

Michigan Supreme Court. 1983. Royal Oak School District v. Cody Park Association. 116 Mich App 103, 1982, Appeal Denied 417 Mich 985, 1983.

———. Charter Township of Northville, et al. v. Northville Public Schools, et al. 469 Mich 285, 2003.

Michigan Surgeon General's Health Status Report. 2004. Healthy Michigan 2010. Michigan Surgeon General. http://www.michigan.gov/documents/Healthy_Michigan_2010_1_88117_7.pdf.

National Civic League. 2007. Healthy communities initiatives. http://www.ncl.org/cs/services/healthy communities.html.

Norton, Richard K. 2007. Planning for school facilities: School board decision-making and local coordination in Michigan. *Journal of Planning Education and Research* 26 (4): 478–96.

Perry, Clarence A. 1929. The neighborhood unit: A scheme of arrangement for the family-life community. In *Regional plan of New York and its environs volume VII: Neighborhood and community planning,* 2–140. New York: Committee on Regional Plan of New York and Its Environs.

Public Act 276 of 2006. Michigan State public law. Michigan Legislature.

Smart Growth Network. 2008. Smart growth online: About smart growth. http://www.smartgrowth.org.

Speicher, Nancy, and Arnold A. Goldstein. 2002. School locale codes 1987–2000. Working Paper No. 2002–02, U.S. Department of Education, National Center for Education Statistics, Washington, DC.

Stevenson, Kenneth R. 2002. *Ten educational trends shaping school planning and design.* Washington, DC: National Clearinghouse for Educational Facilities.

U.S. Census Bureau. 1950. 1950 Census of population and housing: Summary file 1.

———. 1960. 1960 Census of population and housing: Summary file 1.

———. 1970. 1970 Census of population and housing: Summary file 1.

———. 1975. Historical statistics of the U.S.: Colonial times to 1970. Bicentennial Editions. U.S. Department of Commerce.

———. 1980. 1980 Census of population and housing: Summary file 1.

———. 1990. 1990 Census of population and housing: Summary file 1.

———. 2000. 2000 Census of population and housing: Summary file 1.

———. 2005. Population projections to 2030. U.S. Census Bureau.

———. 2006. Population Estimates for 2006. U.S. Census Bureau.

———. 2007. Population Estimates for 2007. U.S. Census Bureau.

U.S. Environmental Protection Agency (EPA). 2003. Travel and environmental implications of school siting. EPA 231-R-03-004. Washington, DC: U.S. EPA. http://www.epa.gov/smartgrowth/pdf/school_travel.pdf.

U.S. National Institute of Environmental Health Sciences. 2005. Obesity and the environment. http://www-apps.niehs.nih.gov/conferences/drcpt/oe2005/factsheet.pdf.

Walters, David. 2007. *Designing community: Charrettes, master plans and form-based codes.* Burlington, MA: Elsevier.

Wilkerson, Risa, and Candance Kohinakis. 2006. Safe routes to school: Planning for a safer and healthier way to school. *Planning & Zoning News* 24, no. 4 (February 5–9): 5–9.

Wyckoff, Mark. 1998. More on schools and local zoning. *Planning & Zoning News*, May 16, no. 7, 14–17.

Wyckoff, Mark, and Jason Cherry. 1998. Are public schools subject to local zoning? *Planning & Zoning News*, January 16, no. 3, 5–10.

Population Effects on School District Structure and Size in Michigan

ADESOJI ADELAJA, MELISSA A. GIBSON, AND YOHANNES HAILU

SCHOOLS SERVE AS SYMBOLS OF COMMUNITY AUTONOMY, VITALITY, INTEGRATION, tradition, and identity, as well as personal control and comfort (Peshkin 1978, 1982). The performance, reputation, and location of schools have a large impact on a community (Orfield 2002). Local property taxes paid by residents to support local education often represent a significant component of all local taxes paid (Murray, Evans, and Schwab 1998; Taylor 1999). Therefore, there is an imperative for schools to deliver tangible community results. In short, the success of a community, be it a city, suburban township, or rural community, is tied to schools all across the United States (Lyson 2002).

Families that can afford to move often flee low-quality urban schools in search of better schools in suburban or rural areas or enroll their children in private schools (see Vincent 2006). It is a widely held notion that young families tend to move out from dense communities (e.g., urban areas) to less dense areas (suburban townships) as they approach childbearing age. In the process, such families target those high-status communities in order to get the best quality education for their children (see Taylor 1999; Haurin and Brasington 1996; Graves and Linneman 1979). Given the role of schools in families' decision to move and their choice of where to eventually reside to meet their needs, schools may represent a significant factor in shaping the landscape of communities.

Given the expected correlation between the number of school-age children and adult parents, school expansion and contraction must be viewed as endogenous to population shifts. When populations grow, school districts with a limited supply of school facilities must accommodate this excess demand by filling up existing schools or by building more schools. Small class size is a status symbol and an indicator of the quality of education that students receive in a school district. Therefore, there may be pressure on schools that lack excess capacity to build new schools in order to reduce the negative consequences of excessive enrollment or overcrowding (either in the schools or in specific classes). Schools have to balance classroom size, district efficiency, crowding, revenues, and the demands of parents in the community. Population, property values and incomes, tax revenues, and the supply of affordable housing obviously enter into the decisions by school districts to build new facilities, accommodate new growth in existing facilities, or close certain existing structures. This decision is obviously constrained by concerns about school quality or reputation, community reputation or status, and other goals and interests of the community. Regardless of what determines facilities' expansion or contraction, such facility decisions obviously affect land use.

New schools consume land and, in some cases, shape community growth patterns, especially if such schools are located on greenfields. The closure of a school not only takes away a central component of community infrastructure but also often leaves behind old school buildings that could add to blight. Communities must carefully weigh decisions to open and close schools and, in many cases, seek voter (community) support before making such decisions. This is especially so in the case of school expansion or the building of new schools, where additional school tax revenues must be approved by voters.

Forward-thinking communities will take a long-term view. Schools should not rush to expand the very same infrastructure that they might have to close down in the future due to economic downturns or population loss. The complexity of the relationships among population, school-age children, land use, schools, and perceived quality of life is obviously an important consideration, especially in metropolitan areas where the overall decline in urban vitality and quality of life is acute.

The issue at hand is even more significant in such metropolitan areas where population has shifted drastically away from central cities over the past five decades. Urban schools have faced the most significant attrition, especially in some of the Rust Belt states, such as Michigan, where state population growth has been limited in recent years and where the populations of some areas of the state have actually declined significantly (U.S. Census Bureau 2009a). An understanding of the distributional and equity impacts of school location and school district structure vis-à-vis critical driving factors such as population, income, and property values will be helpful in developing policies and strategies to guide more efficient management of school location decisions and, therefore, the structure and performance of schools.

STUDY OBJECTIVES

The major goal of this study is to investigate some of the equity implications of the size distribution of schools through the impacts of population and demographic factors on such distribution. We decompose school enrollment in order to explain the impacts of socioeconomic and demographic factors on such enrollment. Michigan is used as a case study. Michigan stands out in terms of the statewide acuteness of its population shifts. Between 2005 and 2008, the state lost approximately 90,000 people, and the losses are progressively worsening (U.S. Census Bureau 2009a). Many urban and rural parts of the state have been losing population to suburban locations for at least a decade (Adelaja, Hailu, and Gibson 2009). Metropolitan areas in the state have been characterized by significant sprawl (Skole et al. 2002). The impacts of such shifts are expected to affect the structure and nature of schools, as well as equity and access by different population groups.

Since Proposal A was passed in Michigan in 1994 (Arsen and Plank 2003), school operations have been financed by the State School Aid Fund, while building and renovation costs for schools are funded through local millage taxes. Proposal A was adopted by the legislature to increase educational equity by distributing finances for the operations of schools on a per-pupil basis. Since communities must balance state revenues (tied to variable enrollment) against local revenues (tied to property-based revenues), the finance of schools is endogenous to local socioeconomic and land use policies and factors (e.g., millage rates, desirability of schools, and property taxes). Therefore, the decisions made by school districts about new buildings, school closure, and school size should be affected by local socioeconomic and land use factors. School financial stability has been cited as one of the most pressing issues facing the state today (Adelaja and Gibson 2008; Wyckoff et al. 2008; Granholm 2008).

The specific objective of this study is to examine the impacts of socioeconomic and demographic factors on such issues as school capacity, school crowding, and other structural school-related factors. Using an enrollment decomposition framework, we decompose total school enrollment per capita (E/P) into two distinct components: (1) enrollment per school (E/S) and (2) schools per capita (S/P). Enrollment per school reflects school district size while schools per capita reflects school availability per district (or number of schools per person). Both of these components were then evaluated in the context of driving factors for enrollment based on a multiple regression model. Since Proposal A created a funding source for schools not tied to local taxing capacity and rewards expanded school enrollment, the enrollment decomposition analysis was conducted for 1990 and 2000 separately, in order to determine the extent to which the structure of schools changed between 1990 and 2000 as a result of Proposal A. Proposal A created a situation where a school must generate new tax revenues to expand its physical capacity (or maintain or upgrade its facilities). Otherwise, increased crowding of schools (or dilapidation of buildings) will occur. Specifics of this model are presented in the following section.

METHODOLOGY AND APPROACH

The underlying framework behind the decomposition analysis of schools is that while schools are an essential feature of every community, their structure, nature, size, scope, and intensity vary across communities due to differences in community economics, politics, preferences, location, and so on. One important element of schools is the agglomeration of grade levels within a given school. Communities vary in terms of how they delineate their high schools (grades 9 to 12 or grades 10 to 12) and how they constitute elementary schools (K–3, K–4, K–5, or K–6).[1] Other important elements are the ratio of students per school (efficiency or crowding) versus the ratio of schools to population. Obviously, some communities want fewer schools that are large (Taj Mahal Syndrome) while others want smaller schools. The term *Taj Mahal* is used to describe the preference for larger schools because the Taj Mahal, a very large structure, is a good analogy for large schools (Arsen 2006).

E denotes school enrollment in a school district, S denotes the number of schools in a school district, and P denotes the total population of residents of the school district. A general expression of enrollment per unit of resident population can be specified as follows:

$$E/P = (E/S) \times (S/P), (1)$$

where E/P is a measure of aggregate student intensity in the school district, E/S is a measure of the size of the average school in the school district and an indicator of school scale, and S/P is a measure of the tendency of a community to have more schools and an indicator of school scope. In other words as enrollment increases, a district can increase school scale (larger schools) or increase school scope (operate more schools). The former can be accomplished through consolidation while the latter can be accomplished through increasing the number of schools. Equation (1) captures the choice of a community to have more schools rather than large schools. In many parts of the United States, school districts have favored new schools that are large. The ability to break E/P down into two structural elements is pivotal. It is hypothesized that such factors as housing affordability, income, wealth, employment, class, and race affect E/P. The same factors should affect E/S and S/P.

To decompose school enrollment–related factors based on the specification in Equation (1), the E/S and S/P equations were estimated. These two elements of school enrollment are regressed against hypothesized determinants of school enrollment. The analysis was done for 1990 (pre-Proposal A) and 2000 (post-Proposal A). This analysis therefore allowed the estimation of the effects of various demographic-type factors on both elements.

Identified determinants include population density (POPDENS), the number of school-age children in the district in 1990 (POP05–18), median household income (MEDHINC), median housing value (MEDHVAL), the percentage of the total population in poverty (%POV), the number of employed people living in the school district (EMPL), percentage of the population that is classified as nonwhite (%NWHITE), and percentage of the population classified as urban (%URBAN).

Obviously there are differences between highly dense communities, including cities and suburbs, and less dense communities, such as townships and rural communities. Our hypothesis is that highly dense school districts have the potential to benefit from economies of scale, and therefore there would be a positive relationship between population density and enrollment per school. Simultaneously, one would expect the number of schools per population to be inversely related to population density if our economies-of-scale argument holds true.

The number of school-age children in the school district in 1990 is included as an explanatory variable to examine the effect of cohort size on school structure. Again, the estimated coefficient of the scale variable would be positive for E/S and negative for S/P. However, in the case of very rural communities, where the critical mass is just not there to fill large schools, one could expect E/S to be high and S/P low. Alternatively, S/P may be low while E/S would also be low.

Median household income (MEDHINC) is included as an explanatory variable to show the income effect on school structure in the community. High income and status communities are often argued to prefer smaller classes and less crowding. Private school attendance is also expected to rise with per capita income, implying lower enrollment per schools. On the other hand, much has been said about the Taj Mahal Syndrome (Arsen and David 2006). An inverse relationship between MEDHINC and E/S would confirm the high-status hypothesis, which proposes that high income schools prefer smaller classes, while a positive relationship would confirm the Taj Mahal Syndrome.

The corollary of the high-status hypothesis is that one should see a positive relationship between MEDHINC and S/P, suggesting higher income communities can afford a high number of schools. We characterize this as the income or status effect on S/P. Of course, the inverse is also possible. As a result of the Taj Mahal Syndrome, high-income school districts want just a few schools with large capacity and state-of-the-art facilities. With respect to MEDHVAL, it is assumed that the effects would be similar to that of MEDHINC.

Employment (EMPL), defined as the number of employed people living in the school district, was included to capture the extent to which the community is a bedroom community where employed people reside, whether or not they work within the community. High employment should indicate greater ability to build schools (greater S/P and reduced E/S). Therefore, we hypothesize a positive S/P effect and a negative E/S effect.

The school district poverty rate (%POV) was included to capture the impact of poverty on enrollment in schools. One might expect high dropout rates in poor school districts and therefore lower actual enrollment. One might also expect that poorer school districts are not able to generate the high taxes required to build new schools. On the other hand, as poverty rises, a school may be able to attract more special grants that target underserved communities from federal and state sources. We therefore expect that districts with a higher proportion of households in poverty will have higher revenues per child. Proposal A, which essentially is a revenue-normalizing state distribution scheme, was passed in order to attempt to equalize funding across the state. However, since such funding only goes to support operations (not buildings), it is possible that Proposal A did not change much in the structure of school districts.

The percentage of the population that is nonwhite (%NWHITE) within a school district is an indicator of the racial diversity of the district. A very high or a very low percentage of nonwhite indicates that a community is not racially diverse. In Michigan nearly 80 percent of the population is white, with just under 14 percent black (U.S. Census Bureau 2009b). A difference in school structure between those communities that have a high percentage nonwhite and a low percentage nonwhite may indicate a difference in preference for small or large classes and small or large schools between various racial groups or a disparity in ability to provide desired schooling.

Population density reflects differences between school districts with high-density and low-density populations. However, it does not necessarily reflect differences between urban and rural school districts. School districts in Michigan are not uniform in size and can encompass large or small areas. For example, a school district in a highly urbanized area may have a low population density due to the large amount of land occupied by industry or business uses and thus draw much of the daytime population from neighboring bedroom communities. By utilizing %URBAN in our estimation, we are able to specifically examine the differences associated with urban and nonurban school districts.

The estimated equations are expressed as follows:

$$\text{Log } (E/S) = \alpha_0 + \alpha_1 \text{ Log } [POPDENS] + \alpha_2 \text{ Log } [MEDHINC] + \alpha_3 \text{ Log } [MEDHVAL] + \alpha_4 \text{ Log } [EMPL] + \alpha_5 \text{ Log } [\%POV] + \alpha_6 \text{ Log } [POP05\text{--}18] + \alpha_7 \text{ Log } [\%NWHITE] + \alpha_8 \text{ Log } [\%URBAN], (2)$$

and

$$\text{Log } (S/P) = \alpha_0 + \alpha_1 \text{ Log } [POPDENS] + \alpha_2 \text{ Log } [MEDHINC] + \alpha_3 \text{ Log } [MEDHVAL] + \alpha_4 \text{ Log } [EMPL] + \alpha_5 \text{ Log } [\%POV] + \alpha_6 \text{ Log } [POP05\text{--}18] + \alpha_7 \text{ Log } [\%NWHITE] + \alpha_8 \text{ Log } [\%URBAN]., (3)$$

From Equations (2) and (3), the following average school enrollment elasticity measures can be estimated: $\varepsilon_{(E/S),(POPDENS)}$; $\varepsilon_{(E/S),(POP05\text{--}18)}$; $\varepsilon_{(E/S),(MEDHINC)}$; $\varepsilon_{(E/S),(MEDHVAL)}$; $\varepsilon_{(E/S),(EMPL)}$; $\varepsilon_{(E/S),(\%POV)}$; $\varepsilon_{(E/S),(\%NWHITE)}$; and $\varepsilon_{(E/S),(\%URBAN)}$, where the ε operator denotes elasticity. Also, the following school presence elasticity measures can be estimated: $\varepsilon_{(S/P),(POPDENS)}$; $\varepsilon_{(S/P),(POP05\text{--}18)}$; $\varepsilon_{(S/P),(MEDHINC)}$;

$\varepsilon_{(S/P),(MEDHVAL)}$; $\varepsilon_{(S/P),(EMPL)}$; $\varepsilon_{(S/P),(\%POV)}$; $\varepsilon_{(S/P),(\%NWHITE)}$; and $\varepsilon_{(S/P),(\%URBAN)}$. From Equation (1), the product of E/S and S/P is E/P. Hence by combining the coefficients of the E/S and S/P regressions from Equations (2) and (3), one can impute the coefficients of E/P as follows:

$$\varepsilon(E/S),(POPDENS) + \varepsilon(S/P),(POPDENS) = \varepsilon(E/P),(POPDENS)$$
$$\varepsilon(E/S),(POP05-18) + \varepsilon(S/P),(POP05-18) = \varepsilon(E/P),(POP05-18)$$
$$\varepsilon(E/S),(MEDHINC) + \varepsilon(S/P),(MEDHINC) = \varepsilon(E/P),(MEDHINC)$$
$$\varepsilon(E/S),(MEDHVAL) + \varepsilon(S/P),(MEDHVAL) = \varepsilon(E/P),(MEDHVAL)$$
$$\varepsilon(E/S),(EMPL) + \varepsilon(S/P),(EMPL) = \varepsilon(E/P),(EMPL)$$
$$\varepsilon(E/S),(\%POV) + \varepsilon(S/P),(\%POV) = \varepsilon(E/P),(\%POV)$$
$$\varepsilon(E/S),(\%NWHITE) + \varepsilon(S/P),(\%NWHITE) = \varepsilon(E/P),(\%NWHITE)$$
$$\varepsilon(E/S),(\%URBAN) + \varepsilon(S/P),(\%URBAN) = \varepsilon(E/P),(\%URBAN), (4)$$

DATA SOURCES

The data were obtained from several sources, including the following:

1. *Demographics.* Data by school district (SD) were obtained from the U.S. Census Bureau for the years 1990 and 2000 (U.S. Census Bureau 1991 and 2001).
2. *School enrollment.* Data were obtained from the National Center for Educational Statistics (NCES) Common Core Data (CCD) build-a-table function for enrollment by school.
3. *School locations.* GIS was utilized to identify the location of school buildings. School building addresses were obtained from the Michigan Education Directory. These data were supplemented with address information from the NCES, phone calls to schools, school districts with a missing or incomplete address, mailed questionnaires to school district with missing addresses, and Library of Michigan files on school directories. The number of school buildings within a district was determined by summing all the data points (address locations) within the district.

The list of variables utilized in this analysis is presented in table 1. Demographic and school district maps have been published in two atlases and show the changes from 1990 to 2000 (Adelaja et al. 2008a, 2008b). All the analyses in this chapter involve school enrollment (population numbers) with respect to such hypothesized drivers as income, poverty, and other demographic factors. The population factors that enrollment-related figures were evaluated against included the log of population density in school district area (POPDENS), the log of population of those ages five to eighteen in the school district area (POP05–18), the log of median household income in school district area (MEDHINC), the log of medium home value for specified owner occupied housing units in school district area (MEDHVAL), the log of employment in school district area (EMPL), the school district poverty rate (%POV), the percentage of nonwhite population in the school district area (%NWHITE), and the percentage of urban population in the school district area (%URBAN). The dependent variables were constructed from data on total enrollment (ENROLTOT), or E; the number of buildings in the school district (BUILDINGS), or S; and the total population in the school district (POP), or P.

The analysis is done for the years 1990 and 2000 in order to allow the identification of population growth or attrition and school growth or attrition. A comparative analysis across

Table 1. Description of Data and Sources

Variable measure for school district area	Variable name	Description	Source
Population density in the school district	POPDENS	Persons per sq. mi.	U.S. Census Bureau 1990, 2000.
Population ages 5–18 in the school district	POP05–18	Persons	U.S. Census Bureau 1990, 2000.
Median household income in the school district	MEDHINC	U.S. dollars	U.S. Census Bureau 1990, 2000
Median home value for specified owner-occupied housing units in the school district	MEDHVAL	U.S. dollars	U.S. Census Bureau 1990, 2000
Number living in the school district who are employed	EMPL	Persons	U.S. Census Bureau 1990, 2000
Percent poor households in the school district	%POV	Percentage	U.S. Census Bureau 1990, 2000
Percentage nonwhite population in the school district	%NWHITE	Percentage	U.S. Census Bureau 1990, 2000
Percent urban population in the school district	%URBAN	Percentage	U.S. Census Bureau 1990, 2000
Average enrollment per school in district	ENROLAVG	Persons	CEPI and NCES/CCD
Total enrollment in the school district	ENROLTOT	Persons	CEPI and NCES/CCD
Number of buildings in the school district (one school = one building)	BUILDINGS	Numbers	Sum of buildings mapped within a school districts boundaries
Total population in the school district	POP	Persons	U.S. Census Bureau 1990, 2000

periods further allowed the evaluation of the effect of time periods on school distribution. The 1990–2000 analysis covered a period of expansion in the state.

RESULTS

The parameter estimates for the enrollment decomposition model are reported in table 2. For cross sectional data, adjusted R-squares of around 70 percent for the E/S model and around 77 percent for the S/P model are impressive. In both equations, population is excluded as an explanatory variable based on the notion discussed earlier that population density is a more appropriate measure, particularly for rural areas. Our examination of the residuals of all final equations suggests that heteroschedasticity was not a concern. The estimated correlation coefficients suggested the absence of multicollinearity.

Recall from Equation (4) that the coefficients of the E/S and the S/P equations for a particular exogenous variable can be multiplied to obtain the impacts on E/P. Therefore, in table 2, the estimated coefficients for E/S are presented, along with the estimated coefficients for the S/P equation. At the bottom of table 2, the imputed impacts of each variable on E/P are calculated. Note that if any coefficient in the E/S or S/P equations is insignificant, we interpreted the impacts to be zero.

Enrollment per School or Average School Size

Enrollment per school (E/S) is essentially a measure of school size. A positive impact of a causal factor on this variable suggests that the response is to encourage larger schools. The results in table 2 suggest that in 1990, enrollment per school was inversely related to median household income, percent poverty, and percent urban but positively related to the number of people aged 5 to 18, that is, the sizes of the schools tended to be lower in high income, high poverty, and urban communities, holding other factors constant. The finding regarding income is consistent with expectations, as one would expect high-income school districts to have a higher proportion of parents that can afford to send their children to private schools. It may also suggest, however, that high-income communities value smaller schools but more schools. The latter is inconsistent with the Taj Mahal Syndrome hypothesis, at least as it relates to income, but suggests that the high-status hypotheses may be true.

The findings that both high poverty and urban school districts had lower average school enrollment suggests that poor urban school districts have lower school enrollment but perhaps more schools. In another chapter by the authors in this book, we highlight the fact that some of the large urban schools had greater infrastructure capacity, which is increasingly burdensome to many of them (Wyckoff, Adelaja, and Gibson 2011). The fact that enrollment per school tends to be higher in places with a high population of 5–18 year olds is consistent with expectations.

The effects of identified independent variables were significantly different for 2000, compared with 1990. For example, the effect of median household income and percentage poverty became insignificant in 2000. This suggests that Proposal A, which was adopted in 1994, may have achieved one element of its intended results, to reduce the disparity in educational access between wealthier school districts and poorer school districts to the extent that school or class size affected educational quality and effectiveness.

The effects of median household value, the percentage of nonwhite persons, and employed persons became significant for 2000. The former two became negative and the latter became positive. These suggest that expensive neighborhoods with high employment (bedroom communities from where people commute to work) featured lower per school enrollment but that those bedroom communities came to feature greater enrollment per school after Proposal A. These also may reflect the incidence of private school enrollment, as it indicates that enrollment per school became affected by a school district's level of poverty by 2000. The total school-age population's effect on enrollment per school became less pronounced from 1990 to 2000, suggesting the movement toward private schooling, home schooling, schools of choice, additional schools or combinations thereof. The remaining variables remained of the same signs and magnitude.

Table 2. Parameter Estimates of the Double Log Models of School Enrollment, 1990 and 2000 Estimates

Dependent variable = Enrollment per school (E/S)
1990: R-squared = 0.706; adjusted R-squared = 0.702; D W Stat = +1.798
2000: R-squared = 0.696; adjusted R-squared = 0.692; D W, Stat = +1.797

Independent variable	Estimated coefficient (1990)	Prob /|Z|>z]	Estimated coefficient (2000)	Prob /|Z|>z]
Intercept	5.923*	0.000	4.574*	0.001
Log [POPDENS]	0.025	0.265	0.024	0.274
Log [POP05–18]	0.632*	0.000	0.228*	0.057
Log [MEDHINC]	−0.326‡	0.034	−0.048	0.783
Log [MEDHVAL]	−0.053	0.579	−0.222‡	0.025
Log [EMPL]	−0.063	0.602	0.337*	0.005
[%POV]	−1.559*	0.005	−0.414	0.559
[%NWHITE]	−0.333	0.111	−0.428‡	0.035
[%URBAN]	−0.472*	0.000	−0.498*	0.000

Dependent variable = Schools per population (S/P)
1990: R-squared = 0.770; adjusted R-squared = 0.766; D W Stat = +1.725
2000: R-squared = 0.772; adjusted R-squared = 0.769; D W, Stat = +1.916

Independent variable	Estimated coefficient (1990)	Prob /|Z|>z]	Estimated coefficient (2000)	Prob /|Z|>z]
Intercept	−7.404*	0.000	−9.484*	0.000
Log [POPDENS]	−0.022	0.211	0.007	0.672
Log [POP05–18]	0.000	0.996	0.030	0.746
Log [MEDHINC]	0.392*	0.001	0.656*	0.000
Log [MEDHVAL]	−0.050	0.510	−0.119	0.120
Log [EMPL]	−0.474*	0.000	−0.525*	0.000
[%POV]	0.731	0.101	2.176*	0.000
[%NWHITE]	0.230	0.167	−0.025	0.874
[%URBAN]	0.233*	0.001	0.216*	0.002

(continued on next page)

Table 2. Parameter Estimates of the Double Log Models of School Enrollment, 1990 and 2000 Estimates *(continued)*

Imputed enrollment per population (E/P)

Independent variable	1990 imputed estimates 1990 imputed coefficient	2000 imputed estimates 2000 imputed coefficient
Log [POPDENS]	0	0
Log [POP05–18]	0.632	0.228
Log [MEDHINC]	0.066	0.656
Log [MEDHVAL]	0	−0.222
Log [EMPL]	−0.474	−0.188
[%POV]	−1.559	2.176
[%NWHITE]	0	−0.428
[%URBAN]	−0.239	−0.282

*Significance at the 1 percent level, †at the 10 percent level, and ‡ at the 5 percent level.

Schools per Population or per Capita

Schools per population (S/P) is essentially a measure of the proliferation of school in a community. A positive impact of a causal factor on this variable suggests that the response of the school district is to expand the number of schools. With respect to S/P, which is reflective of the intensity of school presence in a community, the results suggest that in 1990, this variable was inversely related only to employment but was directly related to median household income and percent of the population of the school district that lived in urban areas. The number of schools per capita was less related to socioeconomic and demographic factors than enrollment per school, as revealed by the sizes of the coefficients. This is consistent with the notion that school establishment decisions are sticky, vis-à-vis the expansion of enrollment per school or school size. Obviously, it is easier to expand enrollment in existing schools than to build new ones as demographics change.

The positive coefficient for median household income and percent urban population in the district suggests that high-income communities and those in relatively more urban areas are the ones more likely to feature a high number of schools per population. The income effect can understandably be attributed to purchasing power, which translates into willingness to pay higher taxes to create new schools. The urban effect suggests that predominantly nonwhite urban schools tend to carry a heavy school facilities burden. On the other hand, high employment locations, such as bedroom communities, tend to feature fewer schools per population.

The findings for 2000 are somewhat similar, except that the schools per population variable was more strongly associated with median household income and employment and less strongly with percentage urban in 2000, compared with 1990. The reduced disparity between urban and nonurban schools is consistent with this result. The almost doubling of the effect of income on the number of schools suggests that while Proposal A may have affected school enrollment, it did not slow down the ability of high-income communities to finance schools.

One unique finding about 2000 is the significant and positive coefficient of percentage of poor households, which was not significant in 1990. This suggests that poverty began to be an indicator of school intensity in the year 2000, possibly as a result of the change in school funding structure brought on by Proposal A. Poorer school districts, which do not have the tax base, may have been aided by Proposal A revenues from the state, which reduced the potential disparity with other school districts. Such schools also do not have the funding to be as flexible with the number and type of schools as wealthier school districts.

Enrollment per Population or per Capita

Enrollment per capita (E/P) is essentially a measure of the average number of children enrolled to total population. A positive impact of a causal factor on this variable suggests that the school district attracts more children per capita. The bottom of table 2 shows the relationships between enrollment and population (E/P), which was decomposed into impacts on the number of schools and impacts on enrollment per school. For example, increased median household income is directly related to E/P, but this manifests through a positive effect on schools per capita, which overshadows the negative impact on enrollment per school. While the effect of median household income on E/P was small for 1990, it was relatively large for 2000. People with greater income may be selecting to send their children to good public schools or they may be having more children. Only the percentage of urban residents and number employed in the school district were negatively related to enrollment per capita in both 1990 and 2000. This indicates that the more urbanized a school district, the less enrollment per capita.

As housing values increase, however, the effects on E/P became more pronounced and negative by 2000. This means that high housing value communities have lower E/P, which could be because they have fewer children or are better able to send their children to private schools. Greater incidence of poverty resulted in lower E/P in 1990, but greater E/P in 2000. This suggests growth in the public school enrollment of kids in poverty.

Holding all else constant, the single factor with the greatest impact on E/P is the percentage of the population in poverty. Interestingly, while poverty was associated with decreased enrollment in 1990, prior to Proposal A, it was associated with increased enrollment in 2000. This may suggest that Proposal A actually contributed to school access for poorer households. This issue should be investigated further. On the other hand, the impact of an increase in school-age population (ages 5–18) on E/P decreased between 1990 and 2000, suggesting pathways other than attending public schools for school-age children. This issue also needs further investigation.

CONCLUSIONS

Our decomposition analysis suggests some unique aspects of school district structure that hitherto have not been confirmed. For example, we confirmed that as a school district's school-age population increases, the increase is absorbed more through increased enrollment per school than through the number of schools. However, as median household income increases, there is a tendency to increase the number of available schools, reducing enrollment per school. This has an overall result of increased enrollment per capita and suggests that the high-income school districts face higher school of choice demands. This tendency became more pronounced in 2000 compared with 1990.

Bedroom communities (with higher employment and high income) are associated with relatively fewer schools and, in 2000, higher enrollment per school. This is consistent with the Taj Mahal Syndrome for 2000. The negative effect of high employment on the number of schools per capita overshadowed the positive effect of median household income, resulting in a net negative effect on schools per capita in 1990 but a net positive effect in 2000. This indicates the increased ability of high-income communities to provide more schools per capita following Proposal A. Proposal A left school building funding to be provided at the local level and operational funding to be supplied centrally by the state school aid fund. This appears to have resulted in high-income communities with a greater funding base potential, being able to better support their school districts through the generation of taxes to support the creation of additional school buildings, while lower income communities were less able to do so.

School districts in urban areas tended to have more schools per capita but less enrollment per school and less enrollment per population. These results indicate that more urban school districts are composed of a greater number of smaller schools, such as multiple neighborhood elementary schools. However, the effect on schools per capita and enrollment per school became less pronounced in 2000. Only percentage urban was consistently a significant factor in enrollment per school and schools per capita, possibly resulting from the historical structure of how urban and rural areas developed differently.

Proposal A made it possible, by law, for school operating costs to come from the state, while buildings were associated with raised local property taxes. It appears that one result of Proposal A (which was passed in 1994) was to make the number of schools per capita more tied to median household income but to decouple the relationship between enrollment per school and median household income. Thus while Proposal A facilitated more equity in enrollment per school across income, it created greater inequity in new facilities. High-income school districts may have been able to develop new schools while lower income schools were not. Simultaneously, school districts with higher property values became associated with lower enrollment after Proposal A. Proposal A may have encouraged private schooling and allowed schools of choice, resulting in lower enrollment per school in places with higher property values.

NOTE

1. Ongoing analysis at the Land Policy Institute involves the evaluation of the impact of socioeconomics and demographics on enrollment distribution by grade.

REFERENCES

Adelaja, Adesoji O., and Melissa A. Gibson. 2008. Municipal land use and the financial viability of schools. Paper presented at the American Agricultural Economics Association Annual Meeting, Orlando, FL, July 27–29.

Adelaja, Adesoji O., Yohannes Hailu, and Melissa A. Gibson. 2009. Economic impacts of county population changes in Michigan. Land Policy Institute Report. East Lansing: Michigan State University.

Adelaja, Adesoji O., Mark A. Wyckoff, Melissa A. Gibson, Charles McKeown, Benjamin Calnin, Tyler Borowy, and Michael Forsyth. 2008a. *The Michigan demographic atlas*. East Lansing: Land Policy Institute, Michigan State University.

———. 2008b. *The Michigan public school location atlas*. East Lansing: Land Policy Institute, Michigan State University.

Arsen, David, and Thomas Davis. 2006. Taj Mahals or decaying shacks: Patterns in local school capital stock and unmet capital need. *Peabody Journal of Education* 81 (4): 1–22.

Arsen, David, and David Plank. 2003. *Michigan school finance under proposal A: State control, local consequences*. East Lansing: The Education Policy Center at Michigan State University. http://www.epc.msu.edu.

Atlanta Regional Commission. 2003. Linking school siting to land use planning. http://www.atlantaregional.com/documents/SCHOOLS_TOOL.pdf.

Granholm, Jennifer. 2008. Michigan State of the state address 2008. The PEW Center on the States. January, 29. http://www.stateline.org/live/details/speech?contentId=276770.

Graves, P., and P. Linneman. 1979. Household migration: Theoretical and empirical results. *Journal of Urban Economics* 38: 383–404.

Haurin, Donald R., and David Brasington. 1996. School quality and real house prices: Inter- and intrametropolitan effects. *Journal of Housing Economics* 5: 351–68.

Lyson, Thomas A. 2002. What does a school mean to a community? Assessing the social and economic benefits of schools to rural villages in New York. *Journal of Research in Rural Education* 17 (3): 131–37.

Murray, S. E., W. B. Evans, and R. M. Schwab. 1998. Education-finance reform and the distribution of education resources. *American Economic Review* 88 (4): 789–812.

Orfield, Myron. 2002. *American metropolitics: The new suburban reality*. Washington, DC: Brookings Institution.

Peshkin, A. 1978. *The imperfect union*. Chicago: University of Chicago Press.

———. 1982. *Growing up American: Schooling and the survival of community*. Chicago: University of Chicago Press.

Skole, David, S. Batzli, S. Gage, B. Pijanowski, W. Chomentowski, and W. Rustem. 2002. Forecast Michigan: Tracking change for land use planning and policy-making. In *Urban Policy Choices for Michigan Leaders*, ed. T. Dozier and C. Weissert, 83–111. East Lansing: Michigan State University Press.

Taylor, L. L. 1999. Government's role in primary and secondary education: *Federal Reserve Bank of Dallas Economic Review* 1, 15–24.

U.S. Census Bureau. 1991. *Summary File 1, 1990 Annual Census*. Accessed 2006 from http://www.census.gov/mp/www/cat/decennial_census_1990/.

U.S. Census Bureau. 2001. *Summary File 1, 2000 Annual Census*. Accessed 2006 from http://www.census.gov/census2000/sumfile1.html.

U.S. Census Bureau. 2009a. *2008 Population Estimates.* Accessed 2009 from http://www.census.gov/popest/states/states.html.

U.S. Census Bureau. 2009b. *2008 American Communities Survey.* Accessed 2009 from http://factfinder.census.gov/servlet/DatasetMainPageServlet?_program=ACS&_submenuId=datasets_2&_lang=en.Vincent, Jeffery M. 2006. Public schools as public infrastructure: Roles for planning researchers. *Journal of Planning Education and Research* 25 (4): 433–37.

Wyckoff, Mark A., Adesoji O. Adelaja, Melissa A. Gibson, and Yohannes Hailu. 2008. Implications of school location change for healthy communities in a slow growth state: A case study of Michigan. Paper presented at the Critical Issues Symposium on School Siting and Healthy Communities Conference, Tallahassee, FL, April 3–4.

Wyckoff, Mark A., Adesoji O. Adelaja, and Melissa A. Gibson. 2011. *The implications of school location change for healthy communities in a slow-growth state: A case study of Michigan.* School Siting and Healthy Communities. MSU Press: East Lansing, MI.

PART 3

Consequences of Location Decisions

School Trips

Analysis of Factors Affecting Mode Choice in Three Metropolitan Areas

REID EWING, MING ZHANG, AND
MICHAEL J. GREENWALD

IN THE NEXT FEW DECADES, COMMUNITIES ACROSS THE UNITED STATES WILL NEED to accommodate substantial increases in student enrollment. The expected boom in school construction and renovation and the related planning decisions have implications for student travel.

National data indicate that nearly one-third of all American youth do not engage in sufficient amounts of vigorous or moderate physical activity (Grunbaum et al. 2002). For the twelve- to nineteen-year-old age group, overweight among teenagers increased from 6 percent in 1971–74 to 17 percent in 2003–4 (Ogden et al. 2006), with similar increases in other age groups. A recent study has linked the probability of being overweight in children to the built environment of their county of residence (Ewing, Brownson, and Berrigan 2006). In cross sectional analyses, these relationships are as strong for children as they are in studies of adults (Ewing et al. 2003, *American Journal of Health Promotion*; Papas et al. 2007).

Simultaneously, public schools have been increasing in size and drawing students from larger areas. Between 1940 and 1990, the total number of elementary and secondary public schools fell by 69 percent, despite a 70 percent increase in the U.S. population (Walberg 1992). Large new schools are typically placed in outlying areas because property is available and land prices are low.

Public policies have also contributed to this trend (Kouri 1999; Beaumont and Pianca 2000; Gurwitt 2004). The funding formulas in many states favor new school construction over renovation. Minimum acreage standards for elementary, middle, and high schools may be met only at greenfield locations because locations close to existing neighborhoods may offer little room for large schools with large athletic and recreational areas. Furthermore, building codes designed for new construction may constrain older schools that could otherwise be renovated. Since school districts are often exempt from local planning and zoning laws and can site new schools without consideration of local policies and plans, they can build new schools on greenfields, where school district managers have carte blanche in building the schools of their preference.

A sharp decline in walking and bicycling to school parallels the trends in childhood obesity and school siting. A recent longitudinal analysis showed a 70 percent drop in walking or biking to school across all grade levels between 1969 and 2001 (McDonald 2007). A recent survey by the Centers for Disease Control and Prevention (CDC) found that only 31 percent of children five to fifteen years old who live within one mile of their school walk or bike to class (Dellinger and Staunton 2002). In 1969 this figure approached 90 percent (NPTS 1972).

Why is this drastic decline in walking and bicycling to school occurring? In the CDC survey, parents cited long distances as the primary barrier. The supersizing of schools has left relatively few students living within comfortable walking or bicycling distance. Nonetheless, even short school trips are usually made by automobile, indicating that other factors are also at work.

The CDC survey observed that danger from traffic was the second most important barrier to walking and bicycling to school. The absence of sidewalks is a risk factor for collisions involving pedestrians, one specifically targeted by Safe Routes to School programs (Knoblauch 1988; Transportation Alternatives 2003). A poor walking environment has been linked to automobile dependence in the general population and would be expected to discourage walking and bicycling to school (Ewing and Cervero 2001; Ewing and Cervero 2010).

The trends in childhood health, school location, and walking and biking to school, described earlier, have led to a series of policy and program responses at the federal, state, and local levels. For example, by 2002, the U.S. Department of Health and Human Services and the CDC had become concerned about childhood inactivity and launched a KidsWalk-to-School campaign, citing rising rates of childhood obesity, diabetes, and asthma as the impetus for the program (CDC 2002). Starting in 1999, several states, led by California, responded to the decline in youth physical activity with Safe Routes to School (SRTS) programs. The California program provides approximately $20 million per year for such physical improvements as sidewalk gap closures, pedestrian warning systems, traffic control, and traffic-calming measures (Boarnet et al. 2005).

In 2005 a federal SRTS program was created by the federal transportation bill, the Safe, Accountable, Flexible, Efficient, Transportation Equity Act (SAFETEA-LU). Housed in Federal Highway Administration, the SRTS program is funded at $612 million over five fiscal years (FY 2005–9). Every state has an allocation of funds, and every state is establishing, or has established, a program.

In a parallel trend, policy makers are reemphasizing smaller, in-neighborhood schools. In 2003 South Carolina eliminated minimum acreage requirements for schools and allowed waivers in school square footage—two steps that the governor predicted would foster neighborhood schools. In 2004 the school siting guidelines of the Council of Educational Facility Planners International were revised to eliminate minimum site size requirements, which had encouraged school districts to build on large outlying sites where land is cheap (McDonald 2008).

It would appear, then, that the issues of school siting and location, trends in walking and bicycling to school, and trends in childhood health are related. The growing policy and program interest in this topic and the significant expenditures in programs and activities to address this issue suggest the need for better information on these relationships. This study examines the relationship between school location, the built environment around schools, and student travel across different metropolitan areas. The results suggest that students with shorter walk and bike times to school are significantly more likely to walk or bike—which argues for neighborhood schools. The results also suggest that students who have access to sidewalks along main roads are more likely to walk—which argues for Safe Routes to School sidewalk improvements. In the rest of this chapter, we explore factors influencing biking and walking to school and their implications for future school siting policies.

Factors Influencing Walking and Bicycling to School

Though the literature has expanded in recent years, research connecting student travel to characteristics of the built environment is still sparse. In one study, the percentage of students walking to school was found to be four times higher for schools built before 1983 than for those built later—an average of 16 percent walked to older schools compared with 4 percent to newer schools (Kouri 1999). School age is not a very good proxy for the complete range of factors that distinguish small schools in walkable neighborhoods from mega schools in remote areas.

M. Braza, W. Shoemaker, and A. Seeley's (2004) study of fifth-grade students at thirty-four California public schools showed that walking and bicycling rates were positively associated with neighborhood population density and negatively with school size, after controlling for the percentage of students on public welfare and for the percentage of ethnic minorities. In their study intersection density was not significant, and distance from home to school was not controlled.

T. McMillan's (2002) study of travel to six California schools found that walking and bicycling were more likely for students living within one mile of the school. Some pedestrian-friendly design features had positive influences on walking and bicycling, such as the presence of street trees within a quarter mile of the school. Other features, such as short blocks and mixed land uses, had negative influences. The limitation of the study to only six school sites meant that there was little variance in built environmental conditions across survey respondents, and the significance of these variables was accordingly limited.

Another study by McMillan (2007), focusing on elementary school students at sixteen California schools, after controlling for family attitudes and socioeconomic variables, found that walking and bicycling to school were more likely when high proportions of street segments within a quarter mile of the school had windows facing the streets and mixed land uses along them. Surprisingly, the choice of walking or biking did not depend on the proportion of street segments with sidewalks on both sides of the street.

A study of middle school students at four Oregon schools showed strong relationships between the likelihood of walking to school and the distance between home and school, the intersection density along the route to school, and (inversely) the density of dead-end streets (Schlossberg et al. 2006). The likelihood of bicycling to school was related only to the distance from home to school. Mode choices were not affected by the presence of major cross streets, railroad crossings, or the directness of the route to school. Land use variables were not controlled.

Kerr et al. (2006) conducting a study of students ages four to eighteen in King County, Washington, concluded that walking or bicycling to school were significantly related to an overall "walkability index" and to three of four individual variables that make up the index—residential density, mixed land use, and intersection density (Kerr et al. 2006). Residential density was the variable most strongly related to active travel to school. The fourth component of the index, retail floor area ratio, was apparently unrelated to active travel. The four variables were not tested simultaneously, and distance to school was not controlled.

Building on the work of Schlossberg and Kerr, Lawrence Frank and Company (2008) analyzed travel diary data for school trips made by students ages five to eighteen in the thirteen county Atlanta metropolitan region. Their results indicate that once trip distance is accounted for, urban form measures such as percentage of routes with sidewalks, higher residential density, and better interconnectedness of streets were all significantly related to walking mode choice for trips to school, particularly for short trips (i.e., up to 1.5 miles).

N. C. McDonald's (2008) study of student travel to schools nationwide, using the National Household Travel Survey (NHTS), found that the likelihood of walking to school was strongly and inversely related to long travel time and weakly and directly related to population density. The data source, NHTS, limited the study to a single built environmental variable: density.

Other studies finding that walking or bicycling to school drops off rapidly with greater distance from home to school include D. Merom et al. (2006), A. Timperio et al. (2006), S. U. Jensen (2008), N. M. Nelson et al. (2008), S. Babey et al. (2009), K. Larsen et al. (2009), and M. A. Napier et al. (2011).

Beyond inferring that the built environment matters, it is difficult to generalize across these studies. Their sampling frames and outcome variables differ, as do their explanatory variables. Some combine walking and bicycling into one mode, others treat them as alternate modes. Some control for the distance from home to school, others do not. Some include land use variables, others do not. Some test explanatory variables individually, others test variables in a multivariate framework, holding other variables constant while looking at the independent effect of each variable on the dependent variable.

In sum, the existing literature—and this is true of the entire literature on the built environment and travel—is weak from the standpoint of external validity because each new study comes with its own unique variable definitions, model specifications, and study areas. What policy makers and practitioners need is more explicit information that can provide a generalized framework for making decisions about schools, active school commuting, and the health of children. The present study operates on the premise that advances in our understanding of this heavily researched subject will require a degree of consistency across study areas; therefore, we applied similar methodology to three case study areas: Gainesville, Florida; Portland, Oregon; and Houston, Texas.

Contrasting Metropolitan Areas

When one thinks of Houston, Texas, the images that come to mind are those of urban sprawl, superhighways, fragmented government, and the largest city in the nation without zoning (as in fig. 1). Portland, Oregon, is the polar opposite, at least in its popular image. What comes to mind when imagining Portland is a strong downtown and vibrant town centers, a rapidly expanding light rail system, metropolitan government, and an urban growth boundary (as in fig. 2). Both of these are large metropolitan areas. Gainesville is small but, like Houston, is characterized by sprawling development patterns.

The popular images are borne out in various ways. Using the same definition of mixed-use development (MXD), our recent survey for the Environmental Protection Agency (EPA) identified twice as many MXDs in Portland as in larger Houston. Satellite images at the same scale and elevation show development in Houston spread out in all directions while development in Portland is much more concentrated (see figs. 3 and 4). By almost every measure in

Figure 1. Houston's Unregulated Freeway Environment
Source: Reid Ewing.

Figure 2. Portland's Well-Designed Downtown Environment
Source: Reid Ewing.

Figures 3 and 4. Portland and Houston Urban Footprints at the Same Scale

the Texas Transportation Institute's mobility database and Smart Growth America's sprawl database, Houston is more automobile-oriented and sprawling (see table 1).

The study by Ewing, Schroeer, and Greene (2003) was the first to examine the relationship between the mode of travel to school and the full range of factors that might affect mode

Table 1. Comparative Land Use and Transportation Statistics for Portland and Houston (Measures Not Available for Gainesville)

	Portland, OR	*Houston, TX*
Density factor[1]	101.3	95.3
Mixed land use factor[1]	102.3	110.1
Centering factor[1]	121.8	87.0
Street accessibility factor[1]	128.0	95.6
Highway lanes per 1,000 population[2]	1.88	2.61
Annual transit passenger miles per capita[2]	249	158
Daily VMT per capita[2]	15.2	23.7

[1] Values for major metropolitan areas are standardized with a mean of 100 and standard deviation of 25. R. Ewing, R. Pendall, and D. Chen. 2002. *Measuring sprawl and its impact*. Washington, DC: Smart Growth America/U.S. Environmental Protection Agency. http://smartgrowthamerica.org/sprawlindex/sprawlindex.html.
[2] Urban mobility database for 2007. D. Schrank and T. Lomax. 2009. *The urban mobility report 2009*. College Station: Texas Transportation Institute. http://mobility.tamu.edu/ums.

choice. The study, conducted for the EPA, utilized data from Gainesville, Florida, in estimating a multinomial logit model to explain school travel mode choice for a sample of K–12 students. Since the Gainesville pilot study, planning methodology has matured in an important respect. It is now recognized that data of this type are hierarchical in nature. When individuals are nested within places (in our case, students nested within school environments), they are best analyzed using hierarchical (multilevel) modeling methods (Ewing et al. 2003; Ewing et al. 2005; Ewing, Brownson, and Berrigan 2006). We therefore extend the Gainesville analysis of mode choice for school trips to two very different metropolitan areas, Portland and Houston.

Portland and Houston are two of six metropolitan areas that are supplying trip records for a multiregion EPA study of trip generation by MXDs (Ewing et al., forthcoming). Prior studies have analyzed the relationships of built environmental variables to adult travel in the two regions (Boarnet and Greenwald 2000; Greenwald and Boarnet 2001; Greenwald 2003, 2006; Greenwald and McNally forthcoming; Zhang 2005). This study extends the analysis to mode choice of student travel. The extension allows us to validate findings of the original pilot study in Gainesville. It also allows us to refine our approach, applying hierarchical modeling methods to this subject for the first time.

ANALYTICAL FRAMEWORK

Conventional Mode Choice Models

In the Gainesville pilot study, two conventional mode choice models were estimated, a multinomial logit (MNL) and a nested logit (NL) model. By "conventional" we mean single-level models that treat all observations as independent. Models were estimated using full information maximum likelihood (FIML) via LIMDEP/NLOGIT software. The multinomial model was selected as more consistent with the data set.

The choice of mode was assumed to depend on characteristics of the trip, traveler, school, and built environment through a relationship of the form of

$$P_k = \exp(U_k)/[\sigma_l \in_K \exp(U_l)], \quad (1)$$

where P_k is the probability of choosing mode k for a school trip and U_k is the utility function for mode k as defined in the following equation:

$$U_k = \alpha_k + \beta T_k^{ij} + \gamma SE^m + \theta SC^n + \delta BE^i + \omega BE^j + \varepsilon_k, \quad (2)$$

- T_k^{ij} and β are trip characteristics and corresponding parameter vectors for trips from i to j by mode k—including travel time
- SE^m and γ are socioeconomic characteristics and corresponding parameter vectors for a student from household m—characteristics such as income and automobile ownership
- SC^n and θ are school characteristics, such as enrollment and corresponding parameter vectors for school n
- BE^i and δ are built environmental characteristics and corresponding parameter vectors for origin i, with i being a neighborhood, census tract, traffic analysis zone, or other small area—the vector may include measures of density, land use mix, walking quality, and site design
- BE^j and ω are built environmental characteristics and corresponding parameter vectors for destination j
- ε_k is an extreme-value error vector specific to mode k

This is the kind of single-level mode choice model that has been estimated for the past two decades by travel researchers. The characteristics of the trip, traveler, school, and built environment are lumped together on the right-hand side of the equation, as if they are uniquely identified with an individual trip. Only recently has the multilevel nature of the data structure been recognized in planning circles.

In the Gainesville analysis, the "universal choice set" for the student population studied consisted of four travel modes: automobile, school bus, walking, and bicycling. Practically speaking, certain modes were unavailable to certain students, and their choice sets had to be restricted. If students had walked to school, the longer trips could have taken as long as eight hours. If they had biked, these trips could have taken as long as two hours. No student would be expected to walk or bike this far. Therefore, an arbitrary cutoff value of sixty minutes was established for travel times by these modes.

Once walk and bike modes were removed from the choice sets for trips having walk and bike travel times in excess of the cutoff value, hundreds of school trips in the sample were restricted to two or three modes. Yet nearly all these trips were by automobiles or school buses anyway, so removing walk or bike modes from the choice sets did not deplete the sample appreciably. The model was estimated with these options eliminated from the available choice set for these individuals.

The opposite situation applied to school bus trips. To qualify for school bus service, students in the Alachua County School District generally must live two or more miles from school.

Accordingly, the school bus mode was initially removed from the choice sets for school trips of less than two miles. However, this restriction was later lifted due to the large number of school bus trips lost to the sample. A review of the school district's policy indicated that exceptions to the minimum distance rule are made when a student faces hazardous walking conditions, qualifies for "courtesy" busing by virtue of living along a bus route, or for other similar reasons.

Travel time estimates were included in the utility functions of walk and bike modes. As there was no reason to assume that time spent walking and bicycling would have the same disutility, travel time coefficients were estimated independently for the walk and bike modes. Travel time was left out of the school bus utility function for lack of any credible estimate of travel time by that mode. All plausible combinations of socioeconomic, school, and built environmental variables were tested as explanatory variables in the utility functions of the walk, bike, and school bus modes. Variables were retained only if they proved significant at the 0.05 probability level.

Hierarchical Model Structure

The study of the Portland and Houston regions uses hierarchical modeling methods. Hierarchical modeling (often abbreviated as HLM) is required to account for dependence among observations, in this case the dependence of trips to a given school on characteristics of the built environment around the school. While mode choice depends on unique characteristics of the trip itself, the student, and the student's household, it also depends on characteristics of the school that are shared by all students going to that school. This interdependence violates the independence assumption of ordinary regression analysis (including multinomial logistic regression of the type in the pilot study). Standard errors of regression coefficients will consequently be underestimated. Moreover, coefficient estimates will be inefficient. Hierarchical (multilevel) modeling overcomes these limitations, accounting for the dependence among observations and producing more accurate standard error estimates.

We initially conceived our data structure as a three-level hierarchy, with trips, and the students making them, nested within households and households nested within schools. In fact, in the initial analysis of mode choice versus distance to school, this was the structure adopted. Students from the same household (who may have very different trip distances to different schools) were treated as nested within their respective households, sharing the characteristics of those households (as in fig. 5).

In a second analysis focusing on the built environments around schools, we found that the data were not so neatly nested. Students from the same households often go to different schools, and these schools are in different built environments. Rather than a three-level hierarchy, the choices facing students (and their parents) have to be modeled in a two-level framework. Individual school trips and the associated characteristics of students and their households form level 1 in the hierarchy, and schools and their environments form level 2 (see fig. 6). If we had more metropolitan areas in our sample, they might constitute a third level in a three-level hierarchy. But with only two metropolitan areas (or three with Gainesville), school travel within each area needs to be analyzed separately.

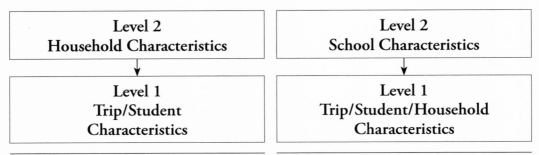

Figure 5. First Hierarchical Mode Choice Model for School Trips

Figure 6. Second Hierarchical Mode Choice Model for School Trips

The D Variables

In the development of a framework for this study, we focus on the "D" variables. In travel research, urban development patterns have come to be characterized by these variables. The original "Three Ds," coined by Cervero and Kockelman (1997), were *density*, *diversity*, and *design*. Two additional Ds have been added since then, *destination accessibility* and *distance to transit* (Ewing and Cervero 2001; Ewing and Cervero 2010). Still one more D is relevant to this analysis: *demographics*.

Density usually is measured in terms of persons, jobs, or dwellings per unit area. Diversity refers to the number of different land uses in an area and the degree to which they are "balanced" in land area, floor area, or employment. Design includes street network characteristics within a neighborhood. Street networks vary from dense urban grids of highly interconnected, straight streets to sparse suburban networks of curving streets forming "loops and lollipops." Street accessibility typically is measured in terms of average block size, proportion of four-way intersections, or number of intersections per square mile. Design, also, is measured in terms of sidewalk coverage, building setbacks, street widths, pedestrian crossings, presence of street trees, and a host of other physical variables that differentiate pedestrian-oriented environments from automobile-oriented ones.

Destination accessibility is measured in terms of the number of jobs or other attractions reachable within a given travel time, which tends to be highest at central locations and lowest at peripheral ones. Distance to transit usually is measured from home or work to the nearest rail station or express bus stop and is sometimes operationalized in terms of transit route or transit stop spacing. Demographic variables (more accurately, sociodemographic variables) commonly used in travel research include life stage, family size, education, employment status, income, and vehicle ownership or vehicle availability.

In this study, all D variables, except distance to transit, are used to explain mode choice on school trips. Distance to transit is omitted because so few school trips, especially in our case study areas, involve public transportation. In the case of school trips, the literature suggests that mode choice may additionally depend on school size and grade level.

Data Sets

The Gainesville data set is richer in one respect than the data sets of these other two regions. More independent variables, both design variables and school-related variables, are available for Gainesville. On the other hand, the Portland and Houston data sets have larger samples of school trips and more precise measures of land use.

For Portland, data came from two main sources: the 1994 Household Activity and Travel Behavior Survey (1994 Travel Diaries) and the associated Regional Land Information System (RLIS) geographic information system (GIS) database files. The 1994 Travel Diaries contain data on 74,399 total trips by 10,048 persons from 4,451 households, collected over two survey days. Due to land use data availability, we focused on the 50,623 trips generated by 4,003 households located within Oregon. Trips by households located in Clark County, Washington, were excluded from the analysis. These two Portland databases together provide the following:

- XY coordinates for trip origins and destinations, so we can zero in on individual sites when studying travel patterns
- Individual parcel data, so we can study land use mix down to the parcel level

Most Houston data were obtained from the Houston-Galveston Area Council (H-GAC). The 1995 Household Activity and Travel Surveys recorded a total of 30,383 trips made by 6,010 persons from 2,443 households for one survey day. The database did not contain XY coordinates for trip ends. However, in most cases, the surveyed individuals provided the street addresses or postal codes of their activity locations. Out of the total 30,383 trips, 22,938 were successfully geocoded by address and 6,612 were approximately geocoded at the zip code or census tract level. The remaining records were spatially unidentifiable.

There was no comprehensive GIS database available for the Houston region. We created one with data files collected from various sources. Traffic analysis zone (TAZ) boundary files and population and employment data at the TAZ level came from H-GAC. H-GAC also provided a land use data set at the grid cell of 1,000 by 1,000 feet for the eight-county area. The street network file was from the Houston regional travel model data CDs. For accessibility calculations skim tables of zonal travel times were obtained from H-GAC.

From the larger Portland and Houston data sets, home-to-school trips were extracted. There were two complicating factors that involved methodological choices. First, because the Portland diary survey covered two days, the data set included more than one observation for many students. The obvious course would have been to eliminate duplicates. However, a review of the data disclosed a surprising number of students using different modes on different days. Thus all records were retained and treated as independent.

Second, some trips to school involved intermediate stops (by a parent, for example, to pick something up) and were coded as two trips: one from home to the intermediate destination, the other from the intermediate destination to school. The latter trip may be short and walkable but as part of a longer trip chain would be made by automobile. All such linked school trips were dropped from the databases, leaving only direct home-to-school trips.

Measures

The variables available at each level are similar for Portland and Houston, though the Portland data set includes two extra environmental variables (shown in italics).

Trip/Student Variables

- WALK—Walked to school (1 = walk, 0 = other)
- BIKE—Biked to school (1 = bike, 0 = other)
- DISTANCE—Road network distance from home to school
- AGE—Age of student in years
- AGE2—Age of student in years squared
- MALE—Dummy variable indicating that a student is a male (1 = male, 0 = female)
- WHITE—Dummy variable indicating that a student is Caucasian (1 = white, 0 = other)
- LICENSE—Dummy variable indicating that the student has a driver's license (1 = licensed, 0 = otherwise)

Household Variables

- HHSIZE—Number of members of the household
- VEHCAP—Number of motorized vehicles per person in the household
- INCOME—Annual household income

School-Level Variables (Level 2)

- POPDEN—Population density (population per square mile) within the one-mile buffer around a school
- EMPDEN—Employment density (employment per square mile) within the one-mile buffer around a school
- ACTDEN—Activity density (population + employment per square mile) within the one-mile buffer around a school
- CEMPDEN—Commercial employment density per net square mile within the one-mile buffer around a school
- DEVLAND—Proportion of developed land within the one-mile buffer around a school
- JOBPOP—Index that measures the balance between employment and resident population in the one-mile buffer around the school

    Index ranges from 0, where only jobs or residents are present in the school buffer—not both—to 1, where the ratio of jobs to residents is the same within the buffer area as in the region as a whole. Values are intermediate when school buffers have both jobs and residents, but one predominates.[1]
- LANDMIX—Diversity index that captures the variety of land uses in the one-mile buffer around the school

    Entropy calculation is based on net acreage in land use categories likely to exchange trips. Slightly different categories of land use were factored into the index in different regions. In Portland, the land uses were single-family residential, multifamily residential, commercial, industrial, and public or semipublic.[2] In Houston, the land uses were residential, commercial, mixed residential and commercial, institutional, and industrial and other. The index varies in value from 0, where all developed land is in one of these categories, to 1, where developed land is evenly divided among these categories.

- STRDEN—Centerline miles of all streets per square mile of land in the one-mile buffer around the school
- INTDEN—Number of intersections per square mile of land in the one-mile buffer around the school
- SIDEWALK—Miles of sidewalk per centerline mile of streets

RESULTS

Descriptive Travel Statistics

Do the macro differences between Portland and Houston (see table 1) translate into different patterns of student travel to school? Descriptive statistics suggest that they do. From travel diary surveys, we have extracted home-to-school trips. The average distance from home to school is a mile longer in Houston (see table 2) than in Portland. And the mode splits are different. About 11 percent of school trips in Houston are walk trips. The comparable figure for Portland is 18 percent, not impressive but better. Nearly all walk trips to school are by students living within two miles of school (see frequency distributions in figs. 7 and 8).

Gainesville is a much smaller metropolitan area than Houston or Portland but actually has longer home-to-school trips than these other metropolitan areas. Apparently, fewer students attend schools within their own neighborhoods. The proportion of students walking to school is correspondingly lower than in Houston and Portland, and the proportion traveling to school in automobiles is correspondingly higher.

MNL Model Results for Gainesville

The best-fit model is presented in tables 3 and 4. These tables present the same basic information in different forms. In table 3 coefficient values and t-statistics indicate the effects of independent variables on mode choice probabilities. The convergence of the MNL model was found to be satisfactory. The log likelihood at convergence is –425, and the log likelihood with constants only in the utility function is –494. The pseudo-R square of the model is thus 1 – (–425/–494) or 0.14 relative to the model with constants only.

Table 2. Length and Mode of Home-to-School Trips (All Trips)

	Gainesville, FL	*Portland, OR*	*Houston, TX*
Sample size (trips)	711	1,220	1,187
Mean home-to-school distance (mi.)	4.85	2.68	3.72
Walk trips (%)	4.5	17.6	10.8
Bicycle trips (%)	3.7	1.8	2.3
School bus trips (%)	14.8	33.5	31.1

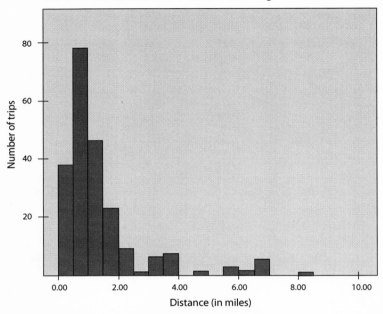

Home-to-school distances for students walking to school in Portland

Figure 7. Plot of Home-to-School Distances for Students Walking to School in Portland

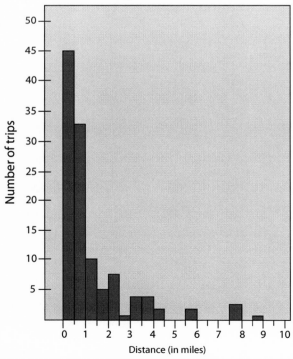

Home-to-school distances for students walking to school in Houston

Figure 8. Plot of Home-to-School Distances for Students Walking to School in Houston

Table 3. Multinomial Mode Choice Model for Gainesville: Log Odds of School Bus, Walk, and Bike Use Relative to Automobile Use

Variable	Bus		Walk		Bike	
	Coeff.	T value	Coeff.	T value	Coeff.	T value
Constant	−1.054	−6.44	2.385	2.40	−1.301	−3.87
Annual household income (in thousands of dollars)			−0.0334	−3.33		
Per capita household auto ownership			−4.570	−3.61		
License ownership indicator (1 if the individual holds a drivers license, 0 otherwise)	−2.513	−4.23				
Walk time for the trip (min.)			−0.0527	−3.98		
Bike time for the trip (min.)					−0.1504	−4.07
Average sidewalk coverage for origin and destination TAZs			1.480	2.09		
Average home-based other accessibilities for origin and destination TAZs	−1.130	−2.37				
Log-likelihood with constants only	−493.9					
Log-likelihood at convergence	−425.4					
Pseudo-R2	0.139					
Number of observations	709					

Table 4. Point Mode Elasticity Estimates for Gainesville, Florida

Variable	Bus	Walk	Bike
Annual household income (in thousands of dollars)		−0.84	
Per capita auto ownership for the household		−1.16	
License ownership indicator (1 if the individual holds a driver's license, 0 otherwise)	−0.91		
Walk time for the trip (min.)		−0.66	
Bike time for the trip (min.)			−2.63
Average sidewalk coverage for origin and destination TAZs		0.42	
Average home-based other accessibilities for origin and destination TAZs	−0.31		

In table 4 the marginal effects of independent variables on mode choice probabilities are expressed as elasticities—that is, as percentage changes in probabilities associated with a 1 percent change in each independent variable. Elasticities are commonly used in travel research to summarize relationships between travel outcomes and explanatory variables. The values presented are point elasticities at the mean values of the independent variables.

As expected, students with shorter walk and bike times to and from school were significantly more likely to walk and bike, respectively. The probability of bicycling is particularly sensitive to travel time; an elasticity value of −2.63 means that students are averse to even small increases in travel time by bicycle. Perhaps this is because even small differences in travel time by bicycle represent large differences in distance traveled (relative to distance traveled on foot). The probability of walking is less sensitive to travel time but still significantly affected by it, with an elasticity value of −0.66.

Of the many built environmental variables, the proportion of arterials and collectors with sidewalks along them proved to be the most significant influence on walking. Values of sidewalk coverage for origin and destination zones are highly correlated for walk trips, precluding the use of both variables in the same utility function. Instead, values of sidewalk coverage for the origin and destination zones were averaged, and the average was used as an explanatory variable. The probability of walking to school has an elasticity of 0.42 with respect to average sidewalk coverage.

Interestingly, the built environment did not have a significant effect on bicycling. Even the proportion of arterials and collectors with bike lanes or paved shoulders along them proved insignificant. The arterials and collectors with paved shoulders tend to be in less developed areas, so this particular variable may not reflect the general bicycle friendliness of the area.

One built environmental variable—regional accessibility for home-based other trips—proved to be related to school bus use. The more accessible the location, the less attractive the school bus relative to other modes, including the automobile. School buses may be serving as a mode of last resort for parents, chosen when parents cannot provide rides themselves due to excessive distances between home and school. As with sidewalk coverage, home-based other accessibilities are correlated for origin and destination zones and, therefore, were averaged to create a single variable that reflects conditions at both origin and destination. The probability of taking a school bus had an elasticity of −0.31 with respect to average regional accessibility.

Students from households with higher incomes and more vehicles per capita were less likely to walk to school compared to taking a car, school bus, or bicycle. The probability of walking is most strongly related to vehicles per capita; its elasticity is −1.16. Less strongly related is household income, with an elasticity of −0.84. It is obvious why greater vehicle availability would make walking less attractive relative to car travel. It is less obvious why greater vehicle availability would make walking less attractive relative to other modes or why higher income would have this effect independent of vehicle availability. These two variables individually and together may have a strong enough influence on mode choice to overwhelm other factors favoring walk trips, such as a short distance to and from school.

Students holding driver's licenses were less likely to take a school bus than those without driver's licenses. This makes perfect sense. Students living too far from school to walk or bike are prime candidates for school bus service until they reach driving age, at which time they become prime candidates for driving themselves if their families' financial situations permit it.

Notably absent from the utility functions of different modes were school variables.

Enrollment did not prove significant after controlling for travel time between home and school. Larger schools may draw students from larger areas and thereby indirectly affect mode choices. But school size did not appear to have a direct effect on mode choices.

Also absent from the utility functions were land use variables such as density and mix. The travel behavior literature emphasizes the importance of such variables in travel decision making. Apparently school trips are different; they tend to be unlinked to other activities, thus reducing the need for proximity to other land uses. They are mandatory, which may render the walking environment less important than with discretionary travel, and they involve children, who may be less sensitive to walking conditions than their adult counterparts.

HLM Results for Portland and Houston

In our analysis of school built environments, we limited the study to students living *within a mile of school* and limited the choice set to walking, bicycling, and other (mostly automobile). Our final samples are as shown in table 5.

Again, the most notable difference between Portland and Houston is in the percentage of walk trips, which is significantly higher for Portland despite marginally longer distances between home and school. This difference suggests that Portland's more pedestrian-oriented urban design may be having an effect on the mode of travel to school beyond any effect of distance to school.

What is the relevant built environment around a school? Is it a quarter mile, a nominal walking distance for adults? Is it a mile, a nominal bicycling distance? At four miles an hour, an older child can cover one mile in fifteen minutes; at three miles an hour, it takes twenty minutes. Neither travel time seems excessive.

Mode choice models were estimated with HLM 6 (Hierarchical Linear and Nonlinear Modeling) software. For reasons that aren't clear, HLM 6 software was unable to estimate multinomial logit models for Portland or Houston. One advantage of the binomial specification is that different explanatory variables could be included in the walk and bike equations, something that HLM 6 does not permit with multinomial models.

Best-fitting binomial logit models of walking and bicycling to school are presented in table 6 (for Portland) and table 7 (for Houston). Table 8 presents elasticities of walking and bicycling with respect to planning-relevant variables.

Tables 6 and 7 come with the following explanatory notes:

Table 5. Length and Mode of Home-to-School Trips in Portland and Houston (Trips by Students Living within a Mile of School)

	Portland, OR	Houston, TX
Sample size (trips)	310	266
Mean home-to-school distance (mi.)	0.66	0.59
Walk trips (%)	38.1	29.3
Bicycle trips (%)	4.2	6.0

Table 6. Log Odds of Walking and Bicycling to School in Portland (1-Mile Buffer)

	Walking			Bicycling		
	Coeff.	*T value*	*P value*	*Coeff.*	*T value*	*P value*
Constant	−0.615			−4.42		
Distance	−1.06	−1.31	0.19	−0.989	−0.78	0.44
Age	0.823	2.11	0.035	2.67	1.88	0.061
Age2	−0.033	−1.82	0.069	−0.139	−2.09	0.037
Sidewalk	0.249	1.53	0.13			
Pseudo-R^2	0.014			0.0		

Table 7. Log Odds of Walking and Bicycling to School in Houston (1-Mile Buffer)

	Walking			Bicycling		
	Coeff.	*T value*	*P value*	*Coeff.*	*T value*	*P value*
Constant	−1.27			−4.57		
Distance	−3.04	−4.23	< 0.001	−2.94	−1.98	0.048
Male				0.99	1.97	0.05
Age				2.21	3.28	0.002
Age2				−0.112	−3.34	0.001
Vehcap	−2.57	−2.30	0.022			
Popden	0.000217	2.67	0.009	−0.000581	−3.11	0.003
Pseudo-R^2	0.032			0.135		

Table 8. Elasticities of Walking and Bicycling to School

	Portland		Houston	
	Walking	*Bicycling*	*Walking*	*Bicycling*
Distance	−0.02	−0.02	−1.71	−1.73
Sidewalk	0.01	—		
Popden	—	—	0.96	−2.68

- The dependent variable is the log odds that a given mode will be used on a home-to-school trip. To compute the probability that the mode would be used, we would first take the antilog and then use the formula p = odds/(1+odds).
- There is not a true R-squared value for a multilevel model. However, there are statistics that represent the proportions of variance explained by the model, and they are often referred to as pseudo–R-squared values. Our ability to explain mean mode shares across schools is limited, particularly for Portland.

- In the final model runs, only the intercepts were allowed to randomly vary across schools. All the regression coefficients at higher levels were treated as fixed. These are referred to as "random intercept" models. We tested for cross-level variable interactions, but none reached the conventional significance level. So all reported results are for random intercept models.

The negative coefficient of the variable DISTANCE in all models for Portland and Houston show behaviorally consistent effect of distance between home and school on walking or biking (tables 6 and 7). However, the coefficients in the Portland walking and biking models are statistically insignificant, suggesting that students in Portland are not very sensitive to distance increases for walking or biking as long as the school or home is located within a one-mile buffer of the home or school. In contrast, Houston students have a relatively low tolerance for distance; an increase in distance between home and school in Houston significantly reduces the odds of walking or biking even within the one-mile range. The effect of distance on the odds of walking or biking between the two regions is clearly shown in elasticity terms (table 8). In Portland, doubling the distance (i.e., a 100 percent increase) between home and school is associated with 2 percent decrease in the probability of walking or biking. In Houston, the decrease in walking or biking probability would be more than 170 percent. Contextual factors such as en route environment, weather, and local culture may explain the difference in distance effects between the two regions.

The odds of walking and biking increase with the student's age. As the student becomes older, toward the end of schooling age, the odds of walking and biking start to decline. This is indicated by the negative coefficient for variable AGE2 (i.e., age squared). Most likely when the student reaches the driving age, he or she is inclined to drive to school if the family's finances permit. To further explore the age effects on walking or biking, one may derive the turning age at which the odds of walking or biking changes from increase to decline with age. For instance, in Portland, the odds of walking decreases with age after he or she becomes twelve years or older (set the marginal odds with respect to AGE to zero—that is, $d(0.823AGE-0.033AGE2)/d(AGE) = 0$; solving for AGE gives AGE = 12.1). For biking, the turning age is 9.6 and 9.9 years for Portland and Houston, respectively.

The effects of gender and vehicle ownership on walking and biking conform to common knowledge. Male students are more likely to bike than female students; high vehicle ownership is associated with low probability of walking. As expected, sidewalk provision and higher population density encourages walking. In Houston, it seems counterintuitive that the higher population density is associated with declined odds of biking. One speculative explanation could be that cyclists used bike trails or parks where population densities tend to be low.

Discussion

Our findings are generally consistent with earlier studies of school mode choice. Distance from home to school was found to be significant in several previous studies. In all three metropolitan areas studied, students living closer to school are more likely to walk or bike. In Houston, walking and bicycling decline rapidly with distance even for those living within a mile of their school. In Portland, the decline is less pronounced, possibly indicating that walk sheds are extended by better walking conditions. This and earlier studies provide support for neighborhood schools serving nearby residential areas.

Elements of the built environment around a school were found to be significant in previous studies as in this study. But determining which built environmental factors influence school mode choice remains an issue. Specifically, neighborhood population density proved important in one earlier study, street tree coverage in the vicinity of school was important in another study, and age of schools (presumably a proxy for traditional neighborhood design, which in turn is a proxy for higher density and finer mixed land use) was important in a third study. Of these variables, only population density proved significant in this study, and then only for Houston. On the other hand, we found sidewalk coverage to be significant in Gainesville and nearly significant in Portland, findings that have not appeared previously (for lack of sidewalk data) in the literature. If confirmed elsewhere, this finding argues for Safe Routes to School sidewalk improvements.

The role of school size in mode choice also requires further study. Student enrollment proved significant in one earlier mode choice study but not in our study of student travel in Gainesville. We are tempted to say that this is because we controlled for travel time to school, while the earlier study did not, but our school size variable proved insignificant in all model specifications. So whether school size has a direct effect on school mode choice, beyond its effect on travel time to school, remains an issue.

NOTES

1. JOBPOP = 1 − [ABS (employment − c × population)/(employment + c × population)]. ABS is the absolute value of the expression in parentheses, where c is the regional ratio of employment to population.
2. LANDMIX = − [single-family share × LN (single-family share) + multifamily share × LN (multifamily share) + commercial share × LN (commercial share) + industrial share × LN (industrial share) + public share × LN (public share)]/ LN (5)—where LN is the natural logarithm of the value in parentheses. These are the active land uses in Portland; the set of active land uses is different in Houston.

REFERENCES

Babey, S. H., T. A. Hastert, W. Huang, E. R. Brown. 2009. Sociodemographic, family, and environmental factors associated with active commuting to school among US adolescents. *Journal of Public Health Policy*, 30 (Suppl 1), S203–S220.

Beaumont, Constance E., and Elizabeth G. Pianca. 2000. *Historic neighborhood schools in the age of sprawl: Why Johnny can't walk to school.* Washington, DC: National Trust for Historic Preservation.

Boarnet, M., and M. Greenwald. 2000. Land use, urban design, and non-work travel: Reproducing for Portland, Oregon empirical tests from other urban areas. *Transportation Research Record* 1722: 27–37.

Boarnet, M. G., C. L. Anderson, K. Day, T. McMillan, and M. Alfonzo. 2005. Evaluation of the California Safe Routes to School legislation: urban form changes and children's active transportation to school. *American Journal of Preventive Medicine* 28 (2 Suppl 2):134–40.

Braza, M., W. Shoemaker, and A. Seeley. 2004. Neighborhood design and rates of walking and biking to elementary school in 34 California communities. *American Journal of Health Promotion* 19 (2): 128–36.

Cervero, R., and K. Kockelman. 1997. Travel demand and the 3Ds: Density, diversity, and design. *Transportation Research Part D* 2: 199–219.

Dellinger, A., and C. Staunton. 2002. Barriers to children walking and bicycling to school: United States. *Morbidity and Mortality Weekly Report* 51 (32): 701–4.

Ewing, R., R. Brownson, and D. Berrigan. 2006. Relationship between urban sprawl and weight of U.S. youth. *American Journal of Preventive Medicine* 31 (6): 464–74.

Ewing, R. and R. Cervero. 2001. Travel and the built environment: A synthesis. In *Transportation Research Record* (1780): 87–114.

Ewing, R. and R. Cervero. 2010. Travel and the built environment: A meta-analysis. *Journal of the American Planning Association* 76, 265–94.

Ewing, R., M. King, S. Raudenbush, and O. Clemente. 2005. Turning highways into main streets: Two innovations in planning methodology. *Journal of the American Planning Association* 71: 269–82.

Ewing, Reid, T. Schmid, R. Killingsworth, A. Zlot, and S. Raudenbush. 2003. Relationship between urban sprawl and physical activity, obesity, and morbidity. *American Journal of Health Promotion* 18 (1): 47–57.

Ewing, R., W. Schroeer, and W. Greene. 2003. *School location and student travel: Analysis of factors affecting mode choice.* Washington, DC: Development, Community and Environment Division, U.S. Environmental Protection Agency.

Ewing, R., M. Greenwald, M. Zhang, et al. forthcoming. Traffic generated by mixed-use developments – A six-region study using consistent built environmental measures, *Journal of the Urban Planning and Development.*

Greenwald, M. J. 2003. The road less traveled: New urbanist inducements to travel mode substitution for nonwork trips. *Journal of Planning Education and Research* 23 (1): 39–57.

———. 2006. The relationship between land use and intrazonal trip making behaviors: Evidence and implications. *Transportation Research D* 11 (6): 432–46.

Greenwald, Michael J., and Marlon G. Boarnet. 2001. Built environment as a determinant of walking behavior: Analyzing non-work pedestrian travel in Portland, Oregon. *Transportation Research Record: Journal of the Transportation Research Board* 1780: 33–43.

Greenwald, M. J., and M. G. McNally. Forthcoming. Testing land use influences on trip chaining behavior in Portland, Oregon. *Proceedings of the Institute for Civil Engineers—Urban Design and Planning.* United Kingdom.

Grunbaum, J., et al. 2002. Youth risk behavior surveillance: United States, 2001. *Morbidity and Mortality Weekly Report—Surveillance Summaries* 51 (SS-4).

Gurwitt, R. 2004. Edge-ucation: What compels communities to build schools in the middle of nowhere? *Governing* 17 (6): 22–26.

Jensen, S. U. 2008. How to obtain a healthy journey to school. *Transportation Research Part A* 42: 475–86.

Kerr, J., D. Rosenberg, J. F. Sallis, B. E Saelens, L. D. Frank, and T. L. Conway. 2006. Active commuting to school: Associations with environment and parental concerns. *Medicine & Science in Sports & Exercise* 38 (4): 787–94.

Knoblauch, R. L. 1998. *Investigation of exposure based pedestrian accident areas: Crosswalks, sidewalks, local streets and major arterials.* Washington, DC: Federal Highway Administration.

Kouri, Christopher. 1999. *Wait for the bus: How low country school site selection and design deter walking to school and contribute to urban sprawl.* Charleston: South Carolina Coastal Conservation League.

Larsen, K., J. Gilliland, P. Hess, P. Tucker, J. Irwin, and M. He. 2009. The influence of the physical environment and sociodemographic characteristics on children's mode of travel to and from school. *American Journal of Public Health* 99 (3): 520–26.

Lawrence Frank and Company. 2008. *Youth travel to school: Community design relationships with mode choice, vehicle emissions, and healthy body weight.* U.S. Environmental Protection Agency.

McDonald, Noreen C. 2007. Active transportation to school: Trends among U.S. schoolchildren, 1969–2001. *American Journal of Preventive Medicine* 32 (6): 509–16.

———. 2008. Children's mode choice for the school trip: The role of distance and school location in walking to school. *Transportation* 35 (1): 23–35.

McMillan, T. 2002. The influence of urban form on a child's trip to school. Paper presented at the Association of Collegiate Schools of Planning Annual Conference, Baltimore, MD.

McMillan, T. E. 2007. The relative influence of urban form on a child's travel mode to school. *Transportation Research Part A* 41 (1): 69–79.

Merom, D., C. Tudor-Locke, A. Bauman, and C. Rissel. 2006. Active commuting to school among NSW primary school children: Implications for public health. *Health & Place* 12: 678–87.

Napier, M. A., B. B. Brown, C. M. Werner, and J. Gallimore. 2011. Walking to school: Community design and child and parent barriers. *Journal of Environmental Psychology* 31(1): 45–51.

Nationwide Personal Transportation Study (NPTS). 1972. *Transportation characteristics of school children, report no. 4.* Washington, DC: Federal Highway Administration.

Nelson, N. M., E. Foley, D. J. O'Gorman, N. M. Moyna, and C. B. Woods. 2008. Active commuting to school: How far is too far? *International Journal of Behavioral Nutrition and Physical Activity* 5: 1–29.

Ogden, C., M. Carroll, L. Curtin, M. McDowell, C. Tabak, and K. Flegal. 2006. Prevalence of overweight and obesity in the United States, 1999–2004. *Journal of the American Medical Association* 295 (13): 1549–55.

Papas, M. A., A. J. Alberg, R. Ewing, K. J. Helzlsouer, T. L. Gary, and A. C. Klassen. 2007. The built environment and obesity: A review of the evidence. *Epidemiologic Reviews*, 1–15.

Schlossberg, M., J. Greene, P. P. Phillips, B. Johnson, and B. Parker. 2006. School trips: Effects of urban form and distance on travel mode. *Journal of the American Planning Association* 72 (3): 337–46.

Timperio, A., K. Ball, J. Salmon, R. Roberts, B. Giles-Corti, D. Simmons et al. 2006. Personal, family, social, and environmental correlates of active commuting to school. *American Journal of Preventive Medicine* 30 (1), 45–51.

Transportation Alternatives. 2003. *The 2002 summary of safe routes to school programs in the United States.* http://www.transact.org/report.asp?id = 49.

Walberg, H. 1992. On local control: Is bigger better? In *Source book on school and district size, cost, and quality*, 118–34. Minneapolis: Hubert H. Humphrey Institute of Public Affairs, University of Minnesota.

Zhang, M. 2005. Intercity variations in the relationship between urban form and automobile dependence: Disaggregate analyses of Boston, Massachusetts; Portland, Oregon; and Houston, Texas. *Transportation Research Record* 1902: 55–62.

Policy Impacts on Mode Choice in School Transportation
An Analysis of Four Florida School Districts

RUTH L. STEINER, ILIR BEJLERI, ALLISON FISCHMAN, RUSSELL E. PROVOST, ABDULNASER A. ARAFAT, MARTIN GUTTENPLAN, AND LINDA B. CRIDER

EVERY SCHOOL DAY, PARENTS ALL OVER THE UNITED STATES WAKE UP AND FOLLOW A pattern of routine activity that could ultimately determine the safety of their neighborhood, the commute times of thousands of other people, and the health of their own children. For many parents, distance or hazardous walking conditions will limit this decision to driving their children to school or sending their children via school bus or carpool. For parents living near a school in a neighborhood with a complete sidewalk network, direct access to the school, and safe walking conditions, their decision will be based on a variety of factors, including their perception of safety, their child's knowledge of traffic conditions, and the relationship between their child's travel and other activities in the household. Nationally, the number of children walking or bicycling to school has declined steadily over the last four decades; in 1969, 48 percent of students walked or bicycled to school, but by 2001, that percentage had declined to 15 percent (BTS 2003; U.S. EPA 2003). In Florida in 1992, for example, only one in six children walked to school daily (Starnes et al. 1992).

Each parent's decision to drive his or her child to school or to send his or her child on the bus can be costly to the community in many ways. The decrease in children walking and bicycling to school has contributed to traffic congestion, air pollution (U.S. EPA 2003), an increased rate of childhood obesity (Ogden et al. 2002; Strauss and Pollack 2001), greater rates of adult-onset—or type 2—diabetes (Flegal 1999; Huang and Goran 2003; Sallis and Owen 1999), and a decrease in children's independence (David and Weinstein 1987; O'Brien 2003; Proshansky and Fabian 1987; Siegl, Kirasic, and Kail 1978).

A major portion of traffic results from the accumulation of decisions by individual parents to drive their child to and from school or to allow their children to drive to school if they have achieved the legal driving age, creating congestion in the community during the morning and afternoon peak commute times. This pattern, termed the "traffic threat multiplier effect," produces a vicious cycle of parents creating additional traffic congestion in cars in order to protect their children from traffic (Appleyard 2003). The greater the traffic congestion near schools, the more likely parents are to feel that the roadways near the school are unsafe and the more likely they are to drive their child to school because they feel walking and bicycling are not safe for their child.

The role of behavioral factors—such as dietary patterns, physical activity, and sedentary behavior patterns—in childhood obesity, are receiving increased attention by researchers (McCann with Glanz 2005). The decrease in the number of children walking and bicycling to school and the reduction in the amount of time children spend in physical education classes both contribute to a reduction in children's physical activity.

Although parents make the final decision on how their children travel to school each day, their decision is constrained or facilitated by factors beyond their control. Contributing decisions made by transportation, land development, and school planners, as well as school administrators and legislators, have not always been coordinated to create a community in which parents are offered reasonable choices about how their children get to school.

Traditionally, school districts have had a great deal of discretion about where schools are located. The changing requirements for school sites have made renovation of existing schools more difficult. The shortage of new school sites in developed areas, the high cost of land in residential neighborhoods, and the difficulty of renovating existing schools have led school districts to locate schools at the edge of the community (Morris 2004). In response to these decisions, parents or children must drive to and from school, or the school district—and all tax payers—must pay to bus children to and from the school. Developers have responded to the location of schools by proposing residential developments around the new school, and local governments have responded to public demand by approving the development even if the schools contribute to sprawl in the community.

The need to coordinate the location of schools with the surrounding residential neighborhoods becomes a decision about the financial health of our communities and our children. Communities can spend scarce public resources building schools that will impose high ongoing transportation costs for the community, or they can build schools that allow parents to choose for their children to walk or bicycle to school. From a policy perspective, the question is "how can we encourage school districts to build schools in a manner that supports greater transportation choice for children and reduces the overall cost of transportation?"

Four counties in Florida were selected as a case study to understand the local implementation of state regulations related to school siting and residential development. Florida is an ideal case study to understand this relationship because it has had continuous growth since the 1950s, with the resultant demand for both residential development and school capacity. Since Florida passed its landmark growth management legislation in 1985, it has increased the requirements for local governments to coordinate with school districts on the siting of schools. This chapter discusses legislative solutions in Florida and then examines the transportation outcomes of these policies in four Central Florida school districts: Hillsborough, Orange, Pasco, and Seminole. These four case studies are employed to begin to measure and understand how policy decisions about school siting and school attendance zone (SAZ) boundaries affect the number of children walking or bicycling to school.

BACKGROUND ON FLORIDA SCHOOL PLANNING,
SITING, AND SAFETY POLICY

When school location is coordinated with land use and transportation planning to create a continuous bicycle and pedestrian network with the most direct connections between residences and schools, there is a greater opportunity for the safe movement of children to and from school. When land use planning, school planning, and transportation planning are not coordinated, the opportunities for walking and bicycling are less available.

As shown in figure 1, the respective overlaps between and among these three types of planning—transportation, land use, and school—represent three areas of coordinated planning: multimodal planning, coordinated school planning, and Safe Routes to School. The first two of these are preemptive measures that set the stage to create the kind of physical environment that supports the education and encouragement activities of the local Safe Routes to School program. The "golden apple" in the center of the diagram represents the area of greatest potential[1] mode shift to walking and bicycling.

Multimodal Planning

Multimodal planning reflects the inherent relationship between land use and transportation, with land uses representing destinations and transportation routes representing the connection between destinations. Multimodal planning involves four guiding principles that create walkable and bikeable environments: (1) a complementary mix of land uses, (2) appropriate density and intensity of development, (3) a high level of network connectivity, and (4) good urban design connecting complementary land uses (Steiner et al. 2006). Multimodal planning encourages a safe, connected, and continuous system of bicycle, pedestrian, and transit facilities (Sokolow, Guttenplan, and Santos 2001) through increased infrastructure and amenities.

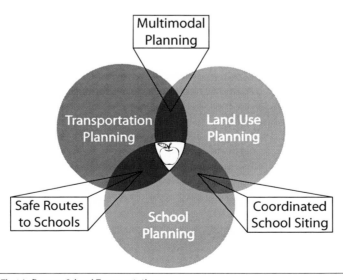

Figure 1. Policy Areas That Influence School Transportation

Florida's 1985 Local Government Comprehensive Planning and Land Development Act incorporated a requirement that local governments provide infrastructure, including transportation, concurrent with the impact of development. The legislation has since been revised to enhance the concurrency system using Multimodal Transportation Districts (MMTDs) and Transportation Concurrency Exception Areas (TCEA), which promote development that factors pedestrian, bicycle, and transit modes over the automobile.[2] Since the mid-1990s, the Florida Department of Community Affairs has encouraged multimodal planning with several publications relating to multimodal planning and design.

Coordinated School Siting

Coordinated school siting is directed at making a pedestrian- and bicycle-friendly connection between schools and the residences where students will live. McMillan, Day, Boarnet, Alfonzo, and Anderson (2006) found that students in California living within a mile of a school are three times more likely to walk or bicycle than those living farther from the school. Coordinated school siting can be seen as an overlap between school planning and land use planning, in that it seeks to locate schools near residential land uses where students will live.

The legal requirements for coordinated school planning have developed gradually. Florida's 1985 Growth Management Act did not require school concurrency. In 1992, legislation was passed allowing school concurrency as an optional element of local comprehensive plans. The 1995 Education Facilities Act required school districts to share the information related to school facilities and development with local governments for use in the comprehensive planning process. Then in 1998, the Florida legislature passed a law that required sharing of planning data and analysis between school districts and planning agencies to ensure that adequate school capacity exists to accommodate new development. In 2002, school boards and local governments were required to negotiate interlocal agreements that allowed both agencies to review school siting comprehensively. In 2005, the legislature passed a law requiring adequate school facilities to be in place within three years of construction of new homes. The state adopted a phased schedule for the adoption of a school concurrency program, with each local government's deadline falling between January 1, 2008, and December 1, 2008.

Safe Routes to School

Safe Routes to School (SRTS) programs are designed to empower communities to make walking and bicycling to school a safe and routine activity. SRTS funding is available for a wide variety of programs and projects, from building safer street crossings to establishing programs that encourage children and their parents to walk and bicycle to school (Federal Highway Administration 2007).

Florida's version of an SRTS program, called Safe Ways to School, has been implemented on a voluntary basis in Florida since 1997, when the Florida Traffic and Bicycle Safety Education Program developed a toolkit and pilot-tested the program in ten schools throughout the state. In 2002, to address school transportation concerns and the need to provide safety for children on their way to school, the Florida legislature passed the Safe Paths to School Bill that requested the Florida Department of Transportation (FDOT) to establish a "Safe Paths" program and consider planning, construction, and funding for that program. In 2005, federal funds were set aside for a new Safe Routes to School program as part of the Safe, Accountable, Flexible, Efficient Transportation Equity Act—A Legacy for Users (SAFETEA-LU) legislation. SAFETEA-LU dedicated approximately $29.1 million over a five-year span, 2005 through 2009, to the FDOT for SRTS-related improvements in Florida. From 10 percent to 30 percent of the funds must be used for noninfrastructure programs, and the rest may be used for the planning, design, and construction of infrastructure improvements supporting the bicycle and pedestrian environment within two miles of a school.

METHODOLOGY

In this study, four Florida school districts—Hillsborough, Orange, Pasco, and Seminole—were examined to observe how multimodal planning, coordinated school siting, and Safe Routes to School programs have impacted children's transportation to school. In Florida, school districts are coterminous with county boundaries. These school districts are in the Tampa Bay and Orlando areas and have high rates of student enrollment and school construction since 1990 and a substantial base of school zones located within mature neighborhoods. Two urban counties (Hillsborough and Orange) and two adjacent suburban counties (Pasco and Seminole) were selected because they have large populations (over 400,000 per county in 2006), high and growing school enrollment (over 30,000 in 2005–6 with over 20 percent growth from 2000 to 2005), and at least thirty elementary schools representing a range of time periods in which schools were built. Additionally, the physical relationship between the counties was considered when making the final selection. The four counties selected represent urban or suburban relationships along the Interstate 4 (I-4) corridor in Central Florida, an area experiencing significant growth. See figure 2 for a general overview of these selected school districts.

For each school district, three analysis areas were explored: policy, potential walkability, and actual levels of walking and bicycling. To understand the respective roles of local governments and school districts, policies relating to school location were researched. In addition, interviews were held with district superintendents or chief school facilities planners. An explanation of the geographic information system (GIS) methodology—potential walkability and actual levels of walking and bicycling—follows.

Potential Walkability

This GIS methodology maps and analyzes SAZs on a countywide scale to better understand institutional impediments to children walking to school. An SAZ exists for each school; students residing within its boundaries must attend that school.[3] This methodology also allows the analysis of the configuration of SAZs, barriers to walking to school introduced by major roads, and residential proximity to schools. While only elementary schools are considered in this analysis, the same methodology could be applied to middle and high schools.

Since the Florida statutes define a two-mile "pedestrian shed" around schools (busing is not available unless hazardous walking conditions exist), two-mile buffers were created around each school using GIS. Because all selected school districts calculate the two-mile pedestrian shed using distances measured along the street network rather than using straight-line distances, these buffers were generated according to the street network. Network distances are used as a more realistic measure of the distance students could be expected to walk. Pedestrian sheds often extend beyond the boundaries of the SAZ and are adjusted to reflect the area contained within the SAZ. For a more detailed explanation of this methodology, please refer to Steiner, Bejleri, Wheelock, Boles, Cahill, and Perez (2008).

A map was created for each school district that includes four data layers: pedestrian shed polygons, SAZ boundaries, residential parcels, and roadway networks (centerlines for all roads in the county). Using these data layers, three criteria are considered:

1. *The percentage of the SAZ area within the pedestrian shed.* Higher percentage values suggest higher potential for walkability. Ideally, the SAZ would fall entirely within the two-mile pedestrian shed.
2. *Impediments to walking introduced by major roads.* Lower percentage values suggest higher potential for walkability. (For the purposes of this study, major roads are those roads identified by the Federal Highway Administration as arterials or collectors. Interstate highways are considered separately.)
3. *The proximity of residential parcels to their zoned school.* Higher percentage values suggest more homes are closer to their zoned school and therefore a higher potential for walkability.

Actual Levels of Walking and Bicycling

To measure actual levels of walking and bicycling in the selected school districts, thirty-two elementary schools were randomly selected to participate in teacher-administered in-school transportation surveys over a three-day period.

The distribution of these thirty-two elementary schools across the four selected counties was determined using SAZ acreage. After eliminating the largest SAZs, where busing is assumed to be unavoidable, schools were randomly selected from a pool of SAZs within a one-half standard deviation of the mean attendance zone acreage across counties. The number of schools selected per county is proportional to the percentage of schools in the selection pool from each county. In order to compare schools built before and after the implementation of school coordination in 1995, schools built before and after 1995 were selected for each county. To prevent oversampling of schools built after 1995, a one-third to two-thirds ratio was used to calculate the number of schools selected prior to 1995 and after 1995, respectively. Fourteen elementary schools were selected from Hillsborough County, eleven from Orange County, three from Pasco County, and four from Seminole County.

Each school was surveyed over a three-day period during the spring of 2008. In most cases, surveys were administered over three consecutive midweek days. Mondays and Fridays were avoided in order to take advantage of maximum student attendance. At the start of each day, the teacher recorded the number of students corresponding to each transportation mode: by foot bicycle, school bus, car, city bus, or other (mixed modes, taxi, etc.). In this chapter, city bus statistics are included with "other" due to negligible numbers of city bus riders.

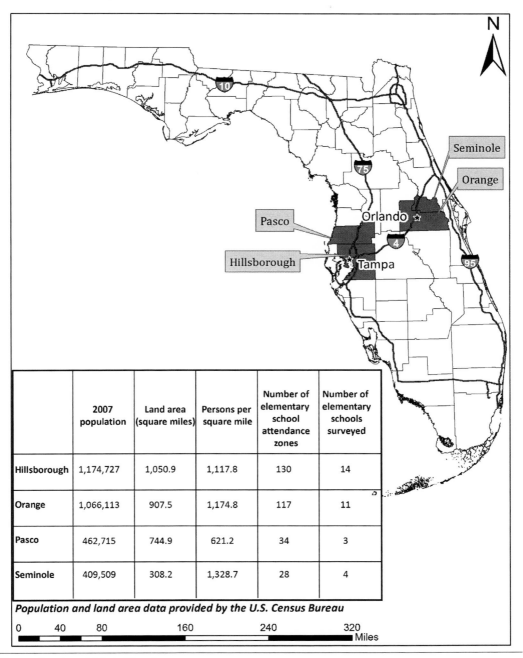

	2007 population	Land area (square miles)	Persons per square mile	Number of elementary school attendance zones	Number of elementary schools surveyed
Hillsborough	1,174,727	1,050.9	1,117.8	130	14
Orange	1,066,113	907.5	1,174.8	117	11
Pasco	462,715	744.9	621.2	34	3
Seminole	409,509	308.2	1,328.7	28	4

Population and land area data provided by the U.S. Census Bureau

Figure 2. Overview of Selected Counties

RESULTS

The schools are classified and compared based on year built: historic (pre-1950), pregrowth management (1950–85), preschool coordination (1986–95), and postschool coordination (post-1995). These time periods are significant due to the 1985 Growth Management Act and the 1995–2005 legislation, requiring coordination between local governments and school boards.

Hillsborough County School District

Hillsborough County's 130 elementary schools illustrate the diversity of situations with respect to impediments to children walking and bicycling to school. Hillsborough—especially the city of Tampa—has a traditional grid street pattern and historic neighborhood schools, comprising one of the oldest inventories of schools in the state. Other parts of the county have suburban patterns and schools sited from the 1960s to the 1990s, while still other areas contain schools built recently under more innovative school planning efforts. Hillsborough was a pilot community for coordinated school planning, and since 1997, the county and the school board have maintained an interlocal agreement to facilitate information sharing between the two entities (Mueller 2004).

Interviews with administrators revealed a commitment to creating neighborhood elementary schools as well as incorporating walking safety considerations into school site plans. However, hazardous walking conditions, as defined in Section 1006.23 of the Florida statute, are more prevalent in Hillsborough County than in any of the other three counties, creating a greater need for courtesy busing. During the 2004–5 school year, over 11,000 students were courtesy bused as compared to less than 1,600 students in each of Pasco, Orange, and Seminole counties (FDOE 2006).

One explanation for the greater prevalence of hazardous walking conditions in Hillsborough is an apparent lack of sidewalks along many major roads in the county. Over the past two decades, Hillsborough has experienced widespread growth with only intermittent attention to infrastructure. In 2006, school impact fees were raised from $196 (the fee since 1989) to $4,000 on average. These fees go, in part, toward on-site infrastructure improvements, such as sidewalks. Off-site improvements, such as traffic signals or connecting sidewalks, are the responsibility of the city or county in which the school resides. With recent budget cuts, the county seeks to fund improvements adjacent to school sites using school impact fees. The county and the school district recently were involved in litigation to determine which party should fund said infrastructure. Battles over infrastructure funding cloud the future of sidewalk availability and pedestrian access in Hillsborough County.

Due to low enrollment growth estimates, the Hillsborough school district plans to build no new schools for three years beginning in 2010. Lower than expected enrollment figures may be attributed to a lack of residential development during the current construction downtrend or to an increasing number of commuters choosing to live in Pasco County but work in Tampa.

Indicators of potential walkability reveal a consistent pattern. For each indicator, generally, historic schools exhibit the highest potential for walkability, followed by a significant drop among pregrowth management schools and a subsequent gradual increase in potential for walkability among schools built since the passage of Florida's Growth Management Act. The presence of major roads and interstates serves as the exception to this pattern, as historic SAZs exhibit the highest percentage of pedestrian sheds intersected by a major road or interstate. One explanation is that schools built prior to 1950 are located primarily in older urban areas, which have been attracting new development and infrastructure for much longer than areas of newer development and, thus, have more roadways. Among fourteen surveyed Hillsborough County elementary schools, 7.6 percent of students walked or bicycled to school. Table 1 provides an overview of findings for Hillsborough County.

Table 1. Potential Walkability Data and Actual Levels of Walking in Hillsborough County

		Historic	*Pregrowth management*	*Preschool coordination*	*Postschool coordination*
Number of SAZs		32	53	18	27
Number of schools surveyed		4	5	0	5
Potential walkability (countywide)					
Walkability indicator	*Measurement(s)*				
Physical relationship between pedestrian shed and SAZ	Average % of SAZ land area located within pedestrian shed	35.6	27.9	28.4	29.4
Impediments to walking introduced by major roads	% of SAZs where major road intersects pedestrian shed	90.6	88.7	55.5	55.5
	% of SAZs where interstate highway intersects pedestrian shed	40.6	17.0	16.7	29.6
Proximity of residential parcels to their zoned school	Average % of residential parcels located within pedestrian shed	81.3	73.6	34.5	48.5

Actual levels of walking and bicycling (survey results for selected schools)

Mode	Total students surveyed				Percentage per mode
Walk (%)	6.2	3.8	9.9	No schools surveyed	3.9
Bicycle (%)	1.4	0.4	1.0		3.1
Bus (%)	34.6	35.1	33.7		35.2
Car (%)	57.6	60.3	55.3		57.7
Other (%)	0.2	0.4	0.2		0.2

Orange County School District

Although it may be more urban at its core than Hillsborough, Pasco, and Seminole counties, sprawl is characteristic of Orange County, due to unbridled growth influenced by the construction of I-4 and the Florida Turnpike. Whereas Orlando exhibits a traditional grid street pattern and historic neighborhood schools, many schools built beyond the city limits are typically in the midst of the curvilinear street patterns and cul-de-sacs of suburbia.

The school board and local governments within Orange County have maintained a formal partnership in planning for schools for at least the past ten years. In 1996, Orange County approved a school siting ordinance, which addresses location, function, and urban design aspects of schools. The ordinance mentions the need to minimize travel distances between home and school and advises that elementary schools be located within neighborhoods. Orange County began tying residential development to school capacity in 2000, upon the adoption of the Martinez Doctrine. This process, called capacity enhancement, is different from state-mandated school concurrency, which all four districts have recently adopted. School concurrency takes place in the planning stage while capacity enhancement takes place during development review.

Indicators of potential walkability suggest historic schools are associated with higher levels of walkability than schools built more recently. Schools built within the past two decades, however, display increased potential for walkability as compared to pregrowth management schools. As with Hillsborough County, impediments to walking introduced by major roads are the exception to this pattern. In general, beginning with pregrowth management schools, there is a gradual increase in the potential for walkability suggested by each indicator. Most schools built since the Growth Management Act went into effect suggest higher potential for walkability than pregrowth management schools. Among eleven surveyed Orange County elementary schools, 15.8 percent of students walked or bicycled to school. Table 2 provides an overview of findings for Orange County.

Pasco County School District

Pasco County is directly adjacent to and north of Hillsborough County. Interstate 75 (I-75) runs along the west coast of Florida connecting the two counties, and in recent years Pasco has become a suburban haven for workers commuting to Tampa using I-75. In 2007, Pasco was ranked the fiftieth fastest-growing county in the country by the U.S. Census Bureau, based on population growth from 2000 to 2006.

Pasco's population boom has led to a school enrollment boom, and, in turn, the school district is handling a backlogged need for school facilities. In the 2008 interlocal agreement between the school district and county and municipal governments, the school district identified an inability to meet their adopted level of service within the next five years for one of its two concurrency service areas. The adopted level of service for elementary schools is 115 percent, meaning that they expect to operate each concurrency service area at 15 percent above state-determined capacity, a figure higher than in any other selected county. In addition, Pasco School District comprises just two concurrency service areas for all elementary schools, compared to one service area per SAZ in Hillsborough and one per up to six SAZs in Orange and Seminole counties. By maintaining a high number of SAZs within each concurrency service

Table 2. Potential Walkability Data and Actual Levels of Walking in Orange County

		Historic	*Pregrowth management*	*Preschool coordination*	*Postschool coordination*
Number of SAZs		8	52	18	39
Number of schools surveyed		0	5	1	5

Potential walkability (countywide)

Walkability indicator	*Measurement(s)*				
Physical relationship between pedestrian shed and SAZ	Average % of SAZ land area located within pedestrian shed	57.1	19.4	30.9	19.4
Impediments to walking introduced by major roads	% of SAZs where major road intersects pedestrian shed	100.0	94.2	94.4	89.7
	% of SAZs where interstate highway intersects pedestrian shed	25.0	9.6	5.5	2.6
Proximity of residential parcels to their zoned school	Average % of residential parcels located within pedestrian shed	86.6	69.0	64.8	64.1

Actual levels of walking and bicycling (survey results for selected schools)

Model	*Total students surveyed*				*Percentage per mode*
Walk (%)	11.4	No schools surveyed	17.7	11.4	7.1
Bicycle (%)	4.4		3.0	4.6	5.2
Bus (%)	21.2		18.5	2.6	28.0
Car (%)	62.0		58.6	81.4	59.3
Other (%)	1		2.2	0.0	0.4

area, the burden of a school capacity need created by a developer can shift more easily from school to school. Even if the district determines that insufficient capacity exists in the concurrency service area in which the school resides, the district will consider whether sufficient capacity exists in an adjacent concurrency service area. All selected counties have adopted this practice, but in Pasco there is only one possible adjacent concurrency service area equal in size to half the county. The effect of Pasco's policy is that each time a residential development is proposed that would create a need for school capacity, the entire county is considered when assigning the needed capacity to a specific school or schools. Pasco's interlocal agreement defines policies that seem to have minimal potential effects on the ever-increasing distances between residences and schools and overcrowding in schools. The agreement, however, does include a financially feasible plan to achieve adopted level-of-service standards within five or ten years (depending on the service area) and procedures for modifying concurrency service areas. These policies are a first step for the district in formally coordinated school planning.

Potential walkability indicators suggest a lower potential for walking and bicycling than any other selected county. The average percentage of SAZ acreage located within the pedestrian shed is consistently below 12 percent for all schools in Pasco County, which may be attributed to the relatively large size of SAZs. A greater percentage of residential parcels are located within the pedestrian shed for schools built after the implementation of the Growth Management Act, but the figure is still low compared to Orange or Seminole school districts. No interstate intersects any of the pedestrian sheds in Pasco County, a fact unique to Pasco among the selected counties. Among three surveyed Pasco County elementary schools, 11 percent of students walked or bicycled to school. Table 3 provides an overview of findings for Pasco County.

Seminole County School District

Seminole County's population is nearly 89 percent of the population size of Pasco County, contained in less than half of Pasco's land area. While large parts of suburban Pasco County are rural in nature, very little land in Seminole County is undeveloped. It is located directly north of Orange County.

Interviews with school district administrators revealed a commitment to coordinated school planning and siting that has been in existence since the early 1990s, earlier than any other selected county. Schools in Seminole County often have several entrances and formal pedestrian paths connecting the school to nearby neighborhoods, a pattern not evident in Hillsborough, Orange, or Pasco counties.

Potential walkability indicators suggest the highest potential for walking and bicycling in pregrowth management schools, a finding inconsistent with patterns observed in other selected counties. This may be due to the fact that pregrowth management schools are significantly larger in number than schools in any other group. Pedestrian sheds in Seminole County generally contain high percentages of residential parcels relative to other selected school districts, a statistic that falls in line with the large number of observed formal pedestrian paths connecting residences to schools. Among four surveyed Seminole County elementary schools, 13.4 percent of students walked or bicycled to school. Table 4 provides an overview of findings for Seminole County.

Summary of Findings

Examining relationships between the Tampa Bay and Orlando areas, Orlando-area school districts (Seminole [13.4 percent] and Orange [15.8 percent]) have greater numbers of students walking or bicycling than Tampa Bay–area school districts (Pasco [11 percent] and Hillsborough [7.6 percent]) among sampled schools. The two suburban counties, Pasco and Seminole, have somewhat higher walk rates among sampled schools than their corresponding more urban counties. However this may be due to the small sample size in these counties. Of

Table 3. Potential Walkability Data and Actual Levels of Walking in Pasco County

		Historic	*Pregrowth management*	*Preschool coordination*	*Postschool coordination*
Number of SAZs		3	18	7	6
Number of schools surveyed		0	1	1	1

Potential walkability (countywide)

Walkability indicator	*Measurement(s)*	*Historic*	*Pregrowth management*	*Preschool coordination*	*Postschool coordination*
Physical relationship between pedestrian shed and SAZ	Average % of SAZ land area located within pedestrian shed	9.4	11.6	10.2	11.8
Impediments to walking introduced by major roads	% of SAZs where major road intersects pedestrian shed	100.0	50.0	57.1	50.0
	% of SAZs where interstate highway intersects pedestrian shed	0	0	0	0
Proximity of residential parcels to their zoned school	Average % of residential parcels located within pedestrian shed	34.7	42.5	48.9	45.0

Actual levels of walking and bicycling (survey results for selected schools)

Model	*Total students surveyed*				*Percentage per mode*
Walk (%)	8.2	No schools surveyed	19.4	5.8	0.1
Bicycle (%)	2.8		1.6	6.4	0.0
Bus (%)	33.0		29.8	19.4	50.8
Car (%)	55.8		48.8	68.2	48.9
Other (%)	0.2		0.4	0.0	0.2

the four counties, Hillsborough has the lowest actual levels of walking and bicycling among sampled schools, which could be, in part, due to its numerous roadways that are hazardous for walkers. Seminole and Orange counties have the highest actual levels of walking and bicycling among sampled schools, which may be the result of early coordinated school planning and greater attention to pedestrian infrastructure than either Pasco or Hillsborough County. Potential walkability indicators suggest that in urban counties, traditional neighborhood schools, built prior to 1950, and schools built since the passage of the Growth Management Act in 1985, tend to exhibit a higher potential for walking and bicycling than schools built between 1950 and 1985. Although the same pattern cannot be observed for actual levels of

Table 4. Potential Walkability Data and Actual Levels of Walking in Seminole County

		Historic	*Pregrowth management*	*Preschool coordination*	*Postschool coordination*
Number of SAZs		1	17	7	3
Number of schools surveyed		0	3	1	0

Potential walkability (countywide)

Walkability indicator	*Measurement(s)*				
Physical relationship between pedestrian shed and SAZ	Average % of SAZ land area located within pedestrian shed	3.2	54.8	36.8	32.3
Impediments to walking introduced by major roads	% of SAZs where major road intersects pedestrian shed	100.0	470.0	14.3	66.7
	% of SAZs where interstate highway intersects pedestrian shed	0	5.9	14.3	0.0
Proximity of residential parcels to their zoned school	Average % of residential parcels located within pedestrian shed	14.4	73.0	58.8	74.4

Actual levels of walking and bicycling (survey results for selected schools)

Model	*Total students surveyed*				*Percentage per mode*
Walk (%)	8.0	No schools surveyed	8.6	6.3	No schools surveyed
Bicycle (%)	5.4		4.7	7.4	
Bus (%)	25.5		29.8	12.7	
Car (%)	60.7		56.6	73.0	
Other (%)	0.4		0.4	0.0	

walking and bicycling among selected schools in the four counties, this may be due to other factors such as small sample size or parental attitudes and perceptions and their socioeconomic status. Comparisons between historic and other schools were difficult, as Hillsborough was the only school district with more than ten historic schools. As Florida's Growth Management Act and school concurrency requirements mature, we will be better able to explore their effects on the potential for children to walk to school.

Results suggest that counties with longer histories of coordinated school siting and multi-modal planning tend to have more students walking and bicycling to school. Data regarding SRTS programs in these selected counties are sparse, making it difficult to ascertain its effect on children's travel to school. It can be deduced, however, that $29.1 million for SRTS programs to be spread across the entire state may be too little to accomplish measurable effects in any single school district.

DISCUSSION AND CONCLUSIONS

This chapter reports on the initial analysis, at the aggregate level, of the potential for walking and bicycling in four Florida counties. As such, it represents a methodology for analyzing the impacts of Florida's Growth Management Legislation and the constraints resulting from decisions by local governments and school districts that affect the potential for children to walk or bicycle to school.

This study uses a two-mile distance to analyze potential walkability because the Florida statutes specify that children living within two miles of a school will receive busing only in the case of hazardous walking conditions. The two-mile distance is used as a starting point for this methodology, but readers should be aware that the two-mile distance, whether a straight line or along the network, is much farther than most children will walk or bicycle to school. Even when conditions appear to be favorable for walking within the two miles surrounding the school, students living on the edge of a two-mile pedestrian shed or pedestrian network shed may still not be walking to school. If no hazardous walking conditions exist, these students will not receive busing. While throughout this chapter the terminology "pedestrian shed" has been used to describe the two-mile walk area, it may be more aptly described as the "parent responsibility zone," as parents are likely to drive their child to school if they feel two miles is too far for their child to walk or bicycle.

Potential walkability indicators used in this study are helpful as tools for determining a general guideline of pedestrian accessibility to schools. They are accurate predictors of walking and bicycling inasmuch as they generally fall in line with survey results. Ongoing research takes advantage of a multitude of indicators to provide a more comprehensive and accurate picture of potential walkability. Such measurements include residential density and street connectivity indicators, such as street density, intersection density, and pedestrian directness ratio. In addition, geocoded student addresses will be used to identify the number of students living within the pedestrian shed for each SAZ.

This study assumes the pedestrian network to be the roadway network. However, pedestrians and bicyclists face barriers and facilitators that cannot be measured using street centerline data. Often, elementary schools are disconnected from adjacent subdivisions along the roadway network but are connected along the pedestrian network due to informal paths and shortcuts. An ideal pedestrian network would consider elements such as sidewalks, crosswalks, speed limits, informal paths, fences, walls, crossing guards, personal safety, and lanes of traffic. The ongoing effort of this research focuses on more accurate modeling of the pedestrian network using field data collection and aerial photography for the same random sample of thirty-two elementary schools whose survey results are presented in this chapter. In addition, eight middle schools are purposefully selected based on feeder patterns from selected elementary schools and analyzed using the same methodology.

Actual levels of walking and bicycling measured in a random sampling of elementary schools across the four counties do not consistently indicate increased walking for schools built after 1995 and decreased levels of walking for schools built between 1950 and 1985. Although these results are contrary to expectations of higher walking levels in more recently built schools, it may be due to parents' perceptions and attitudes, their socioeconomic status, or a small sample size.

Walking to school may be important for children's health, and it may be economical for the state's budget, but walkability is not necessarily a priority in the decision-making process for determining the locations of new schools. Although there are a number of important factors, besides the ability of children to walk to school, that must be considered when siting schools and delineating SAZ boundaries, there may be a methodology that would maximize all these factors, including walkability. Through interviews, surveys, and GIS analyses, we hope to identify those policies that are working to maximize walkability. Future research focuses on examining characteristics of the population and built environment in areas where children are not walking to school.

ACKNOWLEDGMENT

This research was conducted with funding from the Robert Wood Johnson Foundation's Active Living Research Program and the FDOT Research Office. The researchers would like to thank city and county staff, school district staff, and school board members in Orange, Hillsborough, Pasco, and Seminole school districts for their cooperation in providing GIS and other data for this study.

NOTES

1. For the purposes of this chapter, "Safe Routes to School," "Safe Paths to School," and "Safe Ways to School" will all be used to refer to programs that have the shared goal of increasing the number of children who walk or bicycle to school. There are only a few distinctions. "Safe Routes to School" is the national title for such programs and will be used generically to refer to this type of program. "Safe Ways to School" is a local, Florida version of the national Safe Routes to School initiative. "Safe Paths to School" refers to Florida legislation passed in 2002 that assigns the Safe Routes to School program to the Florida Department of Transportation.

2. In its 2009 session, the Florida legislature passed and Governor Crist signed S.B. 360, the Community Renewal Act, which changes the requirements for transportation concurrency exception areas beginning July 1, 2009. All local governments that qualify as dense urban land areas (DULAs), which is designated for municipalities with over 1,000 persons per square mile and over 5,000 in population, are defined as exception areas. A total of eight counties and 238 cities out of sixty-seven counties and 413 cities are eligible defined as DULAs and thus are eligible to define an exception area as a part of their transportation concurrency management system (DCA 2009). Thus two types of TCEAs exist, those defined in DULAs, in which local governments need to define "land use and transportation strategies to support and fund mobility within the exception area, including alternative modes of transportation," and the existing TCEAs, which

are also required to include strategies that "address urban design; appropriate land use mixes, including intensity and density; and network connectivity."

3. In two locations in parts of Seminole County, up to five schools create a single school attendance zone. Within this attendance zone, parents can choose any one of the schools.

REFERENCES

Appleyard, Bruce S. 2003. Planning safe routes to school. *Planning Magazine*, May.

Bureau of Transportation Statistics (BTS). 2003. *Bureau of transportation statistics: National household travel survey—national data and analysis tool CD*. Washington, DC: Bureau of Transportation Statistics. CD-ROM.

David, Thomas. G., and Carol. S. Weinstein. 1987. The built environment and children's development. In *Spaces for children: The built environment and child development*, ed. Thomas G. David and Carol S. Weinstein, 3–20. New York: Plenum.

Federal Highway Administration (FHA). 2007. Safe routes to school. http://safety.fhwa.dot.gov/saferoutes/.

Flegal, Katherine M. 1999. The obesity epidemic in children and adults: Current evidence and research issues. *Medicine & Science in Sports & Exercise* 31 (2S): S509–S514.

Florida Department of Community Affairs (FCDA). 2009. 2009 list of local governments qualifying as dense urban land areas. http://www.dca.state.fl.us/fdcp/dcp/DRIFQD/ DULAList.cfm.

Florida Department of Education (FDOE). 2006. *The quality link: Florida school district transportation profiles, school year 2004-2005*. Tallahassee, FL: FDOE. http://faptflorida.org/Qlinks/2004-2005 Profiles_Complete.pdf.

Huang, Terry T.-K., and Michael I. Goran. 2003. Prevention of type 2 diabetes in young people: A theoretical perspective. *Pediatric Diabetes* 4 (1): 38–56.

McCann, Barbara with Karen Glanz. 2005. *Designing to reduce childhood obesity*. San Diego, CA: Active Living Research. http://www.activelivingresearch.org/files/childhoodobesity021105.pdf.

McMillan, Tracy E., K. M. Day, M. Kristen M., M. G. Boarnet, G. Marlong G., MarielaM. Alfonzo, Mariela, and Craig. Anderson. 2006. Johnny walks to school—does Jane? Sex differences in children's active travel to school. *Children, Youth and Environment* 16 (1): 75–89. http://www.uctc.net/papers/781.pdf.

Morris, Marya. 2004. Rethinking community planning and school siting to address the obesity epidemic. Paper presented at the NIEHS Conference on Obesity and the Built Environment: Improving Public Health through Community Design, Washington, DC, May 24–26.

Mueller, Janet. 2004. Schools planning. Hillsborough County, Florida, Official County Government Online Information Resource. http://www.hillsboroughcounty.org/pgm/communityplanning/school/.

O'Brien, Catherine. 2003. Transportation that's actually good for the soul. *National Center for Bicycling and Walking Forum*, December 2003. http://www.bikewalk.org/pdfs/forumarch0104transportation.pdf.

Ogden, Cynthia L., Katherine M. Flegal, Margaret D. Carroll, and Clifford L. Johnson. 2002. Prevalence and trends in overweight among U.S. children and adolescents, 1999–2000. *Journal of the American Medical Association* 288 (14): 1728–32.

Proshansky, Harold M., and Abbe K. Fabian. 1987. The development of place identity in the child. In *Spaces for children: The built environment and child development*, ed. Thomas G. David and Carol S. Weinstein, 21–40. New York: Plenum.

Sallis, James F., and Neville Owen. 1999. *Physical activity and behavioral medicine*. Thousand Oaks, CA: Sage.

Siegel, Alexander W., Kathleen C. Kirasic, and Robert V. Kail Jr. 1978. *Stalking the elusive cognitive map: The development of children's representations of geographic space*. Edited by Irwin Altman and Joachim F. Wohlwill. New York: Plenum.

Sokolow, Gary, Martin Guttenplan, and Joe Santos. 2001. *Implementing multimodal transportation districts: Connectivity, access management and the FIHS*. Tampa, FL: Publication of the Center for Urban Transportation Research at the University of South Florida.

Starnes, Earl M., Jay M. Stein, Linda B. Crider, Ivonne Audirac, and Allan W. A. Pither. 1992. *Home-to-school transportation study: Executive summary*. Gainesville, FL: Department of Urban and Regional Planning, University of Florida.

Steiner, Ruth L., Ilir Bejleri, Jennifer L. Wheelock, Claude E. Boles, Maria Cahill, and Benito O. Perez. 2008. Understanding and mapping institutional impediments to walking and bicycling to school: A case study of Hillsborough County. *Transportation Research Record: Journal of the Transportation Research Board* 2074: 3–11.

Steiner, Ruth L., Linda B. Crider, and Matthew Betancourt with Amanda K. K. Hall and Tina Perrotta. 2006. *Safe ways to school—The role in multimodal planning*. Prepared for the Florida Department of Transportation (FDOT) Systems Planning Office under Contract #BD545, Project Work Order #32, 2006. Tallahassee, FL: FDOT. http://www.fldoe.org/edfacil/pdf/SAFEWAYS_FINAL_DOCUMENT.pdf

Strauss, Richard S., and Harold A. Pollack. 2001. Epidemic increase in childhood overweight, 1986–1998. *Journal of the American Medical Association* 286 (22): 2845–48.

U.S. Environmental Protection Agency (EPA). 2003. Travel and environmental implications of school siting. EPA 231-R-03-004. Washington, DC: U.S. EPA. http://www.epa.gov/smartgrowth/pdf/school_travel.pdf

Where to Live and How to Get to School
Connecting Residential Location Choice and School Travel Mode Choice

YIZHAO YANG, BETHANY STEINER, BOB PARKER, MARC SCHLOSSBERG, AND SAYAKA FUKAHORI

THE INCIDENCE OF PARENTS DRIVING CHILDREN TO SCHOOL OR ALLOWING OLDER children to drive themselves to school has increased in recent decades. According to the 2001 National Household Travel Survey (NHTS), about 65 percent of all children are transported to school in private automobiles, compared to 18 percent in 1969 (Bureau of Transportation Statistics 2003; U.S. EPA 2003). In some communities, school trips now account for 10 percent of all short trips, and close to 30 percent of morning peak hour traffic is for school-related trips (Dubay 2003). Increased reliance on the private automobile in school travel appears to parallel a general decline in physical activity levels among children and has thus been associated with adverse health impacts on children (Strauss and Pollack 2001; O'Brien 2003; Sallis and Owen 1999). It has also led to concerns about increased pollution and the negative impacts on the environment (U.S. EPA 2003).

Active school commuting (ASC) is defined as the incidence of children walking or biking to school. Increasing the rate of ASC has become one of the national health objectives for 2010 (U.S. Department of Health and Human Services 2001). Programs and campaigns at the federal, state, and local levels have devoted resources to community-based interventions and educational efforts in the hope of changing children's school travel behavior. Recent concerns about higher fuel costs and climate change make ASC an important element of energy conservation strategies.

Parents are the primary decision makers for children's travel, particularly for young children. Whether public interventions affect a shift in school travel from automobile based to walking and biking will, therefore, largely depend on parents' behavior and response. However, our current understanding of the decision process of parents is limited. Much of the existing school travel literature has been devoted to understanding how school travel mode choice is affected by the characteristics of environments in which families live. The literature on the relationships between parental school travel preference, housing location, and school travel behavior patterns is limited. Yet research-based evidence on such relationships is critical to the development of policies and strategies to enhance ASC.

This study contributes to current literature by examining the connection between parents' preference for ASC, residential location choice, and school travel mode choice. We contend that school travel mode choice may be an integral part of families' residential location choice. Specifically, we seek to answer the following three questions:

- Is children's school commuting explicitly considered when households decide where to live?
- To what degree is parents' preference for ASC related to their decisions regarding residential location?
- To what degree is parents' consideration of ASC during the housing location selection process related to later school travel behavioral patterns of their children?

We see these three questions as critical to improved understanding and design of strategies and policies to enhance ASC.

The rest of this chapter is organized in the following way: First, a brief summary outlines current knowledge about the relationship between where people choose to live and how they travel. This is followed by a description of the study area and research methods. We then present the research findings and conclude by summarizing our interpretations of the data and discussing policy implications.

WHAT DO WE KNOW ABOUT RESIDENTIAL LOCATION CHOICE AND TRAVEL BEHAVIOR?

Recent research on travel behavior has drawn attention to the association between people's travel behavior and characteristics of their residential location. Studies have shown that people residing in places with higher population and housing densities, greater land use mix, better street connections, or more public transportation accessibility have fewer automobile trips and more often use other types of travel, such as walking, biking, and public transit (Cervero and Gorham 1995; Friedman, Gordon, and Peers 1992; Newman and Kenworthy 1999; Rutherford, McCormack, and Wilkinson 1996). However, researchers have been cautious about drawing conclusions regarding causal relations between residential location choice and travel behavior (e.g., Crane 2000; Handy, Cao, and Mokhtarian 2006).

Researchers recognize that people with strong preferences for a given travel mode may move to places that can best support the use of that mode (Choocharukul, Van, and Fujii 2008). Thus the observed environment-travel behavior association may merely reflect the fact that residential location choice serves to accommodate a behavioral predisposition rather than prompt the observed travel behavior. Indeed, some studies have shown that residential location exhibits little impact on travel mode choice once the correlation between attitude or lifestyle and location choice has been taken into account (see, for example, Bagley and Mokhtarian 2002). Others suggest that residential location still affects travel behavior even after controlling for travel preference and self-selection, albeit that the effects are, at most, modest (Cao, Handy, and Mokhtarian 2006; Khattak and Rodriguez 2005; Krizek 2000; Schwanen and Mokhtarian 2005).

The current consensus in the literature appears to be that the causal relationship between residential location and travel behavior could be simultaneous. In other words, the type and characteristics of residential location may influence more frequent use of certain travel modes and travel behavioral patterns. On the other hand, people's travel behavior intentions or preference may influence the selection of certain residential environments.

Much of the existing research has focused on studying the first element of this possible causal relationship—that is, how residential location influences travel behavior. Treating the possibility of self-selection as mainly a nuisance, researchers have experimented with increasingly sophisticated methods and instruments in the identification of the "true" relationship between the built environment and travel behavior (Bagley and Mokhtarian 2002; Bhat and Guo 2007; Greenwald and Boarnet 2001; also see a summary by Mokhtarian and Cao 2008).

In contrast, the second relationship, concerning how a person's travel intention or preference may affect residential location choice, has been understudied (Choocharukul Van, and Fujii 2007). One study (Schwanen and Mokhtarian 2005) revealed that people opt for higher-density living, in part because they are concerned about the environment and want to reduce their own automobile travel. In contrast, those who choose lower-density living do so, in part, because it is better suited for fast, flexible, and comfortable automobile travel. Other studies have noted the dissonance between the type of neighborhood people prefer and where they actually live (Schwanen and Mokhtarian 2005) and that the supply of environments that support nonautomobile travel is less than the potential demand (Levine and Inam 2004). These studies suggest that the benefits of modifying our environments would not only "induce" more desirable travel behavior but also "enable" existing travel preferences.

While the general literature on travel has begun to improve our understandings of how people select different residential environments, the school travel literature has not yet addressed this issue. Existing school travel literature has identified a number of factors that impact the choice of travel modes to school. These factors can be grouped into the following categories: built environment (Ewing, Schroeer, and Greene 2004; McMillan 2007; Schlossberg et al. 2006); social environment (McDonald 2006, 2007a, 2007b, 2007c); school characteristics (Wilson 2008); and family or household characteristics (Wen et al. 2008; Black, Collins, and Snell 2001). Even though some researchers have noted the likely dependence of home–school distance and neighborhood walkability on parents' preference for and attitude toward certain school travel means (see, for example, Ewing, Schroeer, and Greene 2004), the conceptual framework that has implicitly or explicitly guided existing school travel studies is based on the notion that parents' school travel decisions are made mainly in reaction to environmental conditions or changes in those conditions (see McMillan 2005), and not the other way around.

In contrast, the more general travel literature previously noted would suggest that, when parents view school travel modes for their children to be important, they will choose a residential location in part to conform to their preference or attitude. While there have been several studies that examined parents' attitudes and preferences, none of them has explicitly connected those variables to the residential location process (Black et al. 2001; McMillan 2007; Wen et al. 2008). Our goal in this chapter is to examine whether and how parents consciously use residential location to obtain the kind of environments congruent with their school travel preferences. We also examine how school travel decisions made during the residential location process are related to later school travel patterns.

RESEARCH DESIGN

To gain a better understanding of the relationship between residential location choice and school travel, we analyzed both quantitative and qualitative data collected through a survey and several focus groups. Our approach is both exploratory and explanatory.

We first attempt to identify the extent to which a preference for ASC is related to residential location choice. We investigate the relative importance people give to different factors when choosing their housing location, and we examine the degree to which parents' preference for ASC is related to how close they live to their school and the perceived walkability of their neighborhood. We then look at the relationship of ASC preference and children's actual travel behavior, including strong controls for household characteristics and neighborhood environment.

The conceptual framework guiding our research design is depicted in figure 1. We contend that parents' preference for ASC will influence their residential location choice and that will then influence the actual travel patterns of their children. In other words, we suggest that parents may explicitly contemplate the available types of school travel when deciding upon their housing location and that their preference for engaging in ASC affects their school travel behavior, independently of the residential location choice. Based on this conceptual framework we test two hypotheses: (1) people's preference for ASC is related to the factors that they consider in making housing decisions and, eventually, in choosing a residential environment that is more conducive to ASC, such as being closer to school and having better environment walkability, and (2) children's actual travel behavior is influenced by parents' preferences regarding ASC, independently of neighborhood environment characteristics.

Study Area and Study Population

Our study area is the 4J school district in Lane County, Oregon. The district spans 155 square miles in the southern Willamette Valley of Oregon, mainly serving the city of Eugene. Twenty-six elementary schools in this district enrolled approximately six thousand students

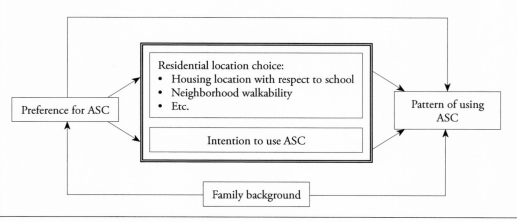

Figure 1. A Conceptual Framework for Understanding Active School Commuting Decisions

in the 2007–8 school year. Among these schools, eighteen are traditional elementary schools, referred to as "neighborhood schools." Eight of the schools are "alternative schools," focusing on special curricular programs such as foreign language education, art, or music. Figure 2 depicts school locations within the district boundaries.

Each of the neighborhood schools has a service zone that defines the area from which a neighborhood school receives its student enrollment. A neighborhood school can accept students outside its service zone if space is available in the school and the students choose to come to the school via the school choice program. The alternative schools do not have defined service zones. They enroll students via a lottery-based, district-wide enrollment policy. In our study we differentiate between "neighborhood schools" and "choice schools," with the latter being either an alternative school or a neighborhood school outside a student's neighborhood.

We limit our study population to parents of young children attending elementary schools. We believe that the school travel decision for children at these young ages is made by their parents or guardians and is thus more reflective of parents' attitudes and intentions (see McMillan 2005). This population group also has a high residential mobility rate, and their residential location process may be more likely to involve the simultaneous consideration of purchasing a house, deciding on schools, and determining travel options.

Survey

In the spring of 2008, the school travel survey was mailed to every household (n = 5,700) with children attending elementary schools (K–5) in the 4J school district and residing within

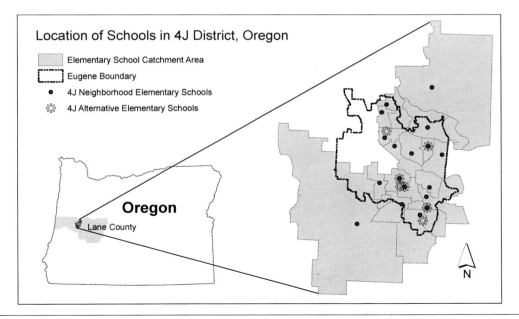

Figure 2. Elementary Schools in the 4J School District

the city boundary of Eugene. Parents were instructed to fill out the survey for their oldest elementary school child if more than one child in the household attended elementary school. The survey was designed to obtain information on school travel behavior, parents' school travel preferences, perceptions about environmental conditions, and the sociodemographic background of recipients. The survey questions about children's school travel behavior are similar to those used in other studies (e.g., Schlossberg et al. 2005). Details on the questions are provided in conjunction with the following discussion of the results.

Parent Focus Groups

To obtain more qualitative data and information that could be useful in our analysis, we supplemented the survey with three parent focus group sessions. These sessions focused more intensely on collecting additional information related to parents' school travel habits and their consideration of school travel in residential location decisions. Parents were recruited from those who indicated in their survey their willingness to participate in focus groups, and an average of ten parents attended each session. Participants were first given a summary of preliminary results from the survey and were then led in a discussion of why they chose their current housing location, their preferred travel modes, and their actual travel behavior.

RESEARCH FINDINGS

We first examine our three research questions using the survey data and then describe how results from the focus groups supplement the quantitative findings.

General Survey Results

Of the 5,700 surveys that were distributed, 1,197 were returned. Discounting the 126 that were nondeliverable, this resulted in a response rate of 21 percent. A comparison of several sociodemographic and housing characteristics of this sample group to the remaining population suggested that the sample was reasonably representative of all households of elementary school students in the school district. Respondents answered most of the questions that were posed, and there did not appear to be a systematic pattern to missing data. All in all, the level of complete survey response was high.

Table 1 provides descriptive data on the sample and the schools that the children attended. The respondents were predominantly white families (80 percent), who owned their homes (75 percent), had two cars (mean = 1.9), and had a mean household income of about $75,000 in 2007 (median income of $60,000). Both parents were employed full-time in almost a third of the homes (30 percent), and at least one parent was not employed in slightly fewer than a third of the homes (28 percent). Slightly more than half of the children attended their neighborhood school (55 percent), and the average distance from their home to school was estimated to be 1.7 miles. Parents were asked to rate the safety and walkability of their

Table 1. Descriptive Statistics

Variable	Mean	Standard error	N
Active school commuting (walking or biking to school)			
3 days or more per week	0.15	0.01	1,195
ASC preference (range: 1–5)	3.99	0.03	1,185
Environmental variables			
Home-school distance (mi.)	1.77	0.06	1,197
Neighborhood walkability (1–5)	3.56	0.04	1,197
Safety concerns (1–5)	2.92	0.05	1,175
School variables			
Total street length within a quarter mile of school (1,000 ft.)	1,500	0.21	1,104
Percentage of residential land within a quarter mile of school	0.63	0.01	1,104
Average lot size within a quarter mile of school	0.24	0.002	1,104
Household variables			
Income	75,455	1,415.0	1,147
Highest education is bachelor or above	0.72	0.01	1,171
White race/ethnicity	0.80	0.01	1,175
Number of cars owned	1.93	0.03	1,197
At least one adult is not employed	0.29	0.01	1,182
Both parents employed fulltime	0.30	0.01	1,182
Child's age	7.91	0.05	1,197
Attending own neighborhood school	0.55	0.01	1,188

neighborhood, using a five-point scale with higher responses reflecting greater perceived safety and greater walkability, respectively. Responses indicated only slight concerns, on average, with safety (mean = 2.9) and moderate levels of perceived walkability (mean = 3.6). Examination of the area directly surrounding the schools (within a quarter mile) using parcel-level data indicated that the neighborhoods were usually highly residential with relatively large home lots and substantial sidewalk access.

To measure parents' preference for ASC, they were asked the extent to which they agreed with the statement "If possible, I'd prefer my child walk or bike to school." The response scale had five levels ranging from strongly disagree to strongly agree. As shown in table 1, the average score on the scale was 4.0, indicating relatively strong levels of agreement. However, the actual level of ASC was substantially smaller. Fewer than one-sixth (15 percent) of the children walked or biked to school at least three days per week.

Is Children's School Commuting Considered
When Families Decide Where to Live?

Parents were asked whether school travel mode was considered when they moved to their current home. We assume that having a particular transportation mode in mind when making a housing location choice indicates that the parents had a certain level of intention to use that mode rather than an alternate one.

Overall, 78 percent of parents indicated that they had thought about school transportation when they chose their current residence. About 60 percent of the parents had just one type of travel mode in mind (e.g., walking or biking, car, or school bus), and 18 percent reported considering more than one type of transportation. Among the respondents who reported considering school travel, 44 percent mentioned walking or biking to school as a considered travel means, followed by private automobile travel (37 percent) and school bus travel (36 percent), respectively.

The survey also asked parents if they chose their housing location because of their interest in a particular school. The data indicate that the order in which parents made their school and housing location choices is related to the extent to which parents think about school travel. For parents who chose a housing location because they were interested in a particular school (i.e., they decided they wanted their child to attend a particular school before deciding on housing location), more than 93 percent thought about their children's school travel. For parents who had not chosen a particular school before moving to their current residence, 80 percent had considered school travel. About 40 percent of respondents who chose their housing location prior to the births of their children considered what travel means they would use for those children to get to school.

To summarize, the survey results indicate that parents in this school district did consider how children would get to school when choosing where to live. This consideration was especially salient for parents who had decided what school they wanted their children to attend before choosing their residential location but also was present for a majority of other parents. We turn now to data regarding the specific factors that parents considered when choosing residential housing and the extent to which children's ability to walk or bike to school (ASC) influenced their residential location decisions.

Is Parents' Preference for ASC Related to Their
Residential Location Decision Making?

We addressed the second research question regarding the relationship of parents' preference for ASC to location decision making in three different analyses. The first examines the importance that parents attached to various factors in the residential location decision-making process, while the second and third use multivariate analyses to examine the relationship of ASC preference to the distance between home and school and perceived walkability of the neighborhood.

ASC Preferences and Important Locational Factors

We asked parents to rank, on a scale from 1 to 5 (with 1 being not important at all and 5 being extremely important), the importance of twenty-one factors involved in the residential location decision-making process. Among those factors, four are directly relevant to ASC: proximity to school, perceived walkability of the neighborhood, pedestrian and biking safety of the environment, and ability for a child to walk or bike to school.

Figure 3 displays the average scale score for each of the twenty-one factors. The results indicate that the most important factors that parents considered in deciding where to live were areas such as safety from crime (particularly for their children), cost of housing, characteristics of the housing unit, and reputation of the neighborhoods. Of the twenty-one factors examined, environmental factors related to ASC, such as pedestrian and biking safety, ease of walking and biking, and proximity to neighborhood school, ranked seventh, eleventh, and twelfth, respectively. Parents' concern over the "ability for my child to walk/bike to school" was of somewhat lower importance, ranked fifteenth out of twenty-one.

The results in figure 3 depict the scores for the entire sample of parents. We would expect, however, that parents who had a greater preference for ASC would be more likely than other parents to rank environmental factors related to ASC more highly. Figure 4 depicts the mean importance scores for the four factors related to ASC within each category of agreement with the ASC preference measure described earlier. Results indicate that parents who have a greater preference for ASC (indicating they would strongly prefer that their child walk or bike to school) are much more likely to rank environmental factors associated with ASC as important when deciding where to live.

For instance, the first set of bars in figure 4 give the scale scores associated with the rated importance of "ease of walking/biking" in choosing where to live. For the total population, as shown in figure 3, the average scale score for this factor was 3.0, exactly in the middle of the five-point scale. However, when the results are presented separately for parents with different preferences regarding ASC, strikingly different results appear. Those with strong preferences

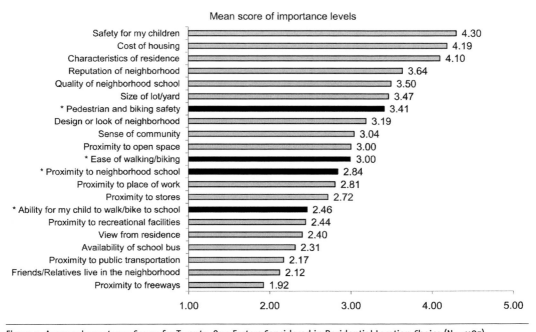

Figure 3. Average Importance Scores for Twenty-One Factors Considered in Residential Location Choice (N = 1185)

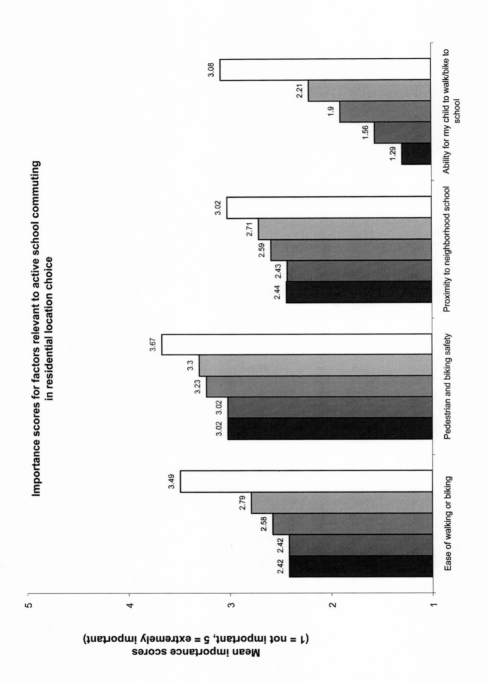

Figure 4. Average Ratings of Importance of Selected Environmental Factors in Housing Decision by Parents' Preference for ASC

for ASC have an average scale score of 3.5, while those without a strong preference have much lower average scale scores (mean = 2.4). Similar results occur with each of the factors. Parents who indicate that they prefer that their children walk or bike to school are much more likely to rate factors related to ASC as important in the residential location decision-making process, although differences are less marked with the importance attached to the proximity to the neighborhood school (see the fourth set of columns in fig. 4.)

ASC Preference and Distance to School

Using our survey data, we used ordinary least squares (OLS) regression to examine the relationship between the parents' report of the distance between home and school and parents' ASC preference while controlling for household characteristics, including whether or not the child attended a neighborhood school and factors related to the school environment. Specifically, we examined the following equation: Distance = a + b(ASC) + b (HDC) + b (SE), where ASC represents preference for ASC, HDC represents the various household demographic characteristics listed in table 1, and SE represents the school environment variables in table 1. Results are given in the first set of columns in table 2.

The R-squared value for this regression was 0.15, indicating that about one-sixth of the variation in home-school distance is explained by variables in the model. Several of the control variables are significantly associated with distance to school. Families with very high incomes (>$100,000), more cars, and both parent(s) employed full time have significantly longer home-school distances, while households with minority member(s) tended to live closer to their children's school. Measures of the built environment around schools were also significantly associated with home-school distance. Schools located in a largely residential neighborhood (with a higher percentage of residential land and thus less "mixed land use") and in lower density areas (with larger lots) had shorter home-school distances for their students, regardless of family characteristics. Finally, children attending their own neighborhood schools lived significantly closer to their schools than those attending other schools.

Even with all these control variables included in the model, parents' preference for ASC is significantly associated with shorter reported distances between home and school. The standardized coefficients (β) may be compared from one variable to another within a model. As would be expected, the largest β is associated with whether or not a child attends a neighborhood school. However, the β associated with ASC preference is second to this value and substantially stronger (by more than twice the magnitude) than the coefficients associated with the various household characteristics.

ASC Preference and Walkability

The second set of columns in table 2 gives results of the regression of perceptions of neighborhood walkability on ASC preference and the control variables. The coefficients indicate that only one household characteristic but all the school environment variables are significantly associated with perceived walkability. Families with fewer cars were significantly more likely to live in more walkable neighborhoods. In addition, those attending schools located on better connected streets (i.e., more streets within a quarter mile of the school site) and in largely residential neighborhoods rated their neighborhoods as more walkable. Respondents whose children attended schools with higher density surrounding a school site rated their environments as more walkable.

Table 2. Regression of Home-School Distance and Neighborhood Walkability on ASC Preference, Household Characteristics, School Environment, and Attendance at Own Neighborhood School

	Home-school distance			Walkability		
	Unstandardized regression coefficient	Standardized regression coefficient		Unstandardized regression coefficient	Standardized regression coefficient	
(Constant)	4.72		***	3.15		***
Preference for ASC (1–5)	-0.25	-0.14	***	0.12	0.11	***
Household characteristics						
Household income below $30,000	0.37	0.07		-0.20	-0.06	
Household income between $30,000 and $59,999	0.06	0.01		-0.15	-0.05	
Household income above $100,000 or more	0.37	0.07	**	-0.05	-0.02	
Number of cars in household	0.14	0.06	**	-0.14	-0.10	***
At least one household member is nonwhite	-0.31	-0.06	**	0.09	0.03	
Highest education: post graduate degree	0.06	0.01		0.03	0.01	
Own the residence (yes = 1)	-0.10	-0.02	**	0.11	0.04	
Parent(s) full time employed	0.30	0.06		0.01	0.00	
Attending own neighborhood school	-1.30	-0.30	***	0.06	0.02	
School environment						
Total street length within a quarter mile of school	-0.12	-0.06		0.10	0.07	*
Percentage of residential land within a quarter mile of school	-1.31	-0.12	***	0.59	0.09	***
Average lot size within a quarter mile of school	-3.27	-0.13	***	-0.73	-0.05	**
Adjusted R-square	0.15			0.07		
N	1,069			1,058		

*p < 0.05, ** p < 0.01, *** p < 0.001

Again, when these control variables were considered, the relationship of ASC preference to the perceived walkability of the neighborhood is statistically significant ($p < 0.001$). Families who indicate a greater preference for ASC are more likely to assess their neighborhoods as walkable. Comparison of the standardized coefficients indicates that ASC preference has a stronger relationship with the measure of walkability than any other variable in the model.

It should be noted that the R-squared associated with the walkability model is 0.07, substantially lower than that obtained for the model of home-school distance. We believe that this largely reflects the differential impact of attendance at a neighborhood school on these two dependent variables. Attendance at a neighborhood school is the most important influence on home-school distance but is unrelated to perceived walkability, relationships that are logical and expected. It should also be noted that the R-squared value of 0.07 in the model of walkability is statistically significant and comparable to many results found within the social sciences. Thus we believe it should not be discounted.

Summary

The results presented earlier appear to indicate that parents' preference for ASC is related to the types of factors that they consider important in choosing a residential location, their reports of how far they live from their child's school, and the perceived walkability of their neighborhoods. These relationships are statistically significant and substantively stronger than the impact of household characteristics and measures of school environments.

To What Degree Does the Consideration of ASC during the Residential Location Process Predict Later Behavior?

While the first two research questions ask if households consider ASC when deciding where to live and if this is related to their location decision-making process, our third research question examines the relationship between considering ASC during the location selection process and children's actual behavior patterns. In other words, do parents who reported considering ASC when choosing where to live have children who are now more likely to use active means to get to school?

To examine this question we used a logistic regression with the parents' report of the "child walking or biking three days or more per week to school" as the dependent variable. Two variables related to views regarding ASC are included: having ASC in mind when choosing one's current residence and stated preference for ASC. Control variables include parents' reports of their neighborhood environment, measures of the school environment, household characteristics, and whether or not the child attends a neighborhood school. Table 3 gives the results of the analysis.

The first two columns in table 3 (the logistic regression coefficients and standard errors) can be used to calculate the t-statistics, testing the null hypothesis that associations with the dependent variable equal zero by simply dividing the regression coefficient by the standard error. It can be seen that several of the control variables are significantly related to children's ASC. Children whose parents rate their neighborhoods as more walkable, live closer to their schools, and have fewer safety concerns are significantly more likely to walk or bike to school. Only one of the school environment variables is significantly related to ASC: students in schools surrounded by more connected street networks are, as would be hypothesized, more

Table 3. Logistic Regression of Children's ASC on Parental Preference, Environmental Descriptors, and Household Characteristics

	Logistic regression coefficient	Standard error		Odds ratio
Parents' views regarding ASC				
ASC in mind when choosing current residence	1.69	0.28	***	5.42
Preference for ASC (1–5)	0.71	0.21	***	2.03
Neighborhood environment				
Neighborhood walkability (1–5)	0.57	0.31	*	1.77
Home-school distance	−1.02	0.18	***	0.36
Safety concern (1–5)	−1.04	0.14	***	0.35
School environment				
Total street length within a quarter mile of school	0.32	0.16	*	1.38
Percentage of residential land within a quarter mile of school	0.57	0.89		1.76
Average lot size within a quarter mile of school	2.08	2.24		7.98
Household characteristics				
Age of child	0.17	0.08	**	1.19
Own the residence (yes = 1)	−0.11	0.36		0.90
At lease one adult not employed	0.69	0.28	*	2.00
Household income below $30,000	−0.86	0.43	**	0.42
Household income between $30,000 and $59,999	−0.47	0.34		0.63
Household income above $100,000 or more	−1.13	0.37	***	0.32
Number of cars in household	−0.30	0.18	*	0.74
At least one household member is nonwhite	0.18	0.32		1.20
Highest education: post graduate degree	0.29	0.28		1.34
Attending own neighborhood school	0.65	0.29	**	1.92
Constant	−5.10	1.66		0.01
−2 log likelihood	420.61			
Quasi R-square (Nagelkerke R-square)	0.62			
N	1,050			

Note: Children's ASC is defined as walking or biking to school at least three times a week.
*p < 0.05, ** p < 0.01, ***p < 0.001

likely to walk or bike. Finally, older children, children attending a neighborhood school, children in homes with at least one adult not employed, and children in homes with fewer family cars are significantly more likely to bike or walk to school. Compared with children in the group of income around $60,000 to $99,999, children in both the lowest and the highest income categories are significantly less likely to walk or bike to school.

Independent of these control measures, both indicators of parents' concern with ASC are significantly associated with children's walking or biking to school. Children whose parents reported that they had ASC in mind when choosing the location of their home and those who report a strong preference for ASC are significantly more likely than other children to walk or bike to school at least three times a week, even when they have household and neighborhood characteristics that are the same as those of other children.

The final column of table 3 reports the odds ratios associated with each variable. For instance, the odds ratio associated with parents considering ASC when selecting their current residence is 5.42 (exp[1.69] = 5.42). This tells us that the odds of a child walking or biking to school at least three days a week increase by a factor of 5.42 if his or her parents considered ASC when selecting their current residence. Notably, this impact is independent of other variables, including the parents' preference for ASC and their perceptions of neighborhood walkability, neighborhood safety, and home-school distance.

To summarize, the results confirmed our hypothesis: Children with parents who had considered ASC when choosing their home and who expressed greater preference for ASC were significantly more likely to walk or bike to school at least three days a week. This relationship holds with extensive controls for household characteristics and measures of the neighborhood and school environment.

Focus Group Results: Qualitative Information

The focus group was designed to enhance results obtained from the survey and to see how a subsample of survey respondents felt about the results we had obtained. Information collected from the three groups provides additional evidence that corroborates the findings from our statistical analysis and also helps us understand our results. As with the survey results, the parents we interviewed emphasized the cost of housing and neighborhood safety in their housing location choice. Proximity to other land uses and services, including schools, was of less importance to them, partly because, they indicated, the community is relatively small and people do not feel that driving is difficult or overly time consuming.

For parents who did use ASC, it was clear that allowing their children the option of walking or biking to school was something they had always intended to do. These parents were willing to pay a premium for shorter home-school distance and good neighborhood walkability. Among those who did not use ASC, a few parents believed that having children walk or bike to school was socially unacceptable. Many participants talked about concerns with distance and safety as a major reason for not using ASC. Yet several acknowledged that some of the reasons they offered for not using ASC were "excuses," such as not wanting to get wet in the rain or not wanting to take the extra time to walk or bike with a child. Quite a few participants acknowledged that they never thought about allowing their children to walk or bike to school, since walking or biking was perceived as a form of recreation but not as an appropriate transportation means for adults or children.

Discussion among the parents also highlighted a general feeling that there was a lack of housing opportunities in the community that would help them fulfill their preference for ASC. Parents also expressed frustration over things out of their control, such as school closures and relocation, which often alter home-school distance and make ASC impossible.

In short, the discussions among the parents, although a self-selected group, confirmed the findings from the survey. They indicated that concerns with ASC can influence housing location choice and subsequent travel behavior.

DISCUSSION AND CONCLUSION

The findings in this study support our contention that residential location choice provides a mechanism by which ASC preference influences later behavioral patterns. While many environmental characteristics, such as the distance between home and school, safety, and walkability, still play a role in parents' decisions, our results suggest that preference for ASC independently influences both residential location choices and later travel behavior. This finding lends credence to the development of targeted education programs aimed at informing parents or young families of these choices before they make long-term housing location decisions.

Integration of the residential location process into a school travel behavior study helps us gain a better understanding of many of the impacts of environmental characteristics on school travel. For example, our research shows that the mix conditions of land use around a school site do not directly influence the likelihood of a household using ASC. This is consistent with other studies (U.S. EPA 2003; McMillan 2007). However, our analysis also reveals that such environmental conditions have a strong influence on whether families live close to school and have a walkable environment in the first place. Thus the actual influence of mixed land use on school travel could be overlooked due to its correlation with other environmental conditions.

The improved understanding of the decision-making process of residential location also helps us to see the limitations in current environment-based strategies for changing school travel behavior. Currently, most Safe Route to School programs devote the majority of their resources to the improvement of physical infrastructure, which is likely to have impacts on parents' perceptions of walkability. Our results indicate that perceived walkability is less important than variables such as home-school distance and ASC preference in explaining travel patterns, and the limited influence of the perceived walkability variable may help explain some of the less encouraging results of the environmental interventions reported in recent studies (see, for example, Boarnet et al. 2005).

Our results suggest that enabling more children to live close to their schools is likely to make a greater difference in school travel behavior than improving environmental walkability. School siting policies have been used to require that schools be located close to residential neighborhoods. While our research findings provide supportive evidence that such policies are likely to be effective, we also note that home-school distance was affected by a number of variables other than school environment characteristics, such as parents' employment status, number of cars owned, and household income. Such findings reflect the many trade-offs that a family faces in determining where to live and suggest that parents' location choice is affected not only by the conditions surrounding a school site but also by the spatial configuration of housing opportunities and land uses in the entire community. This understanding clearly calls for a better collaboration between community land use planning and school planning and a more comprehensive strategy in the use of environmental interventions for changing school travel behavior.

In short, while environmental conditions are necessary for ASC, they are not sufficient. A strong motivation (e.g., strong preference and intention) seems essential for sustaining ASC. Our research shows the strong predictive power of the intention to use ASC on later use of ASC. This finding reinforces the notion that education and encouragement are two critical components, in addition to physical environment, to ensure the success of many programs advocating Safe Routes to School. The greater explanatory power of ASC preference relative to perceived walkability indicates a need to change the existing strategy and invest more resources in changing parent attitudes and preferences.

ACKNOWLEDGMENT

This study was supported by Oregon Transportation Research and Education Center. We thank Community Planning Workshop at the Community Service Center, the University of Oregon, and the 4J school district at Lane County, Oregon, for assistance with conducting the school travel survey, parent focus groups, and interviews with local planners. The authors want to express special thanks to Jean Stockard for her help with analysis and writing.

REFERENCES

Bagley, Michael N., and Patricia L. Mokhtarian. 2002. The impact of residential neighborhood type on travel behavior: A structural equations modeling approach. *The Annals of Regional Science* 36: 279–97.

Bhat, Chandra R., and Jessica Y. Guo. 2007. A comprehensive analysis of built environment characteristics on household residential choice and auto ownership levels. *Transportation Research: Part B* 41: 506–26.

Black, Colin, Alan Collins, and Martin Snell. 2001. Encouraging walking: The case of journey-to-school trips in compact urban areas. *Urban Studies* 38: 1121–41.

Boarnet, Marlon G., Kristen Day, Craig Anderson, Tracy McMillan, and Mariela Alfonzo. 2005. California's *Safe Routes to School* program: Impact on walking, bicycling, and pedestrian safety. *Journal of the American Planning Association* 71 (3): 301–17.

Bureau of Transportation Statistics (BTS). 2003. *Bureau of Transportation Statistics: National household travel survey—national data and analysis tool CD*. Washington, DC: Bureau of Transportation Statistics. CD-ROM.

Cao, Xinyu, Susan L. Handy, and Patricia L. Mokhtarian. 2006. The influences of the built environment and residential self-selection on pedestrian behavior: Evidence from Austin, TX. *Transportation* 33: 1–20.

Cervero, Robert, and Roger Gorham. 1995. Commuting in transit versus automobile neighborhoods. *Journal of the American Planning Association* 61: 210–25.

Choocharukul, Kasem, Hong Tan Van, and Satoshi Fujii. 2008. Psychological effects of travel behavior on preference of residential location choice. *Transportation Research. Part A, Policy and Practice* 42: 116–24.

Crane, Randall. 2000. The influence of urban form on travel: An interpretive review. *Journal of Planning Literature* 15: 3–23.

Dubay, Ann. 2003. See Dick and Jane sit in traffic. *The Press Democrat*, September 7.

Ewing, R., W. Schroeer, and W. Greene. 2004. School location and student travel. *Transportation Research Record* 1895 (1):55–63.

Friedman, Bruce, Stephen P. Gordon, and John B. Peers. 1992. The effect of neotraditional design on travel characteristics. In *Compendium of technical papers, Institute of Transportation Engineers, 1992 District 6 annual meeting*. Anchorage, AK: Institution of Transportation Engineers, Alaska Section.

Greenwald, Michael J., and Marlon G. Boarnet. 2001. Built environment as a determinant of walking behavior: Analyzing non-work pedestrian travel in Portland, Oregon. *Transportation Research Record: Journal of the Transportation Research Board* 1780: 33–42.

Handy, Susan, Xinyu Cao, and Patricia L. Mokhtarian. 2006. Self-selection in the relationship between the built environment and walking. *Journal of the American Planning Association* 72: 55–74.

Kestens, Yan. 2004. Why families move and what do they choose: An analysis of single-family property buyers. Unpublished diss., Laval University, Quebec City, Canada.

Khattak, Assad J., and Daniel Rodriguez. 2005. Travel behavior in neotraditional neighborhood developments: A case study in USA. *Transportation Research Part A: Policy and Practice* 39: 481–500.

Krizek, Kevin J. 2000. Residential relocation and changes in urban travel: Does neighborhood-scale urban form matter? *Journal of the American Planning Association* 69: 265–81.

Landford, H., and J. Wyckoff. 2000. The effect of school choice and residential location on the racial segregation of students. http://www.albany.edu/~wyckoff/segpapr14.PDF.

Levine, Jonathan, and Aseem Inam. 2004. The market for transportation-land use integration: Do developers want smarter growth than regulations allow? *Transportation* 31: 409–27.

McDonald, Noreen C. 2006. Exploratory analysis of children's travel patterns. *Transportation Research Record* 1997 (1): 1–7.

———. 2007a. Active transportation to school: Trends among U.S. schoolchildren, 1969–2001. *American Journal of Preventive Medicine* 32 (6): 509–16.

———. 2007b. Children's mode choice for the school trip: The role of distance and school location in walking to school. *Transportation* 35 (1): 23–35.

———. 2007c. Travel and the social environment: Evidence from Alameda County, California. *Transportation Research Part D: Transport and Environment* 12: 53–63.

McMillan, Tracy E. 2005. Urban form and a child's trip to school: The current literature and a framework for future research. *Journal of Planning Literature* 19: 440–56.

———. 2007. The relative influence of urban form on a child's travel mode to school. *Transportation Research Part A,* 41: 69-79.

Mokhtarian, Patricia L., and Xinyu Cao. 2008. Examining the impacts of residential self-selection on travel behavior: A focus on methodologies. *Transportation Research Part B: Methodological* 43: 204–28.

Newman, Peter W. G., and Jeffrey R. Kenworthy. 1999. *Cities and automobile dependence: An international sourcebook*. Brookfield, VT: Gower.

O'Brien, Catherine. 2003. Transportation that's actually good for the soul. *National Center for Bicycling and Walking Forum*. December 3, 2003. http://www.bikewalk.org/pdfs/forummarch0104transportation.pdf.

Rossi, Peter H. 1980. *Why families move*. Beverly Hills, CA: Sage.

Rutherford, G. Scott, Edward McCormack, and Martina Wilkinson. 1996. Travel impacts of urban form: Implications from an analysis of two Seattle area travel diaries. Paper prepared for the Travel Model Improvement Program Conference on Urban Design, Telecommuting and Travel Behavior, University of Washington, Seattle, October.

Sallis, James F., and Neville Owen. 1999. *Physical activity and behavioral medicine*. Thousand Oaks, CA: Sage.

Schlossberg, Marc, Page Paulsen Philips, Bethany Johnson, and Robert M. Parker. 2005. How do they get there? A spatial analysis of a sprawl school in Oregon. *Planning Practice and Research* 20: 147–62.

Schwanen, Tim, and Patricia L. Mokhtarian. 2005. What affects commute mode choice: Neighborhood physical structure or attitudes toward neighborhoods? *Journal of Transport Geography* 13: 83–99.

Strauss, Richard S., and Harold A. Pollack. 2001. Epidemic increase in childhood overweight 1986–1998. *Journal of the American Medical Association* 286 (22): 2845–48.

U.S. Department of Health and Human Services. 2001. *Health United States, 2001*. Washington, DC: Department of Health and Human Services.

U.S. Environmental Protection Agency (EPA). 2003. Travel and environmental implications of school siting. EPA 231-R-03-004. Washington, DC: U.S. EPA. http://www.epa.gov/smartgrowth/pdf/school_travel.pdf.

Wen, Li Ming, Denise Fry, Chris Rissel, Helen Dirkis, Angela Balafas, and Dafna Merom. 2008. Factors associated with children being driven to school: Implications for walk to school programs. *Health Education Research* 23: 325–34.

Wilson, Ryan Donald. 2008. *Effect of education policy and urban form on elementary-age school travel.* Unpublished Masters thesis, Department of Civil Engineering, University of Minnesota, Master of Science in Civil Engineering.

PART 4

School Siting and Healthy Communities in Practice

Safe Schools

Identifying Potential Threats to the Health and Safety of Schoolchildren in North Carolina

DAVID SALVESEN AND PETER ZAMBITO

IN SEPTEMBER 2010, SCHOOL OFFICIALS AT THE NEW $75-MILLION CARSON-GORE Academy of Environmental Studies in Los Angeles were scrambling to deal with the threat of toxic fumes emanating from beneath the school. The elementary school—named after former vice president and Nobel Prize–winner Al Gore and environmentalist Rachel Carson, author of *Silent Spring*—was built, ironically, on a site where soil was contaminated by a leaking underground gasoline tank at a former gas station and possibly from oil well operations next door. The school district spent $4 million cleaning up the site, including the removal of thousands of square feet of soil. Still, many parents and children's health advocates question official pronouncements that the school is safe. Carson-Gore Academy is not an isolated incident.

Every school day nearly fifty million children spend six hours or more at one of the nation's approximately 97,000 public schools (NCES 2007). Most of these schools are located in safe, healthy environments. However, numerous school campuses are located on or dangerously close to potential environmental threats such as industrial facilities, underground gas pipelines, Superfund sites,[1] railroad tracks, floodplains, or other hazards that threaten the health and safety of children and school employees.

Children are more vulnerable to environmental threats than adults due to their higher respiration rates, higher ratio of skin surface area to body weight, and higher metabolism (Amler et al. 2003). Children consume more calories, drink more water, and breathe more air per pound of body weight than adults. In addition, children absorb, metabolize, detoxify, and excrete poisons differently than adults. Low-income children are at even greater risk. Due to their economic status, children of low-income families have limited or no access to health care. Children spend a large part of their day at school, and several studies have shown that children can be exposed to environmental hazards (e.g., pollution from vehicle exhaust) while there (Appatova et al., 2008). Moreover, a growing body of research demonstrates that low-income and minority children are exposed disproportionately to environmental hazards.

There are no hard figures on the total number of public schools in the United States located near environmental hazards. A few studies exist that focus on just one or two hazards. For example, a 2002 study of public schools in five states (California, Massachusetts, Michigan, New Jersey, and New York) identified 1,195 schools located within a half mile of a state or federal Superfund site (CHEJ 2002). A California study found over 700 public schools located within 150 meters (164 yards) of busy roads—defined as roads with over 25,000 vehicles per day (Green et al. 2004).

PURPOSE

Between 2008 and 2010, the Institute for the Environment at the University of North Carolina-Chapel Hill conducted a study of public schools in North Carolina and their proximity to different environmental hazards such as industrial facilities, Superfund sites, major highways, and railroads. The primary goals of the study were to do the following:

1. Determine the extent to which public schools in North Carolina are located close to environmental hazards, including multiple hazards
2. Assess whether schools located close to environmental hazards in the state are disproportionately attended by racial minorities and the poor
3. Identify how North Carolina's policies for siting schools could be strengthened to reduce the likelihood of schools being built too close to environmental hazards

We chose North Carolina because of our knowledge of the state's policies on school siting, our contacts with state health and environmental officials, the availability of the geographic information system (GIS) databases on environmental hazards in the state, and the proximity of schools for the case study.

NATIONWIDE SCHOOL SITING POLICIES

School location decisions ultimately fall under the jurisdiction of local school boards. In general, such decisions are shaped by a number of factors, including the location of current and future residential growth, land availability and cost, available infrastructure, and state and local policies and practices.[2] Some states preclude local districts from purchasing land within a certain distance from a known environmental hazard. However, there has been no comprehensive analysis of whether state policies are sufficient to prevent schools from locating near environmental hazards or, conversely, to prevent environmental hazards from locating too close to existing schools.

A 2005 survey of state school siting policies found that only twenty-six states have restrictions on siting schools on or near environmental hazards, whereas twenty states have no policies of any kind affecting the siting of schools in relation to environmental hazards. The survey also found that only fourteen states outright prohibit siting schools in locations that pose health and safety risks due to the presence of man-made or natural environmental hazards (Fischbach 2005).

Some states provide specific setbacks and procedures for mitigating a broad range of potential environmental threats, including proximity to highways, railroads, airports, and prior land uses. A few states, notably Kentucky, Mississippi, and West Virginia, ban schools from locating near certain hazards. Others use broad language that is advisory only. For example, California prohibits construction of schools within five hundred feet of a freeway or busy traffic corridor, while North Carolina simply urges local school districts to avoid high-traffic areas.

In addition to existing environmental hazards, schools may be threatened by the arrival of new hazards, such as a new factory or the widening of an existing road. Yet few states have enacted laws preventing new and hazardous uses near schools. Indiana is one of the few states that make reference to *future* uses locating near existing schools.

Interestingly, states generally have authorized local governments to adopt ordinances to protect school children from moral threats such as liquor stores or adult bookstores. For example, Ashe County, North Carolina, prohibits adult businesses (e.g., state-run liquor stores) from locating within 1,320 feet of a public school. However, other than for electric transmission lines, North Carolina's school facility planning guidelines lack specific, measurable standards to ensure that schools are built at safe distances from environmental hazards.

Table 1 provides a summary of state policies on school siting, selected from among the twenty-six states with such policies. The table provides a sample of policies from states with specific, measurable standards for different environmental hazards in contrast to North Carolina's relative lack of strong policies or guidelines on school siting.

ENVIRONMENTAL HAZARDS

We focused our analysis on the types of environmental hazards that are commonly addressed in the states that have adopted standards or guidelines for school siting and that are at least mentioned in the North Carolina school facility guidelines. Although not mentioned in North Carolina's guidelines, we included hog waste lagoons in our analysis as North Carolina is the second leading hog producer in the country (there are over ten thousand hogs in the state), plus the data on their location is readily available electronically. We did not include gasoline or natural gas pipelines or overhead transmission lines because the data was either unavailable or cost prohibitive. Unfortunately, in the post-9/11 world, access to these data is severely limited due to national security concerns.

Major Roads

Emissions from cars and trucks contain a number of substances that can be harmful to human health, including benzene and diesel particulate matter. In recent years, several studies have indicated that living or attending school near major roads can increase exposure to such pollutants and that such exposure is associated with adverse health effects, such as increased risk of heart and lung disease (Green et al. 2004). Major roads for this study were defined as those primary roads that were classified as either an interstate, such as I-40 or I-85, or a U.S. route, such as U.S. 1. Some interstates, for example I-77 near Charlotte, experience traffic volumes of over one hundred thousand vehicles per day. North Carolina primary roads and all secondary roads were omitted, as these tend to be smaller, two-lane roads with relatively low traffic volumes. The data on major roads, including traffic volume as well as shape files for the GIS maps, were obtained from the North Carolina Department of Transportation (NCDOT).

Table 1. Comparison of Selected States' School Siting Policies

Category	Regulation	State	Source
Transportation routes	Noise from air and motor vehicle traffic should not exceed sound decibel level of 65 dB sustained and 75 dB peak	AK	Arkansas Rules and Regulations governing the Minimum Schoolhouse Construction Standards; Arkansas Code 6-20-1406
Transportation routes	No site within 500 ft. of the edge of the closest traffic of a freeway or busy traffic corridor; identify sources of air pollution within ¼ mile of the site that emit hazardous air emissions (including industrial, traffic corridors, agricultural operations, and rail yards)	CA	California Education Code Sections 17072.12, 17072.13, 17072.18, 17210–215.5, 17251, and 17268 (2001)
Transportation routes	Setback of 2,500 ft. for roads where explosive loads are carried and 1,500 ft. for roads where gasoline, diesel, propane, chlorine, and other combustible or poisonous gases are transported	CA	School Site Selection and Approval Guide (2004)
Transportation routes	Risk/hazard analysis required if site is within a 3-mile radius of railroads, major highways, or airport approach or departure paths	GA	A Guide to School Site Selection (2003); Georgia Compilation of Rules and Regulations, Department of Education, School Facilities, and Capital Outlay Management, section 160-6-5-16 (2001)
Transportation routes	Cannot build within 500 ft. of a railroad	IN	Indiana Code section 16-41-21-6, Prohibited Sites; waiver (1993)
Pipes and power	Site must be at least the following distances from electric power line easements: 100 ft. from edge of easement for a 50–133 kV line, 150 ft. for a 220–30 kV line, and 350 ft. for a 500–550 kV line; site cannot be near an above-ground water or fuel storage tank	CA	California Code of Regulations, Title 5 Education, Chapter 13 School Facilities and Equipment, Subchapter 1 School Housing Sections 14001–14012 (2000)
Pipes and power	Risk assessment must be performed if site is within 1,500 ft. of an above-ground or underground pipeline; if risk posed, must abandon site	CA	California Code of Regulations, Title 5 Education, Chapter 13 School Facilities and Equipment, Subchapter 1 School Housing Sections 14001–14012 (2000)
Pipes and power	Risk/hazard analysis required if within 3-mile radius of electrical transmission lines rated at 115 kV or higher, oil or petroleum products transmission lines and storage facilities, hazardous chemical pipelines, etc.	GA	A Guide to School Site Selection (2003); Georgia Compilation of Rules and Regulations, Department of Education, School Facilities and Capital Outlay Management, section 160-6-5-.16 (2001)

(continued on next page)

Table 1. Comparison of Selected States' School Siting Policies (*continued*)

Category	Regulation	State	Source
Pollution	Must consult with air quality management agencies if hazardous air emissions are within ¼ mile of site; must make written finding to acquire site presently zoned for agricultural production; if site is within 2,000 ft. of significant disposal of hazardous waste site school district must contact Dept. of Toxic Substances Control for determination of regulatory status	CA	California Education Code Sections 17072.12, 17072.13, 17072.18, 17210–17215.5, 17251, and 17268 (2001); California Code of Regulations, Title 5 Education, Chapter 13 School Facilities and Equipment, Subchapter 1 School Housing Sections 14001–14012 (2000)
Pollution	Site should not be located in areas zoned for commercial or industrial development; risk/hazard analysis if site is within 3-mile radius of industrial/manufacturing facilities that meet certain conditions	GA	A Guide to School Site Selection (2003); Georgia Compilation of Rules and Regulations, Department of Education, School Facilities and Capital Outlay Management, section 160-6-5-.16 (2001)
Pollution	Not within 500 ft. of a stable or barn for horses, mules, cattle, or used for breeding or any noise-making industry	IN	Indiana Code Section 16-41-21-6, Prohibited Sites; waiver (1993)
Pollution	Must be free of odors, dust, dirt, noise, and smoke from factories; stockyards; railroads; mills; or agricultural, chemical, or aerial spraying, etc.	MS	Mississippi Department of Education, Division of School Building, Evaluation of Proposed School Sites (2004)
Prior land use	Not on current/former hazardous waste disposal site or solid waste disposal site unless site was a former solid waste site and all wastes have been removed	CA	California Education Code Sections 17072.12, 17072.13, 17072.18, 17210–17215.5, 17251, and 17268 (2001)
Prior land use	Analyze climate conditions to identify upwind contamination sources; evaluate ambient air quality and prepare a map of surrounding areas to show existing and potential contamination sources; investigate history of activities and business practices to avoid responsibility and liability for contamination clean up	WA	School Indoor Air Quality Best Management Practices Manual (2003); Superintendent of Public Instruction, School Facilities Manual, Revised 4th Edition, Chapter 5 Site Selection (March 2000)
Natural hazards	No site with radon potential unless project plan incorporates radon mitigation techniques	CT	Connecticut General Statutes Section 10-291, as amended by Section 6 of Public Act No. 03-220 (July 9, 2003)
Natural hazards	Risk/hazard analysis required if proposed site is within 3-mile radius of lakes, rivers, dams, reservoirs, or other bodies of water, within 100-year flood plain, or dam breach zone	GA	A Guide to School Site Selection (2003); Georgia Compilation of Rules and Regulations, Department of Education, School Facilities, and Capital Outlay Management, section 160-6-5-.16 (2001)

Railroads

About 1.8 million carloads of hazardous substances are shipped annually by rail in the United States. Of these carloads, approximately 105,000 contain toxic substances such as chlorine, anhydrous ammonia, and hydrochloric acid (Learn et al. 2007). Although collisions involving trains are relatively rare, when they occur they can cause severe health consequences. For example, a 2005 train collision in Graniteville, South Carolina, released 11,500 gallons of chlorine gas, causing nine deaths and resulting in over five hundred people seeking medical attention (Learn et al. 2007). In North Carolina there are over 3,300 miles of train tracks that are actively used to carry freight. These tracks carry over one hundred million tons of freight per year, including fourteen million tons of chemicals (NCDOT 2001). Since 2000, there have been 254 collisions involving trains in the state, or about 32 per year, excluding highway-rail collisions. Most (169) were from derailments (Federal Railroad Administration 2008).

We obtained the most current GIS database of railroads in North Carolina from "NCo-nemap," which is the official North Carolina GIS data source. The roads and railroads were georeferenced in this database by the United States and NCDOT using a process that relies on digital imagery as the basis for georeferencing. This process yielded lines that accurately represent the centerline of roads and railroads.

Floodplains

Floodplains were included in our study not because they pose an immediate threat to the health and safety of schoolchildren but because we wanted to assess whether schools are vulnerable to flooding—that is, if the schools had been built in floodplains, particularly since they often serve as emergency shelters during disasters. Flooding is the nation's most common natural hazard and the most prevalent in North Carolina. We obtained the most current GIS floodplain database from the Federal Emergency Management Agency (FEMA). At the time of our analysis, this database contained the one hundred–year and five hundred–year floodplains for only two-thirds of the counties in North Carolina, as FEMA was in the process of updating its digital floodplain maps for the state. The coverage of this GIS database is limited to the central and eastern portions of the state but excludes the western counties, including the cities of Charlotte and Asheville. Thus floodplain data for nearly 20 percent of schools were not included in our analysis.

Hog Farms

There are over three thousand industrial hog farms—confined animal feeding operations or CAFOs—in the state. We obtained geospatial data for hog farms in North Carolina from the North Carolina Center for Geographic Information and Analysis (CGIA). This data set represents the center point of hog waste lagoons associated with intensive swine operations in North Carolina. The data set was produced by CGIA in 2003 with the use of digital ortho-photography to verify and update a 1999 North Carolina Department of Natural Resources GIS layer that identified intensive swine operations. Since this data set is seven years old and the hog industry has expanded since then, it likely underestimates the actual number of hog waste lagoons in the state.

Potentially Hazardous Facilities

"Potentially hazardous facilities" refers to any facility, private or public, that produces, stores, or releases one or more of four Environmental Protection Agency (EPA)–designated types of pollution: hazardous waste, toxic substances, air pollution, and wastewater. These facilities include a wide array of entities ranging from power plants, all variety of manufacturing facilities including chemical manufacturers and pulp mills, commercial- and service-oriented businesses, and municipal services such as wastewater treatment plants. Many innocuous facilities are also included in this database such as churches, schools (chemistry labs), and pools (chlorine). We obtained data on potentially hazardous facilities directly from the EPA's unified Envirofacts database.[3]

Under hazardous wastes, the Envirofacts database includes information on brownfield and Superfund sites as well as facilities that treat, store, or dispose of hazardous wastes. For toxic substances, the database includes an inventory, called the Toxic Release Inventory (TRI), which contains detailed information on every facility that uses, manufactures, treats, or transports at least one of 650 chemicals deemed to be toxic by the EPA. Manufacturers and users of these chemicals are required to report the types and quantities of chemicals used or stored on-site to state and local governments, which in turn submit that information to the EPA. The information provided on each facility includes the name of each TRI chemical on the premises but lacks information on the quantity of each chemical.

Based on our review of the literature, industries or facilities that were not likely to pose a major threat to the health and safety of schoolchildren were excluded. These industries include water supply, general services, schools, hospitals, mobile home construction, hotels, grocery stores, places of worship, and general municipal services other than garbage collection. Again, our main focus was on the types of facilities commonly addressed in state policies on school siting and that were at least mentioned in North Carolina's school facility planning guidelines. Determining the exact number of facilities excluded from our analysis is difficult, as each facility often has multiple entries in the Envirofacts database—one for each class of EPA-designated pollution it has a permit to discharge or transport.

METHODS

Our analysis involved six main steps: (1) mapping all public schools in North Carolina, (2) mapping environmental hazards, (3) creating buffers around each of the hazards and identifying schools that were located within the buffers, (4) determining whether racial minorities disproportionately attend schools in close proximity to environmental hazards, (5) assessing the adequacy of North Carolina's policies for siting schools, and (6) preparing case studies of potential exposure of schoolchildren to contaminants from nearby industrial facilities. Each of these steps is described in the following sections.

Identifying and Mapping Schools

There are some 2,551 public schools and 667 private schools in North Carolina, as of the 2008–9 school year, according to the North Carolina CGIA. Using a GIS database obtained from CGIA, we mapped the location of every public school (including charter schools) in the state. We excluded private schools from our analysis since the state's guidelines for siting schools apply only to public schools. In addition to school location, we obtained a description of the demographic makeup for each school from the North Carolina Department of Public Instruction (NCDPI) and joined this data to the database we received from CGIA.

To assess the accuracy of the public schools data set, we randomly selected a sample of one hundred public schools in North Carolina and determined whether the corresponding georeferenced points were accurately placed. To accomplish this, we imported an aerial image mosaic of North Carolina from the ArcGIS online database and overlaid it on top of the sample of georeferenced school points. We then visually identified the extent to which these points accurately represented the actual location of the schools. That is, using the GIS along with aerial photographs from Google Earth, we measured the distance from the georeferenced point of each school to the nearest edge of the main school building and to the building's center point.

The distance from a school's georeferenced point to the nearest face of the main school building ranged from 0 to 1,990 meters (1.18 miles), with a median distance of 105 meters (345 ft.) and a mean of 218 meters (715 ft.). The median distance from a school's georeferenced point to the center of the school's main building was 162 meters (531 ft.), with a mean distance of 335 meters (1,100 ft.). For two-thirds (68) of the 100 schools in the sample, the georeferenced point fell within 150 meters (492 ft.) of the nearest edge of the main school building; 80 were within 300 meters (984 ft.).

With a couple exceptions, the divergence between the actual location of schools and their respective georeferenced points was expected, as many of these schools' georeferenced points were created in the GIS by geocoding, which uses a school's street address to place a point, often at the edge of a property and along a street.

Identifying and Mapping Environmental Hazards

We identified the location of potential environmental hazards in the state, including major roads, floodplains, railroads, confined animal feeding operations (hog farms), and potentially hazardous facilities (e.g., industrial sites, Superfund sites, etc.), and we incorporated these locations into our GIS database.

We imported the Envirofacts database into the GIS using the geospatial information (latitude and longitude) that EPA provides as a field for the majority of facilities within the

Table 2. Actual Distance of Schools from Georeferenced Point (distances in meters)

From georeferenced point to:	*Range*	*Median*	*Mean*
Center of main school building	0–2,005	162	335
Nearest edge of school building	0–1,990	105	218

database. The EPA geocoded the addresses for each facility in the database. This method produced georeferenced point data for around two-thirds of facilities within the database. We were unable to obtain point data for the remaining facilities; as a result, about a third of the facilities in Envirofacts were not geographically represented and consequently were excluded from our GIS analysis.

Using the same methodology for ground truthing the sample of one hundred public schools, we selected a random sample of forty facilities from the Envirofacts database and assessed the extent to which these facilities were georeferenced accurately. Of the forty facilities we selected, thirty-two (80 percent) were accurately represented by a georeferenced point. Using the GIS and aerial photographs, we were unable to find a physical structure or building for eight of the facilities. It appears that the attributed address was wrong in the database or the physical building no longer exists. The average and median distances from the center of the facilities to their georeferenced point in our sample was 105 and 71 meters (115 and 78 yards), respectively, excluding the eight missing facilities. The average and median distance from the nearest building edge or face of these facilities to their georeferenced points in our sample is considerably less at 72 and 49 meters (79 and 54 yards), respectively.

Creating Buffers

With the aid of the GIS, we generated buffers around each of the environmental hazards included in our analysis and identified schools that fell within these defined buffer zones. The size of the buffers varied depending on the type of hazard, for example, 150 meters for major roads and one mile for hog farms (table 3).

The buffer sizes selected were based primarily on previous studies. For example, several studies have found that concentrations of pollutants in vehicular exhaust are high near roadways but decline markedly within 150 to 300 meters (164 to 328 yards) (McConnell et al. 2006; Gilbert et al. 2003; Zhu et al. 2002). For our analysis, we selected a buffer size of 150 and 300 meters from busy roads. In addition, while some studies (CHEJ 2002) of the proximity of schools to potentially hazardous facilities used a half mile as a buffer, we selected a more conservative one-eighth and one-quarter mile for our analysis, since we do not know the hazard profile of these facilities and wanted to avoid overstating the potential risk. Also, in most urban areas, it would be difficult to find a school that was not within a half mile of such a facility.

Table 3. Type of Environmental Hazard and Buffer Size

Type of hazard	Buffer size A	Buffer size B
Major road	150 m	300 m
Hazardous waste facility	⅛ mi.	¼ mi.
Flooding	Within 100-year flood zone	—
Railroad	⅛ mi.	¼ mi.
Hog waste lagoon	1 mi.	2 mi.

For railroads, we chose buffers of one-eighth and one-quarter miles—the same as for potentially hazardous facilities. While diesel exhaust from locomotives can pose a health hazard, particularly at rail yards, the more serious threat is from spills of hazardous chemicals caused by rail collisions or derailments. We chose to treat freight trains as, in essence, rolling industrial facilities that store hazardous chemicals. Approximately 81 percent of hazardous substance releases from rail events occurred in areas with residences within one-quarter mile (MMWR 2007). Following a rail accident that involves the release of hazardous materials, authorities often order an evacuation of a one-mile radius area from the site of the release.

For CAFOs, we chose buffer zones of one and two miles based on previous studies showing an increased risk of breathing difficulties within a few miles of such facilities (Mirabelli et al. 2006) and in consideration of the common practice of spraying hog waste into the air to disperse it over greater areas. Finally, we identified schools located within the one hundred–year floodplain.

A few issues complicated this buffer analysis. The location of the majority of schools and all facilities was determined through geocoding, which is based on an interpolation of street numbers along street segments. The resulting points are often located near an adjacent road far from a particular school or industrial building. This issue is compounded by the fact that most school properties in North Carolina, as well as many industrial facilities, occupy twenty acres or more and buildings are typically set back from adjacent roads. As a result, schools that appear to lie within one of our defined buffers might actually fall outside a buffer and vice versa. Many of the buffers used in this study are a quarter mile or less and some are as small as 150 meters, so the geospatial accuracy of schools and hazardous facilities could alter the results of this study.

In an attempt verify the extent to which geocoding issues could affect the results of this study, we went back to our random sample of one hundred schools and, using GIS and aerial photographs, moved the georeferenced point from their original position to the center of each of the schools—that is, from a point along an adjacent street to the center of the main school building. With the aid of the GIS, we analyzed how many schools, with corrected georeferencing, had georeferenced points that fell within a buffer of each type of environmental hazard. For these one hundred schools, we then compared the results of the buffer analysis for the corrected versus uncorrected georeferencing to determine whether there were any differences in the number of schools within the buffers of the various environmental hazards.

The results of this analysis (table 4) show that fewer schools within the corrected sample fell within the buffers of the environmental hazards compared to the schools in the (uncorrected) database, although the differences are rather small. For example, of the one hundred schools with uncorrected georeferencing, thirty-four fell within the one-quarter mile buffer for hazardous facilities, while thirty-two fell within the buffer for the schools with corrected georeferencing. The numbers in table 4 do not add to one hundred, as some schools fell within a single buffer while some fell within multiple buffers.

Determining Whether Minorities Disproportionately Attend Schools Near Environmental Hazards

Minority students comprise 46 percent of the population of students attending public schools in North Carolina, with the highest percentages found in the northeast corner of the state

Table 4. Comparison of Buffer Analysis of Corrected vs. Uncorrected Georeferenced Schools

	Haz facility 1/4 mi.	Major road 150 m	Major road 300 m	Railroad 1/4 mi.	Hog waste lagoon 1 mi.	Hog waste lagoon 2 mi.	Floodplain N/A
Original	34	12	19	18	2	9	2
Corrected	32	8	16	14	1	9	2
Difference	−2	−4	−3	−4	−1	0	0

(Bertie, Halifax, and Hertford counties). We obtained a database from the NCDPI that includes the racial composition of each public school in North Carolina. The DPI uses the following racial categories: white, black, Asian, Hispanic, and American Indian. There is no "other" category. We also obtained data from the DPI on the number of students, by school, receiving free or reduced-price lunch. Eligibility for these types of lunches is often used as an indicator of poverty.

Using the "select by location" function of the GIS, we identified all public schools that were within at least one of our defined buffer zones and all schools that were outside of these buffers. We then calculated the percentage of students that received free and reduced-price lunches for both sets of schools. We duplicated this process to determine the racial profile of schools within and outside of the buffer zones.

Assessing the Adequacy of North Carolina Policies for Siting Schools

We examined policies and guidelines developed by the NCDPI—the agency charged with implementing the state's public school laws and the North Carolina State Board of Education's policies—to determine the standards or guidelines for siting schools, focusing on any guidelines related to environmental hazards. In North Carolina, DPI establishes standards and guidelines for site selection, planning, and educational facilities. We compared these policies to those found in a sample of other states that have adopted school siting policies with specific policies for avoiding environmental hazards. These states were selected to provide a contrast to North Carolina (table 1). We did not analyze all policies of the state, only those developed to guide local school boards in the selection of sites for new schools.

Case Studies to Assess the Potential Exposure at a Sample of Schools

Finally, we prepared four case studies to illustrate the potential threat to schoolchildren due to the proximity of schools to different types of environmental hazards. For the case studies, we interviewed local planners and emergency managers to collect additional data on particular facilities located near schools and to "ground truth" or verify the accuracy of the data from the EPA. For two of the case studies, we used computer-generated maps that depict the projected area of exposure or plume from environmental hazards located near schools. The case studies are located at the end of the chapter.

FINDINGS

Proximity of Schools to Environmental Hazards

Our analysis identified a total of 1,445 public schools—or more than half of the public schools in the state—that fell within the defined buffer zone of at least one environmental hazard (table 5). Note that the numbers in table 3 are not additive because many schools fall within more than one buffer. For example, three chemical manufacturing plants can be found within a quarter mile of Oak Hill Elementary School in High Point, North Carolina, and two railroad lines skirt within 150 meters of the school. A Superfund site lies across the street (see the case study on Oak Hill Elementary School).

Major Roads

For a variety of reasons, local school districts have favored sites near major roads, perhaps because such sites provide easy access for school buses and teachers and parents driving to and from the schools. Not surprisingly, our analysis identified 521 schools (21 percent) within three hundred meters of a major road and 305 schools (12 percent) within 150 meters. This includes fourteen schools within 150 meters of an interstate highway. For example, Zebulon B. Vance High School in Mecklenburg County, North Carolina, sits along I-85, which runs just north of the city of Charlotte. The school lies within 150 meters of the interstate highway, which carries an estimated 100,000-plus vehicles (cars and trucks) per day (fig. 1). The school's running track is a mere fifty meters (fifty-five yards) from the interstate. Using a larger buffer (a quarter mile), a 2006 study found that a much larger number (about half) of schools in the state were located in close proximity to a major road (EDF 2006).

Potentially Hazardous Facilities

Of all the environmental hazards included in our analysis, potentially hazardous facilities were the ones most frequently found in close proximity to public schools: 891 schools (35 percent) in North Carolina are located within a quarter mile of one of these facilities. This includes

Table 5. Type of Threat, Buffer Size, and Number of Schools Threatened

Type of threat	*Buffer size*	*No. of schools*
Major roads	150 m	305
Major roads	300 m	521
Potentially hazardous facility	⅛ mi.	397
Potentially hazardous facility	¼ mi.	891
Flooding	100-year flood zone	53
Railroad	⅛ mi.	212
Railroad	¼ mi.	490
Hog farm (CAFO)	1 mi.	79
Hog farm (CAFO)	2 mi.	258

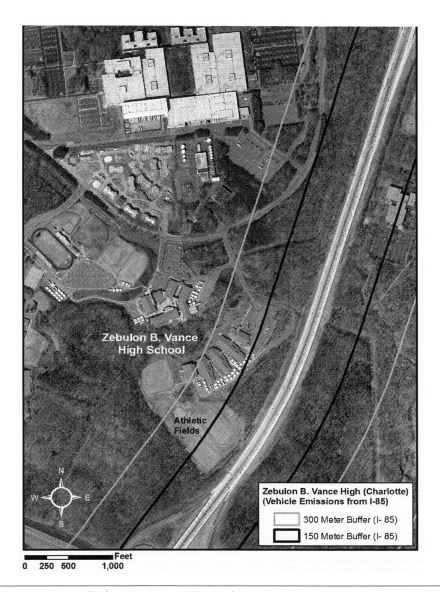

Figure 1. Zebulon B. Vance High School: Proximity to Major Road

thirty-seven schools within 300 meters of a Superfund site and sixteen schools within 150 meters. There are some 884 Superfund sites in North Carolina, thirty-one of which are on the National Priorities List (U.S. EPA 2008).[4]

Railroads

We identified 490 schools within a quarter mile of a railroad and 212 within one-eighth of a mile. While incidents in which hazardous materials are released are uncommon, there have been 254 collisions involving trains in North Carolina since 2000, or about thirty-two per year. This excludes highway-rail collisions. Most (169) were from derailments (Federal

Railroad Administration 2008). North Carolina has no standard or guidelines establishing a minimum setback distance from railroads.

Industrial Hog Facilities

We identified 258 schools within two miles of a CAFO and seventy-nine within one mile. Most of these facilities are clustered in the eastern and south central parts of the state, where the hog industry is concentrated. Surprisingly, despite the abundance of hog farms in the state and recent studies (Mirabelli et al. 2006) suggesting a link between proximity to hog farms and respiratory illnesses, DPI has not adopted any standards or guidelines for building schools a safe distance from these farms.

Floodplains

In the central and eastern parts of the state, some fifty-three schools were built in the one hundred–year flood zone. Since the data on floodplains was not available for the entire state, we have most likely underestimated the total number of schools vulnerable to flooding. It is unclear whether these schools serve as emergency shelters. Locating schools in the floodplain puts buildings at risk of damage but likely poses little risk to students, unless the schools are in an area subject to flash floods.

Environmental Hazards and Inequality

Our analysis suggests that poor and minority students are more likely to attend a school located within one of our environmental hazard buffers. With respect to poverty, on average, 391,458 or 54 percent of students who attended a school within a buffer receive free or reduced- price lunch compared to 48.5 percent of students who attend schools outside of all buffers (table 6). Our findings were statistically significant.[5]

With respect to race, we found that the 1,325 schools located unsafely close to an environmental hazard enroll a total of 727,965 students, about 50 percent of which are minority. By comparison, of the 1,057 schools we found to be located at a safe distance from environmental hazards, only 43.7 percent of students are considered minority (table 7).[6] Unfortunately, data on race was not available for all schools, so the number of schools and associated students were lower when analyzing race (as opposed to poverty).

Adequacy of State Policies and Guidelines on School Siting

According to the DPI's 2003 publication, *School Facilities Guidelines*, site evaluation involves factors such as size, access, traffic, soil conditions, plant life, utilities, security, and cost. The state's policies specifically address four environmental hazards: traffic and roads, industry and manufacturing, topography, and electric power transmission lines. However, most of the guidelines for these hazards use language that is advisory or suggestive rather than mandatory (table 7). For example, local school officials are advised to avoid high traffic areas and noise pollution when selecting a school site. The guidelines are explicit only when it comes to setback distances from power transmission lines. With few exceptions, the guidelines are not sufficiently explicit to offer measurable ways for local school planners to apply them. Lastly, there is no mention of hog waste lagoons, despite the presence of over three thousand waste lagoons and ten million hogs in the state.

Compared to most other states that have adopted policies or guidelines on school siting, North Carolina lacks specific standards for siting schools a safe distance from facilities such as major roads, factories, and railroads. Also, given the number of CAFOs in the state and the threat they pose to public health, it is surprising that North Carolina school siting guidelines are silent on this issue.

Table 6. Schools with Students on Free or Reduced-Price Lunch and Location In/Out of Buffers

	All schools	*Schools within a buffer*	*Schools outside a buffer*
Total number of schools	2,551	1,445	1,107
Mean % of students receiving free or reduced price lunches	51.9	54.4	48.5

Table 7. Nonwhite Student Populations and Location In/Out of Buffers

	All schools	*Schools within a buffer*	*Schools outside a buffer*
Total number of schools	2,382	1,325	1,057
Mean % nonwhite students	47.2	50.0	43.7

Table 8. North Carolina School Facility Planning Guidelines

Type	*Specific guidelines*		
Traffic and roads	Avoid high traffic areas	Avoid locations near large work forces that create heavy traffic	
Industry and manufacturing	Avoid noise pollution	Avoid odor, dust, hazardous materials, or hazardous byproducts and discharges	Reduce potential hazards from industrial accidents
Topography	Allow for natural flow of gravity	Check for wetlands and floodplains	Purchase additional acreage to account for areas that cannot be built upon
Electric transmission lines	100 ft. from edge of easement for 100–110 kV line	150 ft. from edge of easement for a 220–30 kV line	250 ft. from edge of easement for 345 kV line

CONCLUSION

Our study found that 1,445 public schools in North Carolina—nearly half of all schools in the state—are in close proximity to a potential environmental hazard. Our analysis excluded roughly one-third of facilities that are in the EPA's Envirofacts database but lack geocoding. Thus our analysis likely underestimates the number of environmental hazards located near public schools. Unfortunately, the Envirofacts data set does not include information about the size of facilities or the amount or type of pollution emitted, so we were unable to determine whether larger or more polluting facilities were omitted. Furthermore, determining the exact number of facilities excluded from our analysis was difficult, as each facility often has multiple entries in the Envirofacts database—one for each class of EPA-designated pollution it has a permit to discharge or transport.

Our analysis also shows that the geocoding for schools and potentially hazardous facilities can be imprecise. This imprecision can work both ways. For example, we may have included some schools that actually fell outside the buffer of an environmental hazard and excluded others that actually were within the buffer. Our assessment of the accuracy of the geocoding of schools and Envirofacts facilities (using a random sample of one hundred schools and forty Envirofacts facilities), suggests that the imprecision does not appear to have had a major effect on our results: after correcting the georeferencing for the sample of one hundred schools, fifty-three were found to occur within the buffer of at least one of the five environmental hazards. This was consistent with our overall finding of 1,445 out of 2,551 schools falling within a buffer. Ideally, we would have ground truthed every school and Envirofacts facility before conducting the buffer analysis, but we did not have the resources to do that.

Our study supports findings from other researchers who showed that environmental hazards are disproportionately located near schools with a higher percentage of minority or poor students. The study raises questions about the adequacy of state policies guiding local school boards in selecting sites for schools and suggests that some schools were allowed to be constructed too close to environmental hazards and some potential hazards were allowed to be built too close to schools. In many cases, the industrial facilities were built over forty years ago, when the risks to children's health were not as well known. While proximity does not prove that children are at risk (we did not conduct an exposure analysis for the schools we identified nor assess whether the level of exposure is sufficient to cause adverse health impacts), the study nevertheless begs the question, how close is too close? Clearly, some states have found it necessary or prudent to establish minimum setbacks for certain hazards. The precautionary principle would suggest that, given scientific uncertainty about the health risks posed by certain environmental hazards, North Carolina should establish school siting standards sufficient to ensure that schools are kept a safe distance from potential hazards.

At the national level, the EPA is in the process of developing school siting guidelines. The difficulty with national guidelines is that there is no "one size fits all." What works in North Carolina or Arkansas may not work in California or New Jersey. The challenge, of course, even within a single state, is developing standards that apply to all areas: urban, suburban, and rural. Minimum setbacks from certain environmental hazards in rural or suburban areas might not make sense for urban areas. In many cities, school districts would be hard-pressed to find a site that is not within three hundred meters or one-quarter mile of a major road or a small industrial facility. Still, local school boards need simple, affordable, accessible tools to help them make informed decisions about where to locate schools.

Local governments have a role to play as well. At least in North Carolina, local school boards lack the authority to zone land. Thus even if a school board selects a site free from environmental hazards, there is no guarantee that nearby land won't be zoned for industrial development in the future, and facilities that may pose a health threat to schoolchildren will end up locating too close to a school.

Further research is needed in a number of areas. First, it is unclear whether schools were built next to an environmental hazard or vice versa. It may be that more attention should be paid to local land use policies—for example, zoning—to prevent environmental hazards from locating too close to schools.

Second, many smaller hazardous facilities were excluded from our analysis, such as electroplating plants, auto body welding shops, dry cleaners, and waste transfer stations that, unlike TRI facilities, typically are not required to register with the federal government. Yet in many communities, these are the most egregious environmental offenders and could pose a threat to the health and safety of children in nearby schools.

Third, we looked only at the proximity of schools to environmental hazards, not actual exposure. Further study is needed to examine the links between proximity and exposure, particularly for schools facing multiple hazards. Also, for purposes of mapping and identifying facilities within defined buffer areas, we treated all potentially noxious facilities as equal, whereas in reality, the type and amounts of hazardous or toxic materials released and the level of exposure vary considerably from one facility to another. Moreover, using the center point of schools or the building footprint, as opposed to streets adjacent to the school property, would improve the accuracy of the GIS analysis.

Lastly, our study found that minority or low-income students disproportionately are located in close proximity to an environmental hazard. The reasons for this are surely innumerable, though more research could perhaps illuminate the key factors behind this inequality.

ACKNOWLEDGMENTS

This report was made possible by a generous grant from the Wallace Genetic Foundation. We would like to thank Tessa Lee, Dylan McDonnell, and Zoe Hampstead at the University of North Carolina Institute for the Environment for their assistance with the report.

CASE STUDIES

The case studies were designed to illustrate, in greater detail, the kinds of potential hazards faced by schoolchildren attending schools in North Carolina that are located in close proximity to one or more environmental hazards. The case studies include a demographic profile of the school and an assessment of the nature and extent of the potential threat.

For two of the case studies—Jamestown Elementary School and Canton Elementary and Middle Schools—we used a software package called CAMEO (Computer-Aided Management of Emergency Operations), developed by the EPA, to assess the potential exposure of schoolchildren to a release of hazardous or toxic materials from a certain class of environmental hazards—TRI facilities. We used TRI data for this analysis because it is the only easily attainable database, available at the state level, with detailed information on facilities with potentially hazardous chemicals. Other data sets, such as Tier 2[7] data, often require lengthy Freedom of Information Act (FOIA) requests and are only available at the county level. The 650 chemicals on the TRI only account for a small subset of hazardous chemicals that are present at facilities.

CAMEO is designed to manage and model the risk profile of hazardous chemicals. It is used by many emergency managers to assess the level of risk to citizens' health and safety from chemicals stored at industrial facilities. The vast majority of the chemicals on the TRI can easily be modeled with the aid of CAMEO.

CAMEO includes a chemical database of over six thousand hazardous chemicals that are integrated into the modeling of chemical releases from a particular site. Aloha, a component of CAMEO, is an atmospheric air-dispersion model used for evaluating releases of hazardous chemicals. The outputs from Aloha can be graphically represented in the form of a cloud footprint that geographically depicts the projected impact of the chemical release on adjoining areas. Each cloud footprint comprises three zones that represent relative levels of concern ranging from low to high. When modeling chemical spills, each zone is accompanied by a projected concentration of the chemical in the air column. When modeling the explosion of chemicals, each zone represents a possible direct health effect on individuals if exposed for sixty seconds to the heat generated from the explosion, including the potential for pain, second-degree burns, and death. Unfortunately, Aloha is not capable of modeling the resulting blast or shrapnel wave from an explosion of a chemical, which can be equally if not more dangerous than the thermal wave.

Within Aloha, we input the midpoint of the maximum yearly quantity estimates (calculated for each RSEI range) for every hazardous TRI chemical at the facilities we identified in our analyses. We then modeled either a catastrophic release of these chemicals or a catastrophic explosion in instances where chemicals were flammable. Next, we generated a cloud footprint for each chemical. With the aid of the GIS, we overlaid these cloud footprints over aerial images of the adjacent schools. This allowed us to visually assess whether our sample of schools was potentially at risk in the event of a chemical spill or explosion (fig. 1).

Case Study 1

Oak Hill Elementary School
320 Wrightenberry St.
High Point, NC 27260

Student Demographic Profile

Number of students	377
Racial/ethnic composition (%)	
White	15
Minority	85
Students on free or reduced-price lunch (%)	88

Introduction

Oak Hill Elementary School is located in High Point, North Carolina. Most of the land in the immediate vicinity of the school (within a quarter mile) is industrial: 64.8 percent is currently zoned heavy industrial and 17.8 percent is zoned light industrial (fig. A1). Oak Hill

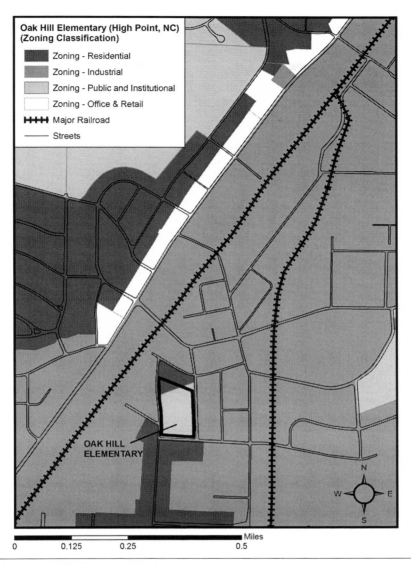

Figure A1. Zoning Near Oak Hill Elementary School

Elementary is in close proximity to several industrial facilities as well as active railways that transport potentially hazardous materials. The school, built in 1960, predates most of the industrial facilities.

Rail transport has been a fixture in High Point since the mid-1800s. Currently, an estimated thirty freight trains pass through the town each day (Maheras 2007). Oak Hill Elementary is located between two active railways, each less than a quarter mile from the school, which transport industrial raw material and finished products. To the east of the school is the High Point Thomasville and Denton Railroad, operated by CSX Transportation. To the west is a line owned by the North Carolina Railroad Company that accommodates both freight (Norfolk-Southern) and passenger (Amtrak) traffic.

Nearby Oak Hill Elementary are seven industrial facilities with potentially hazardous inputs or byproducts (fig. A2). The closest (one-eighth of a mile away) industrial facility is Hexicon Specialty Chemicals, built in 1976. This facility handles hazardous waste and specializes in adhesives and sealants for industrial applications. It is listed on the TRI and has historically emitted formaldehyde and methanol.

Another company, Marlowe Van Loan Corporation, operates two facilities within a quarter mile from the school. One is included in the Envirofacts database by virtue of a National Pollution Discharge Elimination System (NPDES) permit (expired in 2000), while the other manufactures industrial chemicals and is included in the TRI. The latter facility was built in 1989.

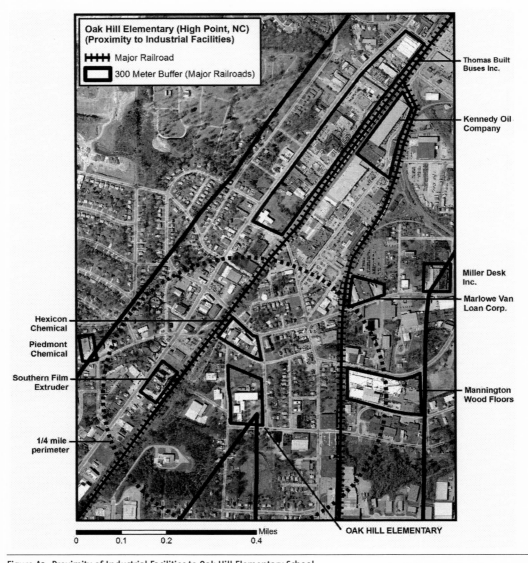

Figure A2. Proximity of Industrial Facilities to Oak Hill Elementary School

Other facilities near the school include Mannington Wood Floors Company, Thomas Built Buses Inc., Piedmont Chemicals, Snyder Paper Corporation, Kennedy Oil Company, and Novachem Corporation. The Kennedy Oil Company, located roughly two-thirds of a mile from Oak Hill Elementary, is listed in the TRI as an emitter of the gasoline additive methyl tertiary butyl ether (MTBE). North Carolina instituted a partial ban on MTBE in 1999 after identifying it as a probable carcinogen. The statewide ban has since become complete as of January 1, 2008 (North Carolina General Statutes § 119–26.3). Piedmont Chemicals, located approximately a half mile from Oak Hill Elementary, is listed on the TRI as an emitter of chemicals into the air and also handles hazardous materials. Built in 1969, the facility made news in 2002 when employees were "evacuated after a chemical-filled drum released a small cloud of vapor," but fortunately, the spill from the drum of acrylic acid and water caused no injuries (*Greensboro News and Record* 2002)

Oak Hill Elementary is an example of where the absence of strong state policies along with lax local regulations allowed several industrial facilities to locate close to the school. The presence of industrial facilities as well as the two rail lines could pose a risk to the health and safety of children attending the school. The school was built in 1960, and many of the industries came along afterward. Were the school to be built today, it is unlikely that it would be located so close to these hazardous industries.

Case Study 2

Lufkin Road Middle School
1002 Lufkin Rd.
Apex, NC 27539

Student Demographic Profile

Number of students	1,025
Racial/ethnic composition (%)	
White	70
Minority	30
Students on free or reduced-price lunch (%)	17

Introduction

Lufkin Road Middle School is located in Apex, North Carolina, within the Wake County Public School District. Based on data from the 1990 and 2000 Decennial Census, Wake County ranked first in North Carolina and twenty-second nationwide in population growth (WCPSS 2005). Enrollment in the Wake County school system grew from 95,000 in 2000 to 134,000 in 2009. This rapid growth has strained the public school system.

In response to this rapid growth, the school system has looked for creative ways to increase its capacity for students, such as adaptive reuse of commercial or industrial buildings. Adaptive reuse schools can provide useable classroom space on a much shorter time horizon than constructing a new facility from the ground up.

Lufkin Road Middle School was constructed in 1998 as an adaptive reuse of a building that had been the home of the American Sterilizer Company. At the time, a typical school in Wake County took roughly two and a half years to complete: twelve months for design and administrative approvals and eighteen months for construction (Spector 2003). Lufkin Road Middle School was brought on line in significantly less time—three months for the design, approval, and bidding processes and only six months for construction.

When the American Sterilizer property was being considered, there were concerns about siting a school within an established industrial area. The twenty-four-acre tract that eventually became Lufkin Road Middle School was located between two facilities that used hazardous chemicals. The vast majority of the quarter-mile area surrounding the school is currently zoned for light industrial uses (fig. B1).

These concerns were not without merit. On the evening of October 5, 2006, an explosion and subsequent fire destroyed a warehouse in Apex owned by EQ Industrial Services and forced the evacuation of roughly four thousand residents. The evacuation area included Lufkin Middle School and Apex Middle School, but school was not in session at the time of the explosion. The EQ facility had been used to store hazardous waste since 1987 and at the time of the explosion stored chemicals such as sulfur, chlorine, polychlorinated biphenyls, and pesticides (WRAL 2007). When the facility opened, it was located on the fringes of town near an asphalt plant, but at the time of the explosion, it was located less than a half mile from

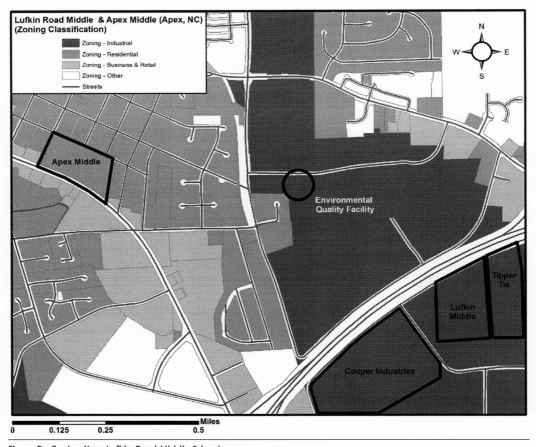

Figure B1. Zoning Near Lufkin Road Middle School

Lufkin Middle School (fig. B1). The site is currently included on the U.S. EPA Superfund list but is not part of the National Priorities List. The EQ Industrial Services fire led the state to enact more stringent regulations of hazardous waste storage facilities—measures that were signed into law in June 2007 (Bonner 2007).

The GIS buffer-proximity analysis conducted as part of this study identified highway and industrial threats in the vicinity of Lufkin Middle School, as well as a CSX-owned railway located approximately half a mile to the west of the school (fig. B2). U.S. 1 lies only seventy-five meters (eighty-two yards) from the school. The stretch of the highway next to the school had an average annual daily traffic (AADT) volume of 18,000 to 41,000 vehicles in 2005. The North Carolina Department of Transportation uses AADT to measure traffic volume along state-maintained highways, and it represents the expected number of vehicles, on average, passing a given point within a twenty-four-hour period. The intersection of Lufkin Road and NC 55 (E. Williams Street) had a 2005 AADT of 36,000 to 38,000 vehicles per day, and the intersection of Lufkin Road and Ten Ten Road (SR 1010) had a 2005 AADT of 18,000 to 24,000 vehicles per day.

Lufkin Road Middle School is an example of a successful adaptive reuse project, one that creatively used vacant industrial property to bring a new school on line quickly to meet the rapidly growing demand for new space. However, it is also a cautionary tale about the potential risks of locating a school in an industrial area, especially one that is so close to a major road. Students at the school could be at risk of exposure from the exhaust of up to 41,000 vehicles per day.

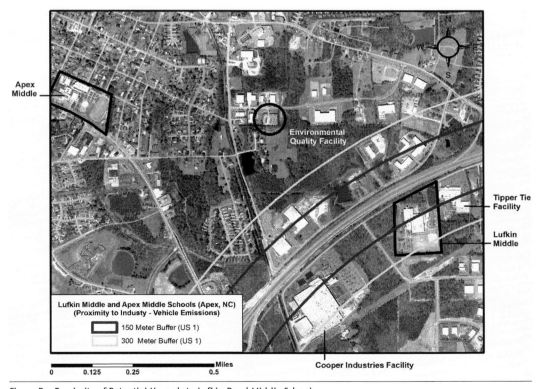

Figure B2. Proximity of Potential Hazards to Lufkin Road Middle School

Case Study 3

Canton Middle School
60 Penland St.
Canton, NC 28716

Student Demographic Profile

Number of students	563
Racial/ethnic composition (%)	
White	94
Black	2
Other	4
Students on free or reduced-price lunch (%)	48

Pisgah High School
1 Black Bear Dr.
Canton, NC 28716

Student Demographic Profile

Number of students	1,001
Racial/ethnic composition (%)	
White	94
Black	3
Other	3
Students on free or reduced-price lunch (%)	37

Introduction

Canton is a small town (population 3,900) located along the banks of the Pigeon River in Haywood County, in the mountains of western North Carolina, approximately twenty miles west of Asheville. Evergreen Packaging is a large pulp paper mill located in the center of Canton, also on the banks of the Pigeon River, with large quantities of potentially hazardous liquids and gases on site, including ammonia, chlorine dioxide, and propane. Both the middle school and high school are located in close proximity to the pulp mill. Canton Middle School lies two-fifths of a mile south of the mill and Pisgah High School is slightly more than a half mile south. While the focus of this study is on public schools, we also included Bethel Christian Academy in our analysis, as it is located adjacent to the mill only a fifth of a mile away.

Although the likelihood is remote, an explosion at the plant that resulted in the release of chlorine dioxide or ammonia could be catastrophic. For years, local (city and county) emergency management officials have played an integral role in addressing the risk associated with the paper mill.

Facility Location Information

Since it opened in 1910, the mill has been the largest employer in town. Because of this, and the fact that the town is small, much of the town has developed around the mill. Also, the mountainous terrain limits where development (including schools) can occur. For all these reasons, the location of the schools in close proximity to the mill is understandable, despite the risks.

Environmental Hazards

Using the RSEI modeling tool, we were able to identify all the chemicals stored on site at the paper mill that are listed on the EPA's TRI as of 2006. Although twenty-two chemicals are listed, it is likely that other chemicals are stored at the mill, since non-TRI chemical inventories are not readily publicized by companies. However, through conversations with local emergency management staff, we gained specific information about two potentially hazardous non-TRI chemicals stored at the mill. First, there are more than one million gallons of propane gas stored in thirty-three tankers in the mill's rail yard. Second, the mill reportedly uses a fuel called black liquor, which is highly reactive and explosive and is stored in amounts greater than five million pounds on site. Of the known chemicals stored at Evergreen Packaging, chlorine dioxide, ammonia, propane, and black liquor pose the greatest risk to students' health and safety.

Ammonia is a colorless gas that is highly corrosive to the mucous membranes of the eyes, nose, and throat and can cause coughing and burns. Exposure to high levels of ammonia gas can cause permanent lung damage and even death. According to the Occupational Safety and Health Administration (OSHA), to avoid any permanent ill effects, the limit for a fifteen-minute exposure to ammonia is thirty-five parts per million (ppm) and twenty-five ppm for an eight-hour exposure. According to the National Institute for Occupational Safety and Health (NIOSH), exposure to ammonia levels greater than or equal to 300 ppm are immediately dangerous to life or health and require special breathing apparatus.

Chlorine dioxide is a powerful oxidizer used as a bleaching agent in the paper industry. It is highly corrosive to the mucous membranes of the eyes, nose, and throat, with an effect similar to that of ozone gas. Both OSHA and NIOSH have set acceptable exposure limits at 0.1 ppm for an eight to ten hour workday at forty hours per week and 0.3 ppm for no more than fifteen minutes. Exposure between 0.1 and 0.25 ppm has been shown to worsen mild respiratory ailments. According to the 2007 Acute Exposure Guideline Levels for Selected Airborne Chemicals by the Board on Environmental Studies and Toxicology (BEST), exposure to chlorine dioxide is lethal at 3 ppm over ten to thirty minutes.

Propane is a highly flammable refined gas widely used as a source of fuel. Although it occurs as a gas at room temperature, it is commonly converted to a liquid in pressurized tanks. According to the National Fire Protection Association, propane has a flammability rating of 4 on a scale of 0 to 4, which qualifies the gas as a severe fire hazard. Propane is prone to vapor

Potentially Hazardous Chemicals at Evergreen Packaging

Chemicals	*Daily Maximum Amount on Site*
Chlorine Dioxide	1 to 9 million lbs.
Formic Acid	100 to 999 million lbs.
Ammonia	10 to 99 thousand lbs.
Methanol	10 to 99 thousand lbs.
Propane (in rail cars)	1 million lbs.
Black Liquor	1 to 10 million lbs.

flashbacks; containers subjected to heat or open flame can result in an explosion and subsequent fire. It is nontoxic but can become an asphyxiant at levels at or greater than the lower flammability limit of propane in air.

Black liquor is a byproduct of the process by which cellulose fibers are extracted from wood pulp in the paper-making process. It is highly alkaline and highly explosive when in contact with water. Because black liquor contains more than half the energy content of the original wood pulp, this byproduct is reprocessed and used as fuel in recovery burners to generate most of the energy needed to power a paper plant. Unfortunately, the software we used was not capable of modeling this chemical, so we do not have a way of assessing the potential impact it would have on the schools and town, should an accident occur at the mill.

Risk to Student Health and Safety

To assess the potential risk to students from these chemicals, we used the GIS along with an EPA chemical air dispersion–modeling program called CAMEO. The model is commonly used by emergency management officials. From our analysis, we identified three chemicals that potentially pose a threat to students' health and safety at some or all the schools in this case study—chlorine dioxide, ammonia, and propane. With respect to black liquor, for which we were unable to generate risk models, local emergency management officials we interviewed stated that black liquor is very safe for use as a fuel, but its explosive potential must be addressed when planning for local emergencies. One local emergency manager said that he considered it a greater concern than the other chemicals stored on site.

According to models generated by CAMEO, there is a significant risk to students' health and safety from a potential catastrophic release of chlorine dioxide at all three schools. According to our analysis, if a storage tank at Evergreen Packaging containing chlorine dioxide was breached significantly, students would be at considerable risk to the resulting plume, provided there is a northeasterly to northwesterly wind. The prevailing winds are predominately from the west, but northern winds are not uncommon in the mountains of North Carolina where the mill is located. The resulting plume would completely engulf all three schools (fig. C1).

The projected concentration of chlorine dioxide at all three schools from the plume would be at least 2.4 ppm. According to OSHA and NIOSH, exposure to this level of chlorine dioxide would have significant impacts on the respiratory system and eyes and could be fatal to healthy individuals if exposure lasts longer than ten minutes. Exposure to this elevated level of chlorine dioxide for shorter durations would likely result in the burning of the respiratory system, eyes, and mucous membranes of the nose, causing significant temporary and possibly permanent reductions in respiratory function. Younger individuals and those with respiratory ailments such as asthma, emphysema, or chronic bronchitis would be adversely affected by such a plume to an even greater degree than healthy persons.

Models generated by CAMEO also reveal a risk to students' health and safety from a catastrophic release of ammonia, but only at the two schools closest to the mill (Bethel Christian and Canton Middle School). According to our analysis, if a storage tank at Evergreen Packaging containing ammonia is significantly breached, students would be at considerable risk to the resulting plume, again provided there is a northeasterly to northwesterly wind. The projected concentration of ammonia at Bethel Christian from the resulting plume would be at least 160 ppm and as high as 1,100 ppm as demonstrated in the map on the following page. Within the highest concentration area, individuals outside could be exposed to

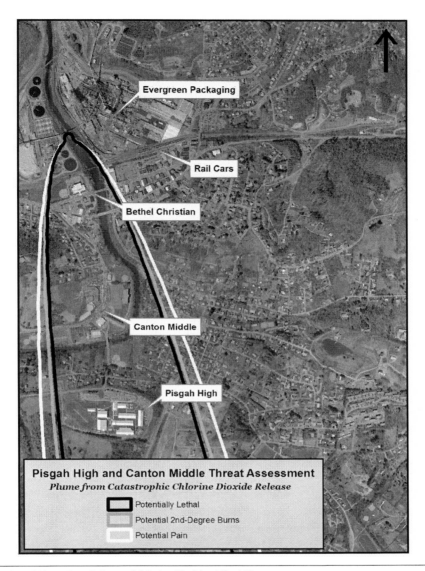

Figure C1. Projected Plume from Release of Chlorine Dioxide at the Mill

approximately 3.7 times the potentially lethal threshold (for a ten-minute exposure) according to NIOSH standards. The projected concentration of ammonia at Canton Middle School from the resulting plume could be at least 160 ppm. At these levels of exposure the effects on students' health are far less critical. Exposure at this level generally tends to result in moderate irritation to the mucous membranes of the eyes, ears, nose, and throat. It is possible that there would be minor skin irritation as well, but the severity would be far less than that experienced closer to the mill at Bethel Christian.

During the course of our research we discovered that Norfolk-Southern Rail Company leases rail space within the Evergreen Packaging rail yard for thirty-three tankers of propane, each holding 33,000 gallons. According to models generated by CAMEO, there is little to no potential adverse effects on students' health and safety from a noncombustible plume resulting from a catastrophic release of propane from these rail cars. The risk in this scenario is reduced because propane dissipates rapidly in the environment and is nontoxic. Models indicate, however, that there is a significant risk to students' health and safety from a catastrophic explosion of propane. According to our analysis, if only a small fraction of these rail cars (eight rail cars or 12.5 percent of all rail cars) were to explode, resulting in complete combustion with 30 percent of propane being consumed in a fireball, students at Bethel Christian and Canton Middle School would be at considerable risk of at least second-degree burns and possibly death if exposed for at least two minutes to the resulting thermal wave (fig. C2). This risk is especially elevated for those caught outside of a building during an explosion.

Interviews with Emergency Management Officials

We interviewed local emergency management officials to get feedback on the output of our models and maps. Emergency management officials stated that our maps were fairly accurate, within limits. The first limit is that the terrain of Canton makes it extremely difficult to determine the exact direction and impact area of a chemical plume, as winds tend to change direction rapidly when moving around mountains and through valleys. The maps that the officials had on hand indicated that the prevailing winds flow west to east, while ours modeled the prevailing winds flowing north to south, since the valley where Canton is located runs along a mostly north-south axis, making it a reasonable assumption that the majority of the chemical would be funneled in this direction.

Regarding the chemicals stored at the mill and the potential risk to children attending adjacent schools, emergency management officials informed us that the assumptions we used for our analysis were reasonable. More specifically, they contended that the scenario we used for a potential propane explosion was plausible, since a primary explosion of just one propane tanker could result in secondary explosions of adjacent rail cars. However, they noted that the greatest threat from such an explosion would be from the resulting shock wave and flying debris. Unfortunately, CAMEO does not have the functionality to model these aspects, so local emergency management suggested that our assessment might be conservative.

Throughout our interviews, local emergency managers reiterated that their cooperative relationship with the mill has greatly benefited the overall preparedness of the town and county. For instance, the county, town, and paper mill jointly developed the comprehensive emergency response plan, which delegates critical responsibilities to all parties, including the mill. This cooperative relationship also has benefited the efforts of the Local Emergency Planning Council (LEPC). LEPCs are mandated by the federal government and required to plan for chemical hazards. In Haywood County, Evergreen Packaging is very involved in the LEPC—the head of environmental health and safety at the mill is the vice chair of the LEPC. This involvement by Evergreen Packaging as an active stakeholder reportedly has improved the effectiveness of the LEPC.

Excellent cooperation also improves emergency response capabilities. In the event of an emergency at Evergreen Packaging, such as an accidental chemical release or explosion, the response strategy (e.g., evacuation) would be jointly determined by the heads of the Haywood County emergency management department, Canton fire department, and Evergreen response team. Evergreen Packaging is involved to such a great degree because the Evergreen

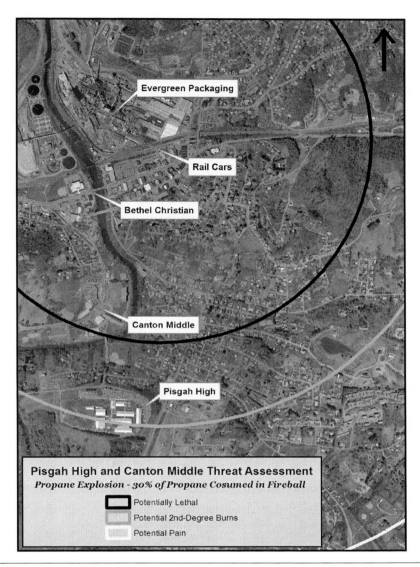

Figure C2. Potential Plume from Explosion of Propane Tanks at the Mill

response team includes four full-time HAZMAT employees that have an expertise in dealing with a wide variety of potential hazards, including hazardous chemical releases and explosions. Local emergency management officials reportedly lack this expertise and knowledge base.

Emergency managers also rely on a network of highly sensitive chemical monitors that surround the mill and are used to detect chemical releases. This network was installed after the attack on the World Trade Center Towers in 2001, when federal funds were made available to emergency management to increase the security around facilities identified as potential terrorist targets. The mill (owned by Blue Ridge Paper at the time) was on this list due to the volume of hazardous chemicals on the premises. Local emergency managers stressed that these chemical monitors are a valuable tool that have increased their ability to quickly detect and respond to hazardous chemical releases.

Case Study 4

Jamestown Elementary
108 Potter Dr.
Jamestown, NC, 27282

Student Demographic Profile

Number of students	541
Racial/ethnic composition (%)	
White	27
Black	52
Other	11
Students on free or reduced-priced lunch (%)	28

Introduction

Jamestown is a small town (population 3,000) in Guilford County, North Carolina. Jamestown Elementary, built in 1960, is situated between the town's residential neighborhood to the north and a small industrial area to the south. Within this industrial area, a quarter mile from the school (fig. D1), is Chemcentral, a chemical manufacturer with large quantities of combustible chemicals including xylene, toluene, and methanol on the premises.

Project History and Site Information

The site where Chemcentral is located was developed in 1957, three years prior to the construction of Jamestown Elementary. Since then, at least five chemical or petroleum companies including Chemcentral (opened in 2005) have operated on this site. The site is zoned for intensive industrial uses. Industrial companies also currently operate on several adjacent parcels south of the school.

Industrial facilities have operated since 1946 on the parcel closest to the school with industrial facilities being developed after the school's construction on the other parcels. Our analysis focuses on Chemcentral as chemical manifests were lacking for these other facilities. Despite the school's proximity to these industrial zones, the majority of land surrounding the school is not zoned for industrial uses but rather as residential land.

Environmental Hazards

Through the use of an EPA program called RSEI, we were able to identify all the chemicals stored at Chemcentral that are on the EPA's TRI as of 2006. This is likely only a fraction of the chemicals used or stored at the facility, as TRI chemicals are a small subset of chemicals used by industrial facilities. Unfortunately, we were not able to obtain information concerning non-TRI chemicals that are used or stored within Chemcentral and adjacent facilities because companies or emergency management officials do not share this information. As a result, our analysis solely considers TRI chemicals, meaning that the potential danger from hazardous chemicals may in fact be greater than we suggest.

Of the TRI chemicals stored at Chemcentral, our analysis indicates that toluene, xylene, and methanol pose the greatest risk to students' health and safety at Jamestown Elementary. Xylene, toluene, and methanol are all colorless, highly flammable liquids with the very low flash points common to explosive chemicals. These chemicals all have a flammability rating of three from the National Fire Protection Association, qualifying them as severe fire hazards. All three chemicals are prone to vapor flashbacks, and containers subjected to heat or open flame can result in an explosion and subsequent fire, which is difficult to extinguish, especially with water. The combustion of xylene, toluene, and methanol produce irritating, corrosive, and toxic gasses, which can cause damage to the mucous membranes and respiratory system. The Emergency Response Guidebook suggests an initial evacuation zone of at least a half mile in all directions from an explosion or fire stemming from a tank containing 9,000 gallons (nearly 65,000 lbs.) of xylene or toluene, which is nearly an order of magnitude less than the 500,000 gallon midpoint volume estimate for both chemicals on hand at Chemcentral. Guilford County Emergency Services officials suggest that an evacuation zone be at least three times larger, or 1.5 miles, if any of these chemicals were to catch fire or explode. Jamestown Elementary School, located only a quarter mile away from Chemcentral, is well within both evacuation zone recommendations.

Risk to Students Health and Safety

To assess the potential risk to students from these chemicals, we used an EPA chemical air dispersion modeling program for chemical plumes and explosions commonly used by emergency management called CAMEO as well as the GIS. From our analysis we identified three chemicals—toluene, xylene, and methanol—that potentially pose a significant threat to students' health at Jamestown Elementary. According to models generated by CAMEO, a noncombustible plume stemming from a catastrophic release of one of these would pose little risk to students as each of these chemicals would dissipate in the environment before reaching the school. On the other hand, there is a significant risk to students' health and safety from a catastrophic explosion of these chemicals. According to our analysis, if a storage tank explodes, with even 30 percent of a chemical being consumed in a fireball, students would be at considerable risk of at least second-degree burns and possibly death if exposed for even two minutes to the resulting thermal wave (see fig. D1). This risk is especially elevated for those caught outside of a building during an explosion. Figure D1 demonstrates the potential risk zone for an explosion of xylene; the risk zones associated with an explosion of toluene and methanol are predicted to be nearly identical in geographic coverage.

In order to validate these findings we presented them to Guilford County Department of Emergency Services. They informed us that the assumptions we used for our analysis were reasonable and that our assessment of risk might be too conservative as CAMEO does not allow for the modeling of multiple chemicals in one scenario. They contend that an explosion considerably larger than the ones we modeled was possible if a primary explosion sparked secondary explosions of other chemicals. Furthermore, CAMEO, like most similar programs, only models the resulting thermal wave of an explosion and not other critical elements such as blast or shrapnel waves, which can be equally dangerous.

During our interview with emergency management, we learned that Guilford County was

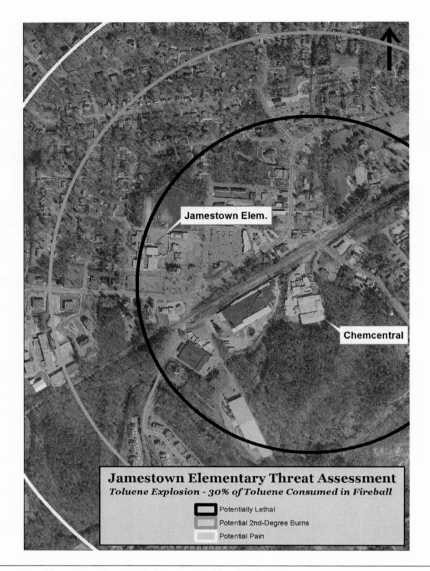

Figure D1. Jamestown Elementary School: Risks from Possible Chemical Explosion

in the process of conducting a risk assessment similar to the one conducted by our study, albeit much more ambitious. Specifically, Guilford County emergency management is embarking on a project to identify critical community facilities including schools and nursing homes that are in close proximity to sources of hazardous chemicals associated mostly with industrial facilities, relying on modeling to determine the potential risk to individuals' health and safety from hazardous chemicals. Since Guilford County Emergency Services has much greater access to the chemical manifests of facilities within the county than we did, their analysis will identify many other chemicals and associated facilities that pose a potential threat to schools. Guilford County suggested that they are ahead of the curve, as most counties still do not conduct assessments this thorough.

NOTES

1. Superfund is the name of the fund established by the Comprehensive Environmental Response, Compensation and Liability Act in 1980 to clean up sites contaminated with hazardous substances as identified by the EPA.

2. Historically, the federal government has played a minor role in school site selection decisions. However, the 2007 federal energy bill (Energy Independence and Security Act of 2007) directs the Environmental Protection Agency (EPA) to develop voluntary guidelines for use by states to help local school districts address environmental hazards when selecting sites for schools. In November 2010, the EPA released its draft school siting guidelines. As of June 2011, final guidelines have not been released.

3. U.S. EPA, Envirofacts, http://www.epa.gov/enviro.

4. The National Priorities List identifies the worst hazardous waste sites in the United States and guides the EPA in deciding which sites warrant additional investigation.

5. It is unlikely that the observed difference between the mean percentage of students receiving free or reduced lunch in school within a buffer and the mean percentage of students attending schools outside of all buffers is strictly due to chance. We used an independent sample t-test to compare the mean percentage of students receiving free or reduced lunch attending schools within a buffer and outside of all buffers. This test is appropriate for a normally distributed interval dependent variable for two independent groups. The t value was -5.3116 with a p value less than 0.001. This p value achieves a traditional level of statistical significance at the 0.05 level.

6. Our numbers indicated that it is unlikely the observed difference between the mean percentage of nonwhite students who attend a school within a buffer and mean percentage of students who attend schools outside of all buffers is strictly due to chance. The t value was -5.5067 with a p value less than 0.001. This p value achieves statistical significance at the 0.05 level.

7. Under the Emergency Planning and Community Right-to-Know Act (EPCRA; Section 312, Public Law 99-499, codified at 42 U.S.C. Section 11022), facilities that store hazardous chemicals above certain thresholds must report the type, amount, and precise location of the chemicals to state and local officials each year. These are called Tier 2 reports. The thresholds for reporting are 10,000 pounds for hazardous chemicals and 500 pounds for extremely hazardous chemicals.

REFERENCES

Amler, S., N. Christopher, T. De Rosa, and M. W. Williams-Johnson. 2003. Risk analysis, uncertainty factors, and the susceptibilities of children. *Human & Ecological Risk Assessment* 9, no. 7:1701-11.

Appatova, Alexandra, Ryan, Patrick, LeMasters, Grace, and Grinshpun, Sergey. 2008. Proximal exposure of public schools and students to major roadways: a nationwide survey. Environmental Planning and Management, 51:5,631-646.

Bonner, Lynn. 2007. State toughens hazardous waste rules. *Raleigh News & Observer*, June 27, 2007.

Environmental Defense Fund (EDF). 2006. *School days & roadways: Protecting North Carolina's school children from automobile pollution.* http://www.edf.org/documents/5255_SchoolDaysRoadways.pdf

Federal Rail Administration, Office of Safety Analysis. 2008. Total train accidents. Washington, DC. http://safetydata.fra.dot.gov/OfficeofSafety/Query/Default.asp?page=stchart.asp.

Fischbach, S. 2005. *Fifty-state survey of school siting laws, regulations, and policies*, Rhode Island Legal Services, Inc. Draft. http://www.childproofing.org.

Gilbert, N. L., S. Woodhouse, D. M. Stieb, J. R. Brook. 2003. Ambient nitrogen dioxide and distance from a major highway. *Science of the Total Environment* 312 (1–3): 43–46.

Green, R. S., S. Smorodinsky, J. J. Kim, R. McLaughlin, and B. Ostro. 2004. Proximity of California public schools to busy roads. *Environmental Health Perspectives* 112 (1): 61–66.

Maheras, N. G. 2007. City's railroad history dates back as far as 1850. *High Point Enterprise*. May 14, 2007, Section A, pg. 2. High Point, North Carolina.

McConnell, R., K. Berhane, L. Yao, M. Jerrett, F. Lurmann, F. Gilliland, N. Künzli, J. Gauderman, E. Avol, D. Thomas, and J. Peters. 2006. Traffic, susceptibility, and childhood asthma. *Environmental Health Perspectives* 114(5): 766–72.

Mirabelli, M., S. Wing, S. Marshall, and T. Wilcosky. 2006. Race, poverty, and potential exposure of middle-school students to air emissions from confined swine feeding operations. *Environmental Health Perspectives* 114 (4): 591–96.

National Center for Education Statistics (NCES). 2007. Digest of Educational Statistics, 2006. Table 3. Enrollment in educational institutions, by level and control of institution: Selected years, 1869–70 through fall 2015. NCES 2007-017. http://nces.ed.gov/programs/digest/d06/tables/dt06_003.asp?referrer=report and Table 83. Number of public school districts and public and private elementary and secondary schools: Selected years, 1869-70 through 2005-06. http://nces.ed.gov/programs/digest/d07/tables/dt07_083.asp

North Carolina Department of Transportation (NCDOT). 2001. North Carolina rail plan 2000. http://www.bytrain.org/quicklinks/reports/railplan2001.pdf.

Spector, Stephen. 2003. Creating schools and strengthening communities through adaptive reuse. *National Clearinghouse for Educational Facilities*, Washington, DC. http://www.ncef.org/pubs/adaptiveuse.pdf

Staff Reports. 2002. "Chemical Cloud Released." Greensboro News and Record, November 13, 2002, page B2. Greensboro, NC.

U.S. Environmental Protection Agency (EPA). 2008. *National priorities list sites in North Carolina.* http://www.epa.gov/superfund/sites/npl/nc.htm#CHATHAM.

Wake County Public School System (WCPSS). 2005. Wake County demographics: growth and diversity. Internal report prepared by Maja Vouk, Director of Demographics, Office of Growth Management, Wake County Public School System, Wake County, North Carolina. May 5, p. 18. http://www.wcpss.net/demographics/reports/Growth2005.pdf.

WRAL News. 2006. Apex mayor: Chemical fire evacuation may last until Saturday morning. October 5.

Zhu, Y., W. C. Hinds, S. Kim, and C. Sioutas. 2002. Concentration and size distribution of ultrafine particles near a major highway. *Journal of the Air & Waste Management Association* 52 (9): 1032–42.

Engaging the Public in Comprehensive Planning and Design for Healthy Schools

ELLEN SHOSHKES

THIS CHAPTER REPORTS ON A PAIR OF NATIONAL SCHOOL DESIGN COMPETITIONS IN New Jersey. The design competitions are for a large new high school in the city of Perth Amboy and for the renovation and expansion of the one-hundred-year-old Robbins Elementary School in a historic neighborhood in Trenton. The overarching goal of these projects was to create a model planning process to engage the public in a comprehensive, efficient design for healthy schools that serve as centers of community life that could be replicated in New Jersey—where an $8 billion court-ordered school construction program was under way—as well as in other places undertaking school construction. This chapter describes that model process, the context in which it evolved, the problems that arose during implementation, how those were addressed, and the lessons for both policy and practice.

In both cases a partnership between the city and the school district, state agencies, and philanthropic foundations sought to integrate public investment in school capital improvements with urban school reform and a broader process of community revitalization. Significantly, these efforts coalesced in the larger context of a statewide strategy to promote smart growth and reduce regional inequities associated with the sprawl system.

PLANNING FOR SCHOOLS AND COMMUNITIES IN NEW JERSEY

State investment in school construction in Perth Amboy and Trenton has its origins in the New Jersey Supreme Court's historic *Abbott v. Burke* set of decisions.[1] In its original ruling in 1985 and subsequent rulings through the 1990s, the court cited the poor condition and overcrowding of school buildings in the state's poorest communities, Perth Amboy and Trenton among them, as evidence of the pervasive inequities of the school finance system. The court directed the state to provide facilities for children in the thirty districts designated in the Abbott ruling "that will be sufficient to enable these students to achieve the substantive standards that now define a thorough and efficient education and the quality of the facilities cannot depend on the district's willingness or ability to raise taxes or to incur debt."[2]

In addition, the court ordered the state to implement whole school reform (WSR)—a comprehensive package of site-based reforms closely aligned with the concept of community schools. To remedy the court order, in July 2000, the state launched an $8.6 billion school construction program—the largest public works program in the state's history. This huge capital investment gave Abbott districts a unique opportunity *to encourage innovation* to integrate comprehensive neighborhood-based school reform with facility design—building schools that serve as centers of community.[3]

There are two ways a school can serve as a community center: (1) reach out and play a more integral role in the community or (2) incorporate local resources into the school environment (USDOE 2000). Either way, the concept of community-centered schools represents a key strategy to achieve the goals of New Jersey's State Development and Redevelopment Plan (SDRP), a blueprint for state investment based on the principles of smart growth—*notably, strategies supporting the revitalization of existing cities and towns.* To raise public awareness about this opportunity to leverage the state's investment in public school construction, the Office of State Planning (OSP), in the New Jersey Department of Community Affairs (DCA), launched the Communities of Learning (COL) campaign—a multiagency team effort including the New Jersey Redevelopment Authority (NJRA), the New Jersey Department of Education (NJDOE), and the New Jersey Economic Development Authority (NJEDA), the agency initially designated to build schools in Abbott districts.

As a result of the short-lived COL campaign (2000–2002)—which sponsored conferences, symposia, outreach programs, technical assistance, and the Community School Smart Growth Planning Grants program—New Jersey served as a laboratory for creative community-based school planning (Shoshkes 2004).

The timing of the COL campaign dovetailed neatly with the U.S. Department of Energy's (USDOE) priority to enhance school design quality, which was supported by National Endowment for the Arts (NEA) funding through its New Civic Works design competition program. With the encouragement of the NEA director of design, the COL staff (this author) approached the Perth Amboy mayor and superintendent of schools about the idea of a partnership to sponsor a school design competition—hopefully the first of many in the state.

PARTNERSHIP WITH PERTH AMBOY

Perth Amboy has been a port of entry since English colonists arrived there in 1664. A spectacular waterfront and its proximity to New York stimulated Perth Amboy's growth as a manufacturing center and its emergent renaissance. After decades of decline, a change in leadership in 1990 stimulated the city's revival. That same year Perth Amboy was designated an Abbott district. Residents did not wait for additional state aid to address their facilities needs, however. In 1992 the district launched a building program that included two new schools and three renovation projects, financed with the proceeds of bond sales. Redevelopment also progressed. In 1997 the mayor inaugurated an ambitious plan to reclaim over one thousand acres of former industrial land, mostly along the waterfront.

Perth Amboy's school construction program was about 75 percent complete in 1998 when the state took over responsibility for these projects as well as a new high school and a new elementary school. All work then stopped, pending state funding. Around that time the district hired a new superintendent, who became an influential advocate of Abbott implementation as president of the state Urban Superintendents Association.

In early spring 2000, the mayor and superintendent of schools welcomed the OSP's suggestion to form the community school partnership and to apply for a grant to support participatory planning for a design competition. The mayor designated the director of the Perth Amboy Redevelopment Agency, whose portfolio included a revision of the city's master plan, to head the planning team. The OSP urban design staff would provide technical assistance. The superintendent saw holding a competition as an opportunity to investigate viable alternatives to the state's restrictive school efficiency facilities standards (FES), also known as "models," which were "developed by non-educators and born out of cost-efficiency goals" but which the NJDOE had transformed into "a set of rigid and conventional design standards" (Education Law Center 2006).

Work began without any new funding thanks to a Columbia University urban design studio, which agreed to explore the opportunities presented by the Perth Amboy community school partnership as its fall-term topic. Meanwhile in July, the state legislature finally authorized funding for Abbott school construction and the DCA announced the Community School Planning Grants, with a November deadline for the first round. The urban design studio now provided a forum that helped crystallize the partnership between the city, the school district, and the OSP and a conceptual approach to the community school planning project. In short, the various individuals involved developed a common language, coalesced into a team and "planned to plan."

This team came up with a two-phase project in which the OSP would be an active partner: the OSP staff would serve as the project director, filling a gap in municipal staffing. In phase one, a $50,000 Community School Smart Growth Planning Grant would support a community-based process to crystallize a vision for the new high school and produce the program and guidelines for the school design competition. In phase two, a $50,000 NEA New Civic Works grant would support the national design competition, which would be articulated with the state school procurement system. The goal was to rethink what a high school for the twenty-first century could look like while accepting the limitations imposed on Abbott funds.

In February 2001, upon invitation by the NEA to submit a full proposal to the New Civic Works program, the team enlisted a professional competition advisor. He recommended a two-stage competition. Stage one would involve a selection process to determine four finalists who would compete at stage two. All qualified architects would be invited to submit a booklet illustrating their conceptual approach to the new Perth Amboy High School (PAHS). The jury would review these submissions and select four finalists to proceed to stage two and receive an honorarium to complete their submissions. The OSP approached the EDA for the funds to pay for stage two expenses, reasoning the competition would advance the project partly through preliminary design, for which Abbott funds were allocated. The executive director of the EDA wrote a letter of support for this proposal, couched in general terms. With the OSP as a member of the Perth Amboy team partners, this level of uncertainty was acceptable.

In October, the NEA director of design publicly announced the award of the New Civic Works grant to Perth Amboy—along with word of a set-aside for school design competitions in the next round of funding—at a COL-sponsored symposium on school design. This inspired the Trenton city planner, who was in the audience, to submit a proposal, building on Trenton's Community Schools Master Plan, a project funded by the DCA as a pilot for the

Community School Smart Growth Planning Grants program in advance of state funding for Abbott construction.

The commissioners of the DCA, EDA, and DOE also held a press conference to announce both the award of the Community School Smart Growth Planning Grant to Perth Amboy—and the matching NEA grant—as well as a their Memorandum of Understanding (MOU) to cooperate on the development of Abbott schools that would serve as a catalyst for community development.

PAHS PHASE ONE: COMMUNITY SCHOOL SMART GROWTH PLANNING STUDY

After a year of incubation, the PAHS Community School Smart Growth Planning study began in November 2001. But despite the support of the mayor and superintendent, the high school principal was wary of the idea. "The high school has not seen a lot of change in curriculum in decades," the president of the board of education (BOE) explained. "The faculty is old and tired. But because the city is landlocked it will be hard to find a site to build a new large high school. We may *have* to do something new, like build a campus with satellites connected by core facilities. The problem is having someone to be in charge of getting it done."

While the superintendent dealt with the high school, the project team's first step was to form an executive committee to guide the planning process, including city and school officials, state agency partners, and civic leaders. They also hired a planning consultant who would be responsible for preparing a technical report to guide the competition. The professional advisor spelled out their charge: "What I need is for you to articulate the goals and objectives of the competition with clarity. Here is our educational philosophy. Here is our community. Here is the site. Here are our goals. Here is a building program sympathetic to our goals and objectives."

Then in February 2002, newly elected Governor James McGreevey disbanded the OSP, ending the Community School Smart Growth Planning Grant program and COL campaign.[4] The Perth Amboy team quickly reorganized, hiring the now former OSP colleague to continue to serve as the project direct as a consultant to the city. Thus began a new phase of this project, along with a new degree of uncertainty about state agency support.

New Partnerships, New Health Priorities

Meanwhile, discussions had already been under way between COL staff and representatives of the Robert Wood Johnson Foundation (RWJF) to explore the possibilities of achieving the goals of a new Active Living program area by building on existing initiatives such as those funded by Community School Smart Growth Planning Grants, which targeted urban minority communities where the population was disproportionately at risk for obesity, overweight, and the associated health risks. With the encouragement of RWJF to submit a proposal for a grant, the Perth Amboy team proposed to take advantage of the high school design competition as an opportunity to raise awareness about the benefits of an active lifestyle and how the design, site planning, and ongoing programming of the school could encourage members of the whole school community to engage in more routine physical activity. RWJF agreed to provide a small albeit nonconforming grant through the NJ Walks and Bikes pilot program.

Inside-Out Planning

Sites to build a large new high school are scarce in Perth Amboy and only one of the three sites the district had proposed suited the city's redevelopment plans. In mid-March 2002, the EDA concluded that it would cost too much to clean that former industrial site for use as a school. While city and district officials regrouped to identify other sites, the school superintendent advised the team to "keep on trucking" and simply begin planning the new high school from the "inside-out."

The high school principal agreed to appoint a group of faculty, staff, and residents to discuss ideas for a new school, skirting the controversial issue of site selection. The president of the board of education urged, "The competition is an opportunity to not just put up four walls and a ceiling, but a different kind of school. The planning team's concern is what goes on in the competition. It is your job to focus on what we want for the education of Perth Amboy's kids." "Let's see what the faculty come up with," the superintendent said, giving the nod to the planning team to start a parallel community-based visioning process.

In April 2002 the planning team organized a Community Steering Committee and invited volunteers to work on one of four subcommittees: Innovative Learning Environments, Special Themed Academies, Community Learning Center, and Healthy Schools and Lifestyles. The subcommittees (including faculty and staff) met weekly and made their recommendations—to organize the three thousand–student school as six small themed academies—to the board of education in June. Paying close attention was the woman who soon would be appointed the new high school principal. Unlike her predecessor, she welcomed the challenge of redesigning the school.

A new wrinkle appeared in June, when Governor McGreevey created a new agency, the Schools Construction Corporation (SCC), as a unit of the EDA to streamline the school construction process. This reorganization added urgency to the need to confirm the EDA/SCC's support for the competition—new alliances would have to be built with new players.

Site Selection

Over the summer, the planning team evaluated three potential sites: a public housing complex already slated for demolition, a vacant factory, and a former petrochemical plant. In September the board of education accepted their recommendation to pursue the fifteen-acre housing site. Thanks to the leadership of the mayor and superintendent, and the no-nonsense attitude of the CEO of the new SCC, by October successful negotiations over a complex strategy for site acquisition—involving a land swap between the city, county, and housing authority; the relocation of 250 households; and the development of 215 units of new housing, including market rate, affordable, and subsidized rentals—also paved the way for resolution of the terms of the SCC's support for the competition, acknowledging it was to be a model for replication in Trenton—for which the NEA had by now invited a full proposal.

The new high school principal now led the faculty, energized by new blood, in planning the academies. The district's liaison with the DOE, who also served on the executive committee, helped translate the faculty, staff, and community's wish list into a realistic program. He also helped expedite the DOE's approval process—complicated by the lack of strict conformance to the school efficiency facility standards—which concluded sufficiently to launch the competition in May 2003.

PAHS PHASE TWO: THE COMPETITION

Anticipating the pending DOE approval, in April 2002 the project team announced the PAHS design competition through a poster and listings in electronic and print media that would point to the competition website. The graphic design consultant, 2 × 4, designed a paired image for the poster and website for both the Perth Amboy and Trenton school competitions to reinforce the programmatic linkage between them. Anyone who visited the PAHS competition website learned that there would soon be a similar competition in Trenton.

Two hundred architects entered the PAHS competition, including many blue-chip firms. In July the task of selecting finalists from 136 eligible submissions fell to a jury including architecture luminaries (Henry Cobb, Toshiko Mori, Michael Hayes, and Carlos Jimenez), as well as the president of the BOE, the mayor, and the DOE's director of facilities (the superintendent had retired in June). Stage one finalists would have to become prequalified by the SCC in order to compete in stage two, which was designed to mimic New Jersey's strict procurement rules in order to make the design competition a replica of the architectural commission. The public met the finalists at a daylong event and studied—and commented on—their proposals during a month-long exhibit, culminating in the final jury in September. Happily, the people's choice corresponded with the jury's selection of John Ronan, a forty-year-old from Chicago, as the winner over renowned competitors Morphosis, Peter Eisenman Architects, and Fox and Fowle. The results of the competition were closely watched in the local press, reported in national and international design and construction media, and exhibited in New York.

Development of the design will evolve along with the execution of the academy plan. The Healthy Schools Committee evolved into a Community School Collaborative for Health under the direction of a youth services program housed at the high school, with funding from state agencies and RWJF. So the competition marked the beginning of a promising process of change.

REHAB IN TRENTON

As a historic city, a river city, a former manufacturing center, and the capital of New Jersey, Trenton has dozens of attributes driving its current renaissance, which follows several decades of decline. As in Perth Amboy, the school superintendent and the mayor recognized the benefits of coordinating school construction with the city's extensive redevelopment initiatives, but neither had the funding for collaborative planning. When approached by COL staff, they readily agreed to form a partnership and received a modest grant to create the Community Schools Master Plan. Directed by a city planner, the partnership hired a team of national experts to orchestrate a participatory process to integrate four new and renovated school facilities and local resources to serve as centers for learning and catalysts for community revitalization. That plan assumed that the one-hundred-year-old Carroll Robbins Elementary School, a three-story brick structure in the historic Greenwood Hamilton neighborhood in Trenton's South Ward, would be demolished, even though it is a city-designated historic landmark. A replacement school was to be located several blocks away, as part of the conversion of the historic Roebling factory into an educational, commercial, and cultural complex.

But the student population in the predominantly Hispanic Greenwood Hamilton neighborhood—one of the fastest growing areas of the city—had been growing significantly, and there was a lack of other schools in the area. Instead of razing the Robbins Elementary School, the district decided to modernize the building. The Trenton superintendent of schools hoped that holding a design competition for the Robbins Elementary School renovation would provoke innovative solutions for the kind of urban school design issues typically faced in Abbott districts, which are mainly densely populated, formerly highly industrialized areas where it is difficult to find affordable and environmentally safe sites for new school construction. The challenges for architects included designing a school that fits in a tight urban space, retaining the interesting character of the building and fitting it into the historic context, and incorporating outdoor play space and parking.

The proposal submitted to the NEA in April 2002 by the Trenton team—which included the same project director and professional advisor who had worked in Perth Amboy—adapted the Perth Amboy model of a two-phased approach: first, a participatory planning study and second, a two-stage national design competition. In lieu of the Community School Smart Growth Planning Grant, municipal and school district resources would provide the matching funds for the $75,000 NEA grant to pay for phase one and the first stage of the competition. Stage two of the competition would be conducted following the award of a predevelopment grant from the SCC.

The Trenton team learned they had been awarded the NEA grant in September, but the mayor and superintendent did not want to move forward before confirming SCC support. The team did receive the CEO of the SCC's "informed consent" to proceed until the following spring, as excitement about the highly visible PAHS competition was building.

PHASE ONE: PARTICIPATORY PLANNING

At the first meeting of the Community Steering Committee for the Robbins Elementary School competition in June 2003, the professional advisor to the team reiterated the charge he had given in Perth Amboy. Planning got under way on several levels to identify community needs and resources: surveys and site visits, review of extant reports and best practices, and focused interviews and visioning workshops conducted in Spanish and English. The goal was to develop a consensus on the education and supplemental programs participants wanted to see at Robbins Elementary School, as well as to generate ideas for community use of the facility. This "wish list" would then be translated into a space program that satisfied state standards for educational adequacy rather than simply applying the state's FES criteria,

In mid-September 2003, in a sign of state support for the project, the NJDOE commissioner joined the Trenton mayor and superintendent in the public kick off at a student assembly and the press conference at Robbins Elementary School. "This is one of the few places in the state where we are asking a lot of people to think about what a school should look like," the NJDOE commissioner confirmed.[5] Surrounded by student drawings of the "school of the future," the mayor spoke directly to the NJDOE commissioner as well as to a larger audience through the press as he proclaimed, "The goal of this project is to make sure that the school's redesign takes into account the needs of the entire community and that we work on design features that will help our children perform better."[6]

The visioning process engaging the Robbins Elementary School faculty was not as layered as the process organized for the much larger PAHS. Instead, a core group of volunteers formed a school design committee, which considered research trends in elementary education and the best practices employed elsewhere to improve teaching and learning. The committee met weekly, and by early December it had articulated a vision that was circulated among and endorsed by the full faculty. Their goal to become a full-service global studies community school was a logical extension of the Comer school reform model the Robbins Elementary School faculty was already successfully implementing.

Site Expansion Needs and Options

Meanwhile the Community Steering Committee began considering options for expansion if the student population was going to increase significantly. The options were extremely limited, and all solutions would be controversial. So before proceeding the city planner advised both the mayor and superintendent, explaining, "The general idea is that we will make the architects aware of the space around the school available for expansion, and let them come up with site planning strategies." Immediately the superintendent e-mailed, "We are VERY comfortable with the directions you're headed." Such communication between city planners and the district, which allowed the project forward while leaving many options on the table, was essential for building public support for difficult site selection decisions in both Perth Amboy and Trenton.

The city planner also made a preliminary presentation of these conceptual expansion plans, including the potential demolition of residential properties, to the City Landmarks Commission. Luckily, the commission recognized the critical need for the school to expand and the positive impact this could have on conserving and revitalizing the historic district as a whole.

Educational Program Drives Facility Programming

By December 2003, community stakeholders had reached a consensus on the programs and features they would like to see. In January the district determined that the enlarged Robbins Elementary School would support a projected enrollment of six hundred in grades pre-K–5 and would serve all students who needed bilingual instruction through the end of elementary school. The next step was to distill the community and faculty wish list into a facility space program that would fit within the constraints on the use of Abbott funds.

The Robbins Elementary School program submitted for NJDOE review called for organizing this large elementary school in three smaller learning communities: the prekindergarten and kindergarten program, grades 1–3, and grades 4–5. Each smaller learning community would be centered on its own instructional commons, a flexible space that could support a range of learning group sizes, from individuals to assemblies of the entire learning community. The NJDOE approval process dragged on for five months, leaving unclear how large of an addition would be eligible for state funds—and whether or not land acquisition would be required for the project.

The team now had to come to grips with the limitations of the site. For a variety of reasons, there were essentially two alternatives: (1) renovate the existing Robbins Elementary School to serve two hundred students and find additional land elsewhere to build a new, four hundred-student school or (2) acquire sites around the existing school sufficient to house the entire six hundred students, which would require demolishing occupied row houses.

The choice was clear, largely because there was no land available nearby to build a new school. A consensus easily formed among members of the Community Steering Committee to recommend the second option. The district quickly agreed because it hoped to preserve Robbins Elementary School as a robust neighborhood school and bilingual center for the growing immigrant population. Fortunately, the adjacent elderly residents that would be displaced welcomed the prospect of state-assisted relocation.

Terms and Conditions of SCC Support Resolved

In March 2004 the SCC—now under a new CEO—agreed to provide a predevelopment grant of $94,000 to support the Robbins Elementary School Design Competition. This decision—which came as the PAHS design competition was concluding with great fanfare—followed an earlier one that specified a cap on design fees, including reimbursable expenses, at 15 percent of construction cost and setting a limit of $200 per gross square foot of renovation and new construction costs.

The SCC liaison to the two competitions called a meeting to discuss lessons learned from the successful Perth Amboy experience. In Perth Amboy, the biggest problem encountered was to ensure that architects who submit proposals in stage one were ready and able to become prequalified according to the SCC procurement criteria. The liaison recommended including more information about the timeframe of the lengthy prequalification process so that applicants would know what to expect. His words proved to be prophetic.

Approval of Facility Program

Throughout the spring, the team sought NJDOE approval of the proposed facilities program, while the NJDOE staff assigned to review the project insisted on an inflexible application of the FES. Finally, the superintendent personally argued the district's case, persuading the agency to adjust the rigid guidelines and approve the itemized space request nearly in its entirety in July 2004. The competition could now proceed. The educational program would indeed drive the design process.

PHASE TWO: THE ROBBINS ELEMENTARY SCHOOL DESIGN COMPETITION

In preparation for launching the competition in mid-September 2004, graphic design consultant, 2x4, produced the poster and completed the website—the primary vehicle for disseminating information about the competition. In mid-December the jury (architects Dana Cuff, Monica Ponce de Leon, Brian Healy, and Jesse Reiser, in addition to the mayor, superintendent, and NJDOE director of facilities) convened to select a set of four finalists and several alternates to proceed to stage two from nearly 140 eligible entries. Their approach was to organize the submissions into typologies and select the strongest proposal in each group. "We wanted to make sure that in the first round there would be broad representation across a typology of solutions to this problem, of how to expand the historic school building on a tight site, in a fragile neighborhood context," one juror recalled.

The four finalists were (in alphabetical order) CR Studio Architects of New York, David Cumby Architect of San Francisco, Ply Architecture of Ann Arbor, and Preston Scott Cohen (PSC) Architect of Boston. The alternates in order of ranking were first, Peter Lee Architect of Los Angeles, second, Magnet Studios of Berkeley, and third, Urban Office Architecture (UUA) of New York. Unlike Perth Amboy, where most of the finalists were prominent architects, the Robbins Elementary School finalists were all relatively young and inexperienced. One benefit of this situation is that fresh talent would have a chance to make their mark, but this situation presented its own set of challenges, compounding the risks involved for the client.

Stage two got under way as the SCC came under a cloud of criticism. A January 2005 report published in New Jersey's leading newspaper alleging mismanagement of the Abbott school construction program spurred the acting governor to ask the state inspector general (IG) to investigate the SCC. In April the IG issued a damning report detailing serious financial and management problems and asking the governor to suspend awards of all new school construction contracts until ten reforms were implemented.[7]

Meanwhile, three competitors—a finalist and two alternates—had to withdraw due to difficulties with prequalification. It was nearly April by the time the third alternate entered stage two. Then in early April SCC officials announced that funds for Abbott schools would be depleted by January 2006. Trenton district officials immediately began to lobby for Robbins Elementary School to be included on the list of projects earmarked to receive the remaining funds. Given the delays due to prequalification and the moratorium on school construction funding, the sponsors postponed the final jury until early October. In July the SCC announced the last projects for which there would be funding; Robbins Elementary School was not among them.

The creative ideas on display at the public exhibit preceding the final jury raised hope for the future of New Jersey schools, even as the SCC was developing new, cost-cutting design standards that angered school districts and education advocates.[8] When the jurors convened in October, the SCC liaison clarified the significance of their deliberations. "The intent of the SCC was to solicit nationally good ideas for this type of project, ideas that would be replicable throughout urban districts. These ideas might be incorporated in one of the agency's new design manuals and as such perhaps even form part of a vehicle for architect procurement," he explained. This competition process itself could very well serve as a model for the state, and the superintendent added,

A loud argument is being made that excluding the district and the city from the procurement process has led to all kinds of problems that collaborative planning would have helped avoid. One of the intriguing things about this project is that it is much like the situation faced in many urban districts, where there is limited space for school expansion or replacement. As a result of the partnership between the city and the district, the neighbors accepted the need to acquire some of the adjacent homes. They took a mature look: we want a good school. But the confined site requires of necessity a certain footprint.

In fact, the winning proposal by Preston Scott Cohen is a sleek, linear form that serves as a colorful *medium-rise* backdrop for the site. The jury also awarded honorable mention to Ply Architects, whose proposal intertwines the public spaces and classrooms around a series of outdoor courtyards and playgrounds that can be securely accessed for community use.

LESSONS AND CONCLUSIONS

The success of the Robbins Elementary School/PAHS model in achieving most of its objectives suggests that it offers a very useful tool to integrate school reform, facility design, and neighborhood planning and to generate creative design solutions for tight urban sites. New Jersey's Abbott school construction program shaped the particular goals and structure for this model, and different political and economic circumstances will influence its replication elsewhere. But the Abbott reforms herald a greater state role in public school finance, involving standards-based, district-wide reform, along with increasing calls for site-based governance and community-school partnerships. Thus lessons learned in these projects apply not only in New Jersey but also in other cities undertaking school construction programs—and other states concerned with smart growth.

Political and Economic Considerations

The story of the Robbins Elementary School and PAHS design competitions confirms that it takes a lot of effort to cultivate a constituency and mobilize resources, both political and financial, for such projects. The statewide Community of Learners (COL) campaign created the framework for a serious discussion within a public forum about the problems and potentials for planning and designing schools that serve as centers of community. This conversation helped sway allies within state government and enabled the launch of the Community School Smart Growth Planning Grant program. Availability of state planning funds, in turn, got the attention of school district superintendents and mayors and facilitated collaboration among public entities accustomed to a high degree of autonomy. Moreover, planning money, which is typically not part of a capital budget, allowed the partnership between the city and school district to look at the big picture and cultivate a framework within which an innovative project—and public support for it—could emerge.

State planning funds and the partnership of state and local officials along with the statewide COL campaign earned the support of the NEA, which was convinced that the model for the PAHS design competition would succeed and could be replicated. The competition offered a cost-effective, transparent method to ensure a level playing field among architects and an incentive for innovative ideas that would raise the bar for design excellence in public schools. Thus strategic investment by federal and state agencies brought design to the fore and instituted the use of design competitions as a public forum as well as a procurement method.

The competition, and community-based planning for the competition, situated school design in a broader social context that brought a civic perspective to bear on the questions raised—such as those regarding site acquisition—and how those questions were framed and the input received. This underscores the importance of the partnership between the mayor and the superintendent of schools as cosponsors of the competition. This meant not only that the mayor and superintendent were "on the same page" but also that they understood the need to communicate with a single voice. As the top elected official, the mayor has to be the lead spokesperson for the school district as well as the community. Thus prestige associated with the NEA grants gave the community a voice it otherwise would not have had in the Abbott school design process and also helped give state agencies permission to fulfill their responsibilities—apply the FES, hire architects—in new, more flexible, and collaborative ways. That permitted the architects to be more innovative.

The success of the PAHS design competition established an informal pattern of accomplishment and cooperation among a range of stakeholders that enabled the adaptation of the model in Trenton. Equally important, the PAHS precedent created a sense among the jurors and competitors that the Robbins Elementary School project would really happen.

A clear lesson from the New Jersey design competitions, though, is that there is no guarantee that the winning design will be built. There are many risks, and many factors are out of the sponsor's control: unexpected turnover of elected and appointed officials, bureaucratic resistance to change, and loss of what appeared to be assured funding. Savvy leadership by the mayor and superintendent of schools and their unwavering commitment to the design competition were essential in keeping the project moving forward despite the uncertainties and pitfalls along the way. But given the length of time it can take to bring such a project to fruition, it is equally important to have as advocates energetic and experienced midlevel bureaucrats, both in city hall and the school district, who are likely to be around after the mayor and superintendent have left office. How can this be achieved?

It is necessary to institutionalize the partnership to keep alliances in place for a sustained effort. This is not easy to initiate or to maintain. At the local level, one strategy might be to create an office of community school partnerships that reports to both the mayor and superintendent. Ideally, the community-school partnership will become embedded in a supportive network of relationships that link agencies at many levels of government and the community and that share overlapping reform objectives related to school funding, governance, educational programs, and facilities. In this way, leadership can shift from the state to the local level and back as political circumstances change, as they did in New Jersey.

Likewise, the winning architect will "need to see themselves as actors in a political system, not floating above it as an artist or a neutral professional," as advised by the political economist Lynn Sagalyn (2006, 48). "Without political skills, they will find their efforts outflanked by those accustomed to acting in the political arena."

Planning

The competition clearly served as a catalyst for public participation in the school planning and design process, but the consultant who served as project director actually made it happen. "We couldn't have done it without . . . an external facilitator," the superintendent confirmed. "Districts don't have that capacity." A key role of the project director was to open up the school planning and design process to include other important community stakeholders.

The participatory planning process and design competition did not prolong the school procurement process (which hinges on the legislature allocating more funds for Abbott school construction). The significant amount of predesign planning would not otherwise have occurred at this stage in the standard state procurement process, yet it added tremendous value to the final product, in addition to the innovative designs elicited by the competition. The NJDOE director of facilities admitted, "In the end, the competition was better thought out than the non-competition process, and accomplished a lot of the things that should be part of the school construction program: engaging input from the school, the district, and the town from the beginning; and tying the education program to the facilities planning." Funding for such planning should be part of any schools construction program, no matter what method is used for architect selection.

Jury Process

A competition is only as good as its program and its jury. Together a well-written and carefully researched program and a notable jury enhance the credibility and professionalism of the competition but do not guarantee a successful outcome. Inclusion of the second stage of the competition provided an opportunity for the finalists to meet the client—sponsors and various stakeholder groups—and get a better feel for the project. However, there was no mechanism for providing the finalists input from the jury or the public concerning their proposals. In retrospect, it would have been useful to provide the finalists with a report of the jury's comments, including, perhaps, recommendations for how they might improve their scheme.

To provide the finalists with meaningful community input about their proposals would require first educating the public about the alternatives and the role of public opinion in the jury process. Various methods of doing this are possible. So enhanced, the competition would serve as a tool for public education about the value of public design and the design process.

With careful attention to the program, structure of the jury, and the jury process, a design competition can ensure that the process is informative, transparent, and fair. "Using the competition builds community support, and credibility," the superintendent stated. "You can see the project as it takes shape, as decisions are made." Given the long gestation period for these projects and the uncertainties about whether or not they will be built, it is important that the process engenders such trust and pragmatic optimism.

Implementation

The Robbins Elementary School and PAHS design competitions were designed to mimic New Jersey's strict procurement rules, replicating the architectural commission process.

"Procedurally we did well," the SCC liaison confirmed. It remains to be seen whether or not the winning designs for the Robbins Elementary School and PAHS can be built within budget. But as one juror noted, "No interesting project starts within the budget. It's always a matter of engineering it down. The jury selects not just a design concept, but also the framework for the conversation that begins following the competition, about how to solve the problem. As a result of a competition you are hiring an architect who thinks along those lines as much as the solution itself. Their scheme reflects their creative problem solving bent."

The real obstacle to the implementation of the Robbins Elementary School and PAHS design competition model is what planner Don Schön (1971) referred to as the "dynamic conservatism" of institutions: "a tendency to fight to remain the same." The rules of the game—facilities standards, procurement guidelines, funding formulas, and so on, may present obstacles along the way, but they are also constantly evolving. Schön advises, "We must become able not only to transform our institutions, in response to changing situations and requirements; we must invent and develop institutions which are 'learning systems,' that is to say, systems capable of bringing about their own continuing transformation."

The COL campaign and the Community School Smart Growth Planning Grant program proved to be an effective way to encourage local experimentation with creative approaches, design competitions among them, to integrate school reform, school facility design, and neighborhood revitalization. It is only through such a systemic effort—operating at many levels of government, in the private sector, in academia, and at the grassroots—that it is possible to create schools and communities capable of planning and designing their own continuous improvement. In addition, there needs to be an incentive for innovation so that local state agencies do not simply replicate what has been done in the past. NEA support for public design competitions provided such an incentive and should be continued and expanded. Finally, for innovative projects such as the PAHS Robbins Elementary School design competition to benefit the system as a whole, there is a need for continuing evaluation through case studies and the exchange of information.

NOTES

1. A series of ten decisions from 1990 to 2003. For case summaries and citations see New Jersey Department of Education website: http://www.state.nj.us/education/abbotts/dec/#4.
2. New Jersey Supreme Court ruling, Abbott v. Burke V, May 21, 1998
3. For an overview of the history, challenges, and lessons learned from implementation of the Abbott school construction program from 1998 to 2004, see the Education Law Center's report, *Breaking Ground: Rebuilding New Jersey's Urban Schools*.
4. In response to widespread criticism of this decision, the governor established a new Office of Smart Growth (OSG) and Smart Future Planning grant program, which did not, however, continue its predecessor's support of interagency cooperation in planning for community-based schools.
5. As Albert Raboteau reported in the *Trenton Times* on September 16, 2003.
6. Ibid.
7. Dunstan McNichol, Inspector flunks school building agency, *Star Ledger*, October 20, 2005.
8. Dunstan McNichol and Steve Chambers, Educators pan SCC's new guidelines, *Star Ledger*, October 20, 2005.

REFERENCES

Education Law Center. March 2006. Facilities efficiency standards: An analysis. http://www.Edlaw center.org.

Ponessa, Joan. 2004. *Breaking ground: Rebuilding New Jersey's urban schools*. Newark: Education Law Center. http://edlawcenter.org.

Sagalyn, Lynn. 2006. The political fabric of design competitions. In *Politics of design: Competitions for public projects*, ed. Catherine Malmberg, 29–52. Philadelphia: Policy Institute for the Region. http://repository.upenn.edu/penniur_papers/19.

Schön, Don. 1971. *Beyond the stable state*. New York: Random House.

Shoshkes, Ellen. 2004. *Creating communities of learning: Schools and smart growth*. Newark: Education Law Center. http://edlawcenter.org.

U.S. Department of Energy (USDOE). 2000. *Citizens guide for planning and designing schools as centers of community*. Washington, DC: U.S. Government Printing Office.

Conclusion

REBECCA MILES, ADESOJI ADELAJA,
AND MARK A. WYCKOFF

THE CHAPTERS OF THIS BOOK POINT TO A NUMBER OF IMPORTANT GAPS NOT ONLY IN the literature on the role of schools in communities but also in the way decisions are made about where to invest in schools. Contributors draw attention to compelling issues that are seldom considered when making decisions such as where to locate new schools, whether to upgrade existing facilities, or whether to create magnet programs in underenrolled schools. An important consequence of these gaps is that society misses out on real opportunities for schools to add more value to the quality of life in communities. School district–level decision makers work independently for the most part when deciding about school siting and facilities. Local officials, likewise, work independently. The result is a number of missed opportunities, many of which have important implications for population health and quality of life. By focusing on such issues, this book adds significantly to the body of literature on the role of schools in the community. More importantly, however, it provides insights for policy makers and the public on why it is important for government, school districts, and citizen groups to work together on school siting and capital expenditures and how these will contribute toward better local and regional outcomes.

Some of the issues raised here are not new. However, in many cases they are observed through a different lens that illuminates the health consequences of current practices and helps policy makers and the public understand the importance of collaborative planning. Considering the marked difference between high-growth states, where school expansions are frequent, and low-growth states, where school consolidation and closure are more the norm, this book also highlights the structural and contextual differences between high-growth and low-growth school environments and the implications of school siting decisions under these unique scenarios.

The multicity study featured in "School Trips: Analysis of Factors Affecting Mode Choice in Three Metropolitan Areas" confirms that the distance between schools and residences is the aspect of school siting that matters most for active travel to school. This finding provides support for coordinating school siting and land use planning. Along with the discussion of the consequences of school siting on physical activity, weight status, risk of injury, and respiratory ailments, it provides further support for the need for new schools to be built close to residences. "Policy Impacts on Mode Choice in School Transportation: An Analysis of Four Florida School Districts" finds that state and local policy can help make this happen. While a quality education is central in the minds of parents, if given a choice, they probably would also prefer that schools contribute to the health of communities.

"Where to Live and How to Get to School: Connecting Residential Location Choice and School Travel Mode Choice" provides new insights into the extent to which parents' preference for active travel to school affects both their choice of where to live and their support for their children walking or cycling to school and further highlights the importance of these issues. Such insights provide further support for the need to coordinate school siting with land use planning and in particular the need for more residences at all affordability levels near schools. School siting decisions that offer parents more options than currently exist in most places will help them optimize other dimensions of their quality of life.

Other issues raised by contributors to this volume have heretofore received little attention in academic and policy-oriented literatures. The case study featured here that documents the presence of a range of environmental hazards near public schools in North Carolina is the first of its kind. It presents the various types of state-level policies that could be implemented to protect schoolchildren. Actual implementation of policies to address the environmental hazard implications of school siting may be difficult, given the fact that adequate scientific evidence on which to base standards for all potential hazards does not yet exist.

The case studies of how external factors and different policies affect school capital expenditure patterns represent important additions to a limited body of literature. They show that the factors that have influenced where investments in existing schools have been made and the opportunities and challenges for transforming the way investments in school facilities are made differ from state to state in important ways and are complex and ever-changing. For example, since April 2008 when chapter authors gathered in Tallahassee for Florida State University's School Siting and Healthy Communities symposium, one of Florida's largest school districts announced it had put plans for building new schools on hold in the face of declining enrollments and budget shortfalls. Under conditions such as these, opportunities for transforming the way school investments are made are unlikely to involve new school construction. Instead, they may consist of upgrading existing schools, changing enrollment zones, or creating schools of choice and considering innovative school transportation options such as collaborating with mass transit to provide for older students' travel to school. Some of these changes may be unpopular and are likely to create challenges for local governments and school districts not used to working together.

Findings and discussions presented in this book point to a number of avenues for future research. Because clear evidence of the effects of the school community environment on population health does not yet exist for most of the relevant aspects—land use, services, transportation systems, community composition, condition of school buildings, there is a need to "grow" the evidence base by investigating the potential size and direction of impacts on population health as a result of different combinations of school facilities investment policies and practices. The proliferation of programs with non-place-based eligibility for school attendance, such as magnet and charter schools, and school choice options of various kinds points to a rich area for future research investigating the potential health impacts of alternative scenarios.

More studies are needed that use a healthy communities lens to evaluate how decisions about where to invest in schools are made and the criteria that are used. The impacts that are of interest should include educational outcomes since they are critical to any discussion of school quality in the United States today. Studies comparing metropolitan areas with many small school districts versus areas with large school districts such as counties; studies of school districts facing expanding versus declining enrollment; and studies of areas with different policy approaches to school siting would be particularly useful. From this research, better practices in school district asset management could be developed—ones that support school district fiscal responsibility and principles of smart growth, healthy communities, and social equity.

A related focus for future research is the role of schools in the emerging knowledge economy. We need a better understanding of how choices related to school siting affect the quality of life in the surrounding communities; for example, the extent to which the integration of school facilities and buildings into key elements of social and cultural community development enhances long-term community character. Schools represent an important dimension of communities. In the emerging knowledge economy, effective planning and management of schools is important for the success of communities, and residents need to expand their view of schools and increase their expectations of the aesthetic and health contributions that schools can make to the community.

Studies are needed that focus on how information about adjacent land uses factor into school siting decision making and whether there are processes to protect schools from future land uses that place school occupants at risk. Some schools in the United States today were allowed to be constructed too close to environmental hazards; and in an unknown number of cases, environmental hazards were allowed to be located too close to schools.

There is also a need for research focused on investigating outcomes. For example, although scientific information is not available on which to base standards for all environmental hazards that have been found to threaten the health of school users, some states or localities may choose to establish school siting standards sufficient to ensure at least a bare minimum of safety for schoolchildren. Studies that investigate whether siting outcomes in such places are substantially different from others in ways that are likely to affect health would be useful.

To facilitate further research and activism, there is a need for publicly accessible information on the physical conditions, qualities, and facility spending of schools. This would contribute to needed research into how school construction investment coincides with, and impacts, school, neighborhood, city, and regional change. It would also facilitate greater accountability for how and where school construction monies are spent.

Again, schools are important and their location has a significant impact on the quality of life. Schools can be built anywhere. However, when such decisions involve a more comprehensive look at potential impacts, schools may add even more value to the community. The collective evidence presented in the chapters of this book shows that society can do much better. This book, and the symposium it builds on, represents the tip of the iceberg with regards to the possibility in the future of having schools contribute more effectively to the overall health and quality of life.

Index

Abbott schools, 221–24, 227–28, 230–33
Abbott v. Burke, 47, 62n5, 221–23, 224, 234n1
ACBM. *See* asbestos-containing building materials
ACS. *See* active school commuting
active school commuting (ACS), 165–66, 168, 171–73, 175–77, 179–80
ADA. *See* Americans with Disabilities Act
adaptive reuse of buildings, 207–9, 225
Adequate Public Facilities Ordinances (APFO), 75–76, 156, 189; effects of, 32–33; Maryland, 6, 8, 31, 32, 36; Virginia, 28, 31, 36
AHERA. *See* Asbestos Hazard Emergency Response Act
Aloha software, 204
American Institute of Architects Communities by Design Initiative, 70
American Planning Association, 77
American Society of Civil Engineers (ASCE), 45, 59
Americans with Disabilities Act (ADA), 46, 47
APFO. *See* Adequate Public Facilities Ordinances (APFO)
ArcGis database, 194
asbestos, 46
asbestos-containing building materials (ACBM), 46
Asbestos-Containing Materials in Schools Rule, 46
Asbestos Hazard Emergency Response Act (AHERA), 46
ASCE. *See* American Society of Civil Engineers
associations, role of, 8; web of, 14–16
Atlanta, Georgia, schools, 128

BEST. *See* Board on Environmental Studies and Toxicology (BEST); Building Educational Success Together (BEST)
bicycling, 58, 140, 238, 162n1; decline, 125–26, 147; density and, 59; distance and, 141; Florida, 9, 132, 133, 148–52, 154–56, 158–61; influences on, 127–28; Lane County survey and, 172, 173, 177, 179; Oregon, 141–43; safety of, 148; siting and, 9, 148; sprawl and, 60; Texas, 141–43; traffic and, 7, 126
Board on Environmental Studies and Toxicology (BEST), 212
Build a Table (BAT) function, 105n19, 114

Building Educational Success Together (BEST), 41, 48, 67n1
built environment: alternate uses for, 60–61; bicycles and, 140; building condition, 3, 13, 18, 21, 45–49, 61n4; building condition and performance, 57, 60; buildings, physical quality, 57–58, 60, 61n4; community composition and, 18–19; construction types, 51–52; defined, 13; environment and, 239; fixtures, 3, 13; health and, 4–5, 13–14, 18; HLM and, 133; injuries and, 17; investment, 58; neighborhood income and, 57–58; obesity and, 125, 126, 127, 131; parks and recreation, 3, 13; reconstruction, 51–52, 77; renovations, 3, 5–6, 28, 34, 41, 51–52, 148; residential choice and, 3, 13, 17, 167; roads, 3, 13; safety perceptions, 21; schools, 13; sidewalks, 140, 144; student travel in, 9, 17, 20–21, 125–27, 131, 133; travel mode choice and, 125–26, 132, 133, 134, 140; urban, 13; utilities, 13; walkability, 125–44; workplaces, 3, 13. *See also* school trips and travel modes
Bulletin 412, 77, 104n15
Burton, Jim, 33
buses, 132–33, 140, 172; Florida, 147, 148, 152, 154, 161

CAFO. *See* confined animal feeding operations
California: *Eliezer Williams, et al., v. State of California, et al.*, 49, 58; Belmont High School, 51, 52; construction spending, 59; coordinated siting, 150; disinvestment in, 56; enrollment growth, 44–45; environment, 187; Field Act, 47; infrastructure, 45–46; labor costs, 61n3; neighborhood income, 51, 52, 57; neighborhood types, 54; school construction, 27, 52, 53; school costs, 8, 42–48; school districts, 51, 52, 60, 187; school growth, 56–59; school investment, 49–45, 56; siting, 189; spending per pupil, 54, 57; SRTS program, 126; urban schools, 56; walkability, 127, 150
CAMEO. *See* Computer-Aided Management of Emergency Operations software
Canada, 4
CCD. *See* Common Core Data
CDC. *See* Centers for Disease Control and Prevention

241

urban areas (*continued*):
and, 65–66; minority grants, 224; neighborhood population decrease, 3, 8; revitalization, 5; schools, 68, 76; school segregation, 3; school services, 47; sprawl, 5; travel in, 9
urban planning and development, 13, 134
U.S. Census Bureau: construction data, 48; income, 50–54, 62n6; Michigan population changes, 65–66, 78–81, 102n2; tracts, 132, 135
U.S. Census of Governments, 42, 48–49; capital outlay data, 61n2
U.S. Department of Education. *See* National Center for Education Statistics
U.S. Department of Energy (USDOE), 222
U.S. Department of Health and Human Services, 126
USDOE. *See* U.S. Department of Energy
U.S. General Accounting Office (GAO, USGAO), 41, 45, 59, 61n4
U.S. Housing and Urban Development (HUD) Healthy Communities Transformation Initiative, 4

Vermont, 77
Virginia: acreage guidelines, 28, 30, 33, 37; APFOs, 28, 31, 36; comprehensive plans, 31, 33, 34; Fairfax County, 28–30, 32, 33, 36; Fauquier County, 28, 29; land allotment per student, 28–20; land use

policies, 27–28, 30, 32; large sites in, 34; Loudoun County, 28, 29, 33; Prince William County, 28, 29; proffer system, 30; pupil transportation policies, 30; School Impact methodology, 30; school renovation, 34; site acquisition in, 28, 30; siting practices, 8, 27; Stafford County, 28, 29; zoning, 30, 31

walkability: decline, 125–26, 143, 147, 148; downtowns, 104n7; Florida, 147–48, 151–52, 154, 158–62; Houston, 143, 144; impediments to, 152; income and, 140; index, 127; Kids Walk-to-School, 126; neighborhood, 69–71; New Jersey Walks and Bikes, 225; Oregon survey, 170–71, 173, 175–77, 179–81; population density and, 127; Portland, 141, 143; residence choice and, 238; Washington (state), 127. *See also* bicycling
Washington (state), 77; King County, 127; walkability index, 127
Washington, DC, 27, 28, 48
Wayne State University, 66
West Virginia, 188
whole school reform (WSR), 222
WSR. *See* whole school reform

zoning, 17–18, 74, 76, 203